Mastering Argo Workflows
Advanced Techniques for Kubernetes-Native Pipeline Automation

Nova Trex

© 2024 by Wang Press. All rights reserved.

No part of this publication may be reproduced, distributed, or transmitted in any form or by any means, including photocopying, recording, or other electronic or mechanical methods, without the prior written permission of the publisher, except in the case of brief quotations embodied in critical reviews and certain other noncommercial uses permitted by copyright law.

Published by Wang Press

For permissions and other inquiries, write to:
P.O. Box 3132, Framingham, MA 01701, USA

Contents

1 Introduction to Kubernetes and Argo Workflows — 9
- 1.1 Understanding Kubernetes Fundamentals — 10
- 1.2 What is Argo Workflows? — 14
- 1.3 Argo Workflows in the Ecosystem — 18
- 1.4 Key Benefits of Using Argo Workflows — 21
- 1.5 Comparing Traditional Workflow Tools with Argo — 25
- 1.6 Industry Adoption and Use Cases — 29

2 Setting Up Your Environment: Kubernetes and Argo — 35
- 2.1 Installing Kubernetes Locally — 36
- 2.2 Deploying Kubernetes in the Cloud — 39
- 2.3 Getting Started with kubectl — 43
- 2.4 Installing and Configuring Argo Workflows — 48
- 2.5 Exploring the Argo CLI — 53
- 2.6 Verifying Your Setup — 58

3 Understanding Argo Workflow Concepts — 65
- 3.1 Basic Workflow Terminology — 65
- 3.2 Argo Workflow Architecture — 70

3.3 Defining Templates and Tasks 76
3.4 Using Parameters and Artifacts 81
3.5 Conditional Execution and Loops 88
3.6 Events and Signals in Argo Workflows 94
3.7 Visualization and Management with Argo UI 100

4 Creating Your First Argo Workflow — 107
4.1 Setting the Stage for Your First Workflow 107
4.2 Defining a Simple Workflow Template 111
4.3 Submitting Your Workflow to Kubernetes 116
4.4 Monitoring Workflow Execution 120
4.5 Handling Errors and Retries 124
4.6 Exploring Workflow Status and Outputs 129
4.7 Iterating and Improving Your Workflow 134

5 Managing Data Pipelines with Argo — 141
5.1 Understanding Data Pipelines 141
5.2 Designing Workflows for Data Pipelines 145
5.3 Managing Data Flow with Parameters and Artifacts . . 150
5.4 Scheduling Data Pipelines 155
5.5 Implementing ETL Processes 159
5.6 Data Validation and Quality Checks 164
5.7 Integrating External Data Sources 169

6 Advanced Workflow Features and Patterns — 175
6.1 Parallel Task Execution 175
6.2 Workflow DAG Patterns 180
6.3 Using Workflow Templates 186
6.4 Retry Strategies and Error Handling 193

CONTENTS

    6.5   Workflow Resumability and Recovery 199

    6.6   Multi-Step Workflow Synchronization 204

7 Integrating Argo Workflows with CI/CD Pipelines   211

    7.1   Understanding CI/CD and Its Importance 212

    7.2   Role of Argo Workflows in CI/CD 215

    7.3   Setting Up a CI/CD Environment 219

    7.4   Automating Builds and Tests with Argo 224

    7.5   Continuous Deployment with Argo 230

    7.6   Integrating Argo with Popular CI/CD Tools 236

    7.7   Managing Environment Configurations 240

8 Monitoring and Debugging Argo Workflows   247

    8.1   Essential Monitoring Practices 248

    8.2   Using Argo UI for Monitoring 251

    8.3   Configuring Alerts and Notifications 254

    8.4   Debugging Failed Workflows 256

    8.5   Leveraging Workflow Logs 259

    8.6   Integrating Third-Party Monitoring Tools 262

    8.7   Optimizing Workflow Performance 265

9 Security and Best Practices in Argo Workflows   269

    9.1   Understanding Security in Argo Workflows 270

    9.2   Securing Workflow Credentials 274

    9.3   Role-Based Access Control (RBAC) in Argo 278

    9.4   Network Policies and Isolation 282

    9.5   Best Practices for Workflow Design 286

    9.6   Audit Logging and Compliance 291

    9.7   Securing Data in Transit and at Rest 296

10 Real-World Use Cases and Examples · · · · · · · · · · · · · · 301
10.1 Data Processing and ETL Pipelines 301
10.2 Machine Learning Model Training 306
10.3 Microservices and Serverless Orchestration 310
10.4 Continuous Deployment in Production 315
10.5 Compliance and Auditing Automation 320
10.6 Batch Processing and Scheduling 325
10.7 Real-Time Data Streaming Pipelines 329

Introduction

In the rapidly transforming landscape of cloud-native development, automation and efficiency have emerged as essential elements in managing modern infrastructure and applications. Kubernetes, a trailblazing open-source platform, has redefined how organizations deploy and scale containerized workloads and services, enabling tremendous advancements in operational efficiency. As Kubernetes becomes more prevalent, the need for a robust orchestration engine capable of managing workflows and data pipelines natively within this ecosystem has grown exponentially. In this setting, Argo Workflows has emerged as a frontrunner, providing precise and powerful orchestration capabilities.

Argo Workflows is a Kubernetes-native engine designed with the flexibility and scalability needed to define, execute, and manage complex workflows directly on Kubernetes. By aligning with the volatile and dynamic nature of cloud infrastructures, Argo Workflows introduces effective automation, opening doors to operational excellence and innovative solutions. The book "Mastering Argo Workflows: Advanced Techniques for Kubernetes-Native Pipeline Automation" endeavors to provide a deep dive into this powerful tool, connecting Kubernetes users with the sophisticated automation offered by Argo Workflows.

Structured to cater to both novice and seasoned practitioners alike, this book aims to impart a holistic understanding of Argo Workflows, while honing the reader's skills in utilizing this tool to its full potential. It begins with a thorough review of Kubernetes and the foundational principles of Argo Workflows, ensuring readers have the necessary groundwork before progressing to more advanced topics. From setup processes to the development of fundamental workflows, the book meticulously leads readers through the essentials. Special attention is given to the integration of Argo Workflows into data pipelines and continuous integration/continuous deployment (CI/CD) frameworks, underscoring the tool's versatility and the substantial efficiency benefits it brings.

As readers advance through the content, they are introduced to more sophisticated techniques in Argo Workflows. This includes exploration of various workflow patterns, strategies for parallel task executions, and methods for dynamic workflow generation. Critical aspects such as security, monitoring, and debugging are addressed comprehensively, equipping readers with the knowledge required to maintain and troubleshoot workflows effectively in production environments. The inclusion of real-world use cases serves to illustrate the practical applications of Argo Workflows across diverse sectors, enabling readers to contextualize and implement the concepts and strategies discussed in the book.

Ultimately, "Mastering Argo Workflows: Advanced Techniques for Kubernetes-Native Pipeline Automation" aspires to stand as a definitive guide for those seeking to master Kubernetes-native workflow orchestration through Argo Workflows. Blending in-depth technical discussion with actionable insights, this book empowers readers to unleash the full potential of Argo Workflows, optimizing and automating their workflows within the expansive Kubernetes landscape.

Chapter 1

Introduction to Kubernetes and Argo Workflows

Kubernetes and Argo Workflows are essential components in modern cloud-native ecosystems, enabling efficient management and automation of containerized applications and complex workflows. This chapter lays the foundation by exploring Kubernetes fundamentals, which include clusters, nodes, pods, and services, to provide a clear understanding of how these elements work together. It also highlights the role and significance of Argo Workflows in orchestrating tasks within Kubernetes environments, focusing on their deployment and execution advantages. By examining how Argo integrates within the broader Kubernetes ecosystem, this chapter sets the stage for appreciating the technological synergy that supports scalable, automated data pipeline orchestration.

1.1 Understanding Kubernetes Fundamentals

Kubernetes has become a cornerstone in cloud-native infrastructure, offering a robust platform for deploying, scaling, and managing containerized applications. Understanding its fundamental components is crucial for leveraging its full potential. This section delves into the core elements of Kubernetes, namely clusters, nodes, pods, and services, forming the basis for comprehending advanced tools like Argo Workflows.

A Kubernetes cluster is the backbone of a Kubernetes deployment, encapsulating an entire ecosystem within which applications run. A cluster comprises two main parts: the control plane and the node pool. The control plane is responsible for maintaining the desired state of the cluster, making decisions regarding the deployment, and managing the lifecycle of applications. It consists of components such as the API server, etcd, the scheduler, and the controller manager.

Nodes are the worker machines, either virtual or physical, that perform the tasks assigned by the control plane. Each node contains the necessary services to run certain containers, such as the kubelet, a container runtime, and a kube-proxy. The kubelet is a crucial component that communicates with the control plane and ensures that the containers are running in the desired state.

Pods represent the smallest deployable unit in Kubernetes. A pod can host one or more containers, which share network namespaces and storage resources. They provide a higher-level abstraction that allows users to package their applications more comprehensively. Pods hold a group of one or more tightly coupled application containers. These containers are managed together to ensure that they operate correctly and can scale successfully.

In a Kubernetes setup, services facilitate the communication between different pods. They provide stable endpoints by abstracting the set of pods and other resources, keeping the communication seamless even as Kubernetes dynamically schedules or reschedules containers across nodes. Services are often exposed through LoadBalancer or NodePort, offering a reliable method to direct traffic to the underlying pods.

1.1. UNDERSTANDING KUBERNETES FUNDAMENTALS

The following examples illustrate how these components interact within a Kubernetes cluster.

```
apiVersion: apps/v1
kind: Deployment
metadata:
  name: nginx-deployment
spec:
  replicas: 3
  selector:
    matchLabels:
      app: nginx
  template:
    metadata:
      labels:
        app: nginx
    spec:
      containers:
      - name: nginx
        image: nginx:1.21.3
        ports:
        - containerPort: 80
```

This deployment creates three replicas of an Nginx server. The deployment object manages the lifecycle of a set of identical pods, ensuring there are always three pods running. If one fails, the deployment will spin up a new pod to replace the failed one.

Another crucial concept is the Service, which maintains a consistent interface to a pod or group of pods. Here's how a simple service manifest might look:

```
apiVersion: v1
kind: Service
metadata:
  name: nginx-service
spec:
  selector:
    app: nginx
  ports:
    - protocol: TCP
      port: 80
      targetPort: 80
  type: LoadBalancer
```

This service manifest defines a 'LoadBalancer' that will expose the Nginx deployment to external traffic on port 80. The service selector corresponds to the labels specified in the pod template, ensuring that the correct pods receive the traffic.

The architecture of Kubernetes adopts the principle of desired state management, where the user declares the intended state of the system, and Kubernetes brings the current state into alignment with this desired condition. The Kubernetes control plane continually maintains this desired state through features like the replication controller, which is integral for scaling the number of pod replicas.

For managing configurations, Kubernetes uses ConfigMaps and Secrets. ConfigMaps allow storage of non-confidential data in key-value pairs for use within pods. Secrets, on the other hand, provide similar functionality but are suited for sensitive information, such as passwords and API keys.

```
apiVersion: v1
kind: ConfigMap
metadata:
  name: example-config
data:
  database-host: localhost
  database-port: "5432"
```

ConfigMaps can be injected into pods as environment variables, or mounted as volumes, providing a flexible mechanism for managing application configurations. The same paradigm applies to Secrets, though they require the use of base64 encoding for their values.

Networking in Kubernetes builds upon several sophisticated mechanisms to deliver seamless connectivity. The Kubernetes networking model is flat, allowing all pods to communicate with each other without network address translation (NAT). This is achieved through the use of a Container Network Interface (CNI), which is a pluggable architecture that supports multiple networking solutions like Calico, Flannel, and others.

The concept of Network Policies in Kubernetes adds a security layer, allowing users to define how pods communicate with each other and other network endpoints. With policies, you can restrict ingress or egress traffic based on rules defined by the user.

```
apiVersion: networking.k8s.io/v1
kind: NetworkPolicy
metadata:
  name: allow-nginx-ingress
spec:
  podSelector:
    matchLabels:
      app: nginx
  ingress:
```

1.1. UNDERSTANDING KUBERNETES FUNDAMENTALS

```
  - from:
    - podSelector:
        matchLabels:
          access: "true"
    ports:
    - protocol: TCP
      port: 80
```

This policy limits ingress traffic to pods labeled 'app: nginx', allowing only traffic from other pods with the label 'access: "true"'.

Storage within Kubernetes is managed using volumes. Although containers are ephemeral in nature—meaning data is lost if they crash—Kubernetes offers persistent storage options such as Persistent Volumes (PVs) and Persistent Volume Claims (PVCs). PVCs are requests for storage by a user, and PVs are pieces of storage in the cluster that have been provisioned by an administrator or dynamically provisioned using StorageClasses.

```
apiVersion: v1
kind: PersistentVolume
metadata:
  name: example-pv
spec:
  capacity:
    storage: 1Gi
  accessModes:
  - ReadWriteOnce
  persistentVolumeReclaimPolicy: Recycle
  hostPath:
    path: "/mnt/data"

---

apiVersion: v1
kind: PersistentVolumeClaim
metadata:
  name: example-pvc
spec:
  accessModes:
  - ReadWriteOnce
  resources:
    requests:
      storage: 1Gi
```

The described PV and PVC manifest provide a simple setup for persistent storage, ensuring that data replicated across pods is secure and retained independently of pod lifecycle. This is particularly pertinent in databases and stateful applications where data consistency is paramount.

Security is a critical component of Kubernetes and is maintained through various built-in mechanisms like Role-Based Access Control (RBAC), which allows administrators to tightly control who can access specific resources within the cluster. RBAC within Kubernetes lets you define fine-grained access policies by permitting users to execute only the actions they are allowed to, providing an additional layer of protection against unauthorized access.

The understanding of these components—clusters, nodes, pods, services, deployments, networking, storage, and security—is fundamental in mastering Kubernetes. Journeying through these basics equips the user to effectively deploy applications and orchestrate containers not just within a Kubernetes environment, but across a multi-cloud and hybrid deployment architecture. With Kubernetes as the underlying platform, technologies like Argo Workflows can be integrated with ease to provide scalable automation, enabling efficient management of complex workflows. These combinations emphasize the strength of Kubernetes as a versatile platform for cloud-native applications.

1.2 What is Argo Workflows?

Argo Workflows is a Kubernetes-native workflow engine designed to orchestrate parallel and distributed tasks at scale. Developed as part of the Argo Project, Argo Workflows leverages Kubernetes' inherently scalable and resilient architecture to automate the execution of complex workflows that encompass tasks varying in scale, complexity, and duration. It is particularly suited for handling use cases in machine learning, data orchestration, continuous integration/continuous deployment (CI/CD), and other complex task management scenarios.

Argo Workflows provides users with a declarative way to define workflows, allowing them to specify a sequence of tasks and their interdependencies. The workflows are defined using YAML files, which detail the sequence of steps and their conditions. Each task within a workflow is a containerized step, running within Kubernetes pods, allowing Argo to parallelize tasks when dependencies permit.

One of the fundamental concepts of Argo Workflows is the Directed Acyclic Graph (DAG), which models workflows as graphs, enabling the

1.2. WHAT IS ARGO WORKFLOWS?

expression of complex relationships between tasks. This allows workflows to encompass conditional logic, looping, and branching based on task outputs.

```yaml
apiVersion: argoproj.io/v1alpha1
kind: Workflow
metadata:
  generateName: hello-world-
spec:
  entrypoint: hello-world
  templates:
  - name: hello-world
    dag:
      tasks:
      - name: hello
        template: whalesay
      - name: world
        dependencies: [hello]
        template: whalesay

  - name: whalesay
    container:
      image: docker/whalesay
      command: [cowsay]
      args: ["hello world"]
```

In the above workflow, the task 'world' is dependent on the successful execution of the 'hello' task, forming a basic DAG. Each task is linked to a template that defines a containerized execution environment.

Argo Workflows provides advanced features like artifact management, parameterization, and cron scheduling, enhancing its utility for complex applications. Artifacts, such as files or data sets used or produced by workflows, are managed through an artifact repository, often using solutions like Amazon S3 or Google Cloud Storage. Artifacts from one task can be used in subsequent tasks, facilitating data continuity and integration.

```yaml
apiVersion: argoproj.io/v1alpha1
kind: Workflow
metadata:
  generateName: artifact-example-
spec:
  entrypoint: artifact-example
  templates:
  - name: artifact-example
    dag:
      tasks:
      - name: generate-artifact
        template: generate
      - name: use-artifact
        dependencies: [generate-artifact]
```

```
            template: use
            arguments:
              artifacts:
              - name: message
                from: "{{tasks.generate-artifact.outputs.artifacts.message}}"
    - name: generate
      container:
        image: alpine
        command: [sh, -c]
        args: ["echo 'Hello, Argo!' > /tmp/message"]
      outputs:
        artifacts:
        - name: message
          path: /tmp/message
    - name: use
      container:
        image: alpine
        command: [sh, -c]
        args: ["cat /tmp/message"]
      inputs:
        artifacts:
        - name: message
          path: /tmp/message
```

This workflow generates a message in the 'generate' task and consumes it in the 'use' task, demonstrating the use of artifacts in Argo Workflows. Parameterization allows workflows to adapt based on inputs provided at runtime, enhancing flexibility and reusability.

Argo Workflows are run within the context of a Kubernetes namespace, and they integrate seamlessly with Kubernetes-native security and permissions. Role-Based Access Control (RBAC) is often configured to control permission to execute or modify workflows, ensuring that only authorized users and services can initiate workflows or manage resources.

Argo Workflows also support cron scheduling, enabling workflows to be triggered on a regular interval, similar to traditional cron jobs in Unix systems. This makes it ideal for tasks that need to be executed periodically or on a defined schedule.

```
apiVersion: argoproj.io/v1alpha1
kind: CronWorkflow
metadata:
  name: hello-cron
spec:
  schedule: "0 * * * *" % Runs every hour
  workflowSpec:
    entrypoint: whalesay
```

1.2. WHAT IS ARGO WORKFLOWS?

```
templates:
- name: whalesay
  container:
    image: docker/whalesay
    command: [cowsay]
    args: ["Automation made simple!"]
```

This manifest schedules a 'CronWorkflow' to run every hour. Cron workflows are managed by the Kubernetes operator for Argo, which schedules jobs based on the defined cron expression.

During execution, Argo provides detailed status information and logs, which can be accessed via the Argo CLI or web interface. This monitoring capability simplifies troubleshooting and ensures workflow transparency, offering a clear overview of workflow progression and potential issues.

Operating in a Kubernetes-controlled environment, Argo Workflows benefit from Kubernetes' intrinsic scalability and reliability features, such as auto-scaling nodes as needed and ensuring application resilience through redundancy and failover practices.

The ability to integrate with a cloud-native infrastructure equips Argo Workflows with elastic capabilities, where additional compute resources and services can be provisioned dynamically to accommodate workflow demands. This autonomy greatly enhances compute resource utilization, reducing operational overhead while ensuring continual system performance and responsiveness.

Managing complex workflows often requires integration with various services, data sources, and external APIs. Argo Workflows provides custom resource definitions (CRDs) and hooks that allow seamless integration and interaction with these external components, providing ample flexibility to implement complex, multi-step tasks.

Argo Workflows' design and approach are informed by microservices and containerization principles, making it not only a tool for orchestrating workflows but also a catalyst for embracing a cloud-native ethos. Its architectural decisions reflect an alignment with goals of strategic automation, empowering DevOps teams to define, execute, and manage task pipelines intuitively.

In summary, Argo Workflows empowers organizations to harness the power of Kubernetes for workflow automation by providing a robust, flexible system to define operational dependencies and task orchestration. It caters to modern application needs where reliability, scalability, and automation are paramount. By integrating deeply with Kubernetes, Argo Workflow stands as a testament to the potential of microservice-driven cloud-native solutions, paving the way for efficient, automated infrastructure and application management. This makes it an invaluable tool in the evolving toolkit of cloud-native technologies.

1.3 Argo Workflows in the Ecosystem

Argo Workflows plays a pivotal role within the Kubernetes ecosystem, providing a versatile toolset that integrates and extends the capabilities of Kubernetes for orchestrating complex, distributed tasks. This section examines how Argo Workflows complements the existing Kubernetes infrastructure, alongside its interplay with other tools and solutions that form the backbone of modern cloud-native environments.

First and foremost, Argo Workflows is a Kubernetes-native workflow engine, leveraging the intrinsic features of Kubernetes, such as its distributed architecture, scalability, and resource management capabilities. By utilizing Kubernetes as its underlying platform, Argo allows for seamless deployment and scaling of workflows, capitalizing on the cluster's dynamic scheduling and networking features. This native integration ensures that Argo Workflows naturally aligns with Kubernetes' operational paradigms, providing an out-of-the-box solution for automating complex workflows without necessitating an additional layer of infrastructure management.

Argo Workflows integrates closely with Kubernetes' scheduling capabilities, permitting the orchestration of tasks that require varying computational resources. This is especially beneficial for organizations deploying machine learning models, big data processing tasks, or CI/CD pipelines, as their computational demands can dynamically fluctuate. By utilizing Kubernetes' horizontal pod autoscaler, workflows can automatically scale to accommodate spikes in resource needs, ensuring efficient load distribution and optimal resource utilization.

In addition, Argo Workflows interacts seamlessly with other components of the Kubernetes ecosystem. One such integration is with Prometheus, a popular open-source monitoring and alerting toolkit. By incorporating Prometheus, users can track and monitor the performance and health of their workflows in real time, setting up alerts for potential issues to intervene promptly. Prometheus metrics can be exposed using exporters within Argo tasks, providing detailed insights into task execution times, resource consumption, and failure rates. This monitoring capability is crucial for maintaining high availability and reliability in production environments.

Moreover, Argo Workflows can be augmented with Istio, a service mesh that provides a uniform way to secure, connect, and observe microservices. Istio allows for advanced networking capabilities, such as intelligent traffic routing, load balancing, and comprehensive telemetry, which can bolster Argo's workflow capabilities by providing reliable service-to-service communications and enhanced tracing within interconnected tasks. The synergy between Argo Workflows and Istio is particularly evident in complex microservices architectures where fine-grained control over network behaviors is required.

In addition to these integrations, Argo Workflows often collaborates with cloud-native storage solutions to manage artifacts and data continuity across workflows. Solutions such as MinIO or Ceph provide high-performance object storage that integrates well with Kubernetes, enabling efficient data handling from one task to the next. Using these storage solutions, Argo Workflows can maintain a consistent data layer, ensuring tasks executing within different nodes can access the data they need seamlessly.

Argo Workflows' extensibility is further exemplified through its collaboration with Tekton, a Kubernetes-native CI/CD pipeline tool. This integration highlights Argo Workflows' versatility in managing diverse use cases within the DevOps pipeline. While Tekton provides a focused approach to CI/CD with its task and pipeline abstraction, Argo Workflows can manage broader, more complex workflows involving multi-step dependencies beyond CI/CD, serving as a higher-level orchestrator in heterogeneous environments.

An illustrative example of an Argo workflow integrated with Tekton can be showcased as follows:

```
apiVersion: argoproj.io/v1alpha1
```

```yaml
kind: Workflow
metadata:
  generateName: tekton-pipeline-
spec:
  entrypoint: tekton-ci
  templates:
  - name: tekton-ci
    steps:
    - - name: clone-repo
        template: clone
    - - name: build-image
        template: build
      - name: deploy
        template: deploy

  - name: clone
    container:
      image: bitnami/git
      command: [sh, -c]
      args: ["git clone https://github.com/org/repo.git /workspace"]

  - name: build
    container:
      image: kaniko-project/executor:latest
      command:
      - /kaniko/executor
      args:
      - "--dockerfile=/workspace/Dockerfile"
      - "--context=/workspace"
      - "--destination=registry/repo:latest"

  - name: deploy
    container:
      image: kubectl
      command: ["kubectl", "apply", "-f", "/workspace/deployment.yaml"]
```

This manifest defines a workflow comprising three steps: 'clone-repo', 'build-image', and 'deploy'. It utilizes tools like Kaniko for building container images in a Kubernetes-native way, demonstrating how Argo Workflows can facilitate CI/CD alongside Tekton's specialized tasks.

Argo Workflows is also pivotal in machine learning workflows where data preprocessing, model training, and validation tasks can be time-intensive and resource-demanding. Integrating with machine learning platforms such as Kubeflow, which provides machine learning operations (MLOps) orchestration on Kubernetes, Argo Workflows enables reproducible and scalable ML pipelines. Through this integration, Argo plays a strategic role in building, training, and deploying ML models efficiently.

Furthermore, Argo Workflows can form part of a broader observability solution when integrated with Elastic Stack (ELK) or other log management tools, enabling teams to perform detailed log analysis and troubleshooting. These integrations ensure capturing detailed execution logs and other critical data related to workflow execution, which can be further enhanced using visualization tools like Grafana for graphical representation and dashboards.

In security contexts, Argo Workflows align with tools like Open Policy Agent (OPA), which provide policy-based control points in the cloud-native infrastructure. Using OPA, organizations can enforce policies that limit or restrict task executions based on various criteria, enhancing security and compliance.

The evolution of Argo Workflows and its seamless integration within the Kubernetes ecosystem illustrate its adaptability and robustness. It effectively simplifies orchestration, improves operational efficiency, and allows developers and operations teams to focus on developing value-driven applications rather than managing complex infrastructure.

Embracing Argo Workflows means adopting a cloud-native mindset wherein workflows can be abstracted from the underlying hardware and location dependencies. The combination of Kubernetes' orchestration with Argo's workflow engine provides a strong foundation for developing resilient, scalable applications, and contributes to a harmonious and efficient ecosystem suitable for modern application demands. By offering a comprehensive solution for integrating critical components and managing complex workflows in cloud-native environments, Argo Workflows exemplifies the innovations within the Kubernetes ecosystem that continue to drive transformative improvements across technology stacks globally.

1.4 Key Benefits of Using Argo Workflows

Argo Workflows stands out as a robust Kubernetes-native workflow orchestrator, offering a myriad of benefits that streamline the management of complex processing tasks in cloud-native environments. Its design and capabilities provide several crucial advantages that cater to modern application needs, enhancing productivity, resource efficiency, and operational simplicity. This section elucidates these benefits, providing detailed insights into why Argo Workflows has captured widespread adoption in numerous technical domains.

One of the foremost benefits of Argo Workflows is its seamless integration with Kubernetes, capitalizing on Kubernetes' inherent capabilities for container orchestration. This integration allows Argo Workflows to leverage Kubernetes' robust scheduling, resource management, and auto-scaling features, providing workflows with a resilient backbone that can dynamically adapt to workload fluctuations. The distributed nature of Kubernetes ensures that workflow tasks can be scaled horizontally without compromising performance or reliability, making it possible to handle large-scale, compute-intensive processes effectively.

This Kubernetes-native architecture of Argo Workflows translates to a consistent, unified environment where infrastructure and application-level workflows coexist without the need for disparate management systems. Having workflows run directly on Kubernetes offers the advantage of simplifying infrastructure management while empowering teams to define repeatable processes that are independent of specific hardware or cloud providers.

Another significant advantage of Argo Workflows is its declarative configuration through YAML manifests. This approach aligns with the Infrastructure as Code (IaC) paradigm, allowing complex workflows to be described, versioned, and shared akin to application code. The declarative syntax simplifies the maintenance and evolution of workflows, facilitating collaboration among development and operations teams. YAML templates provide users the flexibility to define multi-step processes with conditional logic, loops, and parameterization, creating sophisticated workflows that can meet specific application requirements.

Below is an example demonstrating the declarative nature of Argo Workflows with advanced parameterization:

```yaml
apiVersion: argoproj.io/v1alpha1
kind: Workflow
metadata:
  generateName: parameterized-workflow-
spec:
  entrypoint: parameter-example
  arguments:
    parameters:
    - name: message
```

1.4. KEY BENEFITS OF USING ARGO WORKFLOWS

```
    value: "Welcome to Argo Workflows"
templates:
- name: parameter-example
  inputs:
    parameters:
    - name: message
  container:
    image: alpine
    command: ["sh", "-c"]
    args: ["echo {{inputs.parameters.message}}"]
```

This example showcases how parameters can be passed into workflows, allowing for dynamic modification of execution behavior based on provided inputs, thus increasing reusability and clarity.

Argo Workflows offers unparalleled scalability, a critical factor as enterprises expand and their processing demands grow. Efficiently managing workloads across a distributed architecture requires tools that can provision resources dynamically, minimizing waste while maximizing throughput. The ability of Argo Workflows to scale with Kubernetes ensures that resources are optimized according to task requirements, minimizing overhead and enabling seamless handling of both routine and peak loads.

In addition to scalability, Argo Workflows supports a high degree of automation. Automation is a cornerstone of cloud-native architectures, reducing the overhead of manual intervention and enabling rapid iteration. Through features like cron-based scheduling and event-driven triggers, Argo Workflows can automate complex processes, from ETL pipelines and machine learning model training to CI/CD deployments.

```
apiVersion: argoproj.io/v1alpha1
kind: CronWorkflow
metadata:
  name: nightly-data-pipeline
spec:
  schedule: "0 0 * * *" # Executes daily at midnight
  workflowSpec:
    entrypoint: data-pipeline
    templates:
    - name: data-pipeline
      steps:
      - - name: extract
          template: data-extract
      - - name: transform
          template: data-transform
      - - name: load
          template: data-load

    - name: data-extract
```

```
        container:
          image: company/data-tool
          command: ["extract"]
      - name: data-transform
        container:
          image: company/data-tool
          command: ["transform"]
      - name: data-load
        container:
          image: company/data-tool
          command: ["load"]
```

This CronWorkflow defines a nightly data pipeline that automates data extraction, transformation, and loading processes, illustrating how scheduling ensures regular execution without manual input.

Argo Workflows also excels in terms of agility and developer productivity. By abstracting complex orchestration logic and providing an intuitive user interface, including a web-based dashboard, Argo accelerates the development cycle. Developers can visualize task dependencies and track execution status in real-time, facilitating rapid feedback and reducing the mean time to resolve issues (MTTR).

Through self-service capabilities and ease of use, Argo Workflows enhances the ability of teams to innovate without waiting for dedicated resources or infrastructure provisioning. This developer-centric approach empowers technical teams to rapidly prototype and deploy workflows, accelerating the time to market for new features and applications.

The declarative syntax and self-documenting nature of Argo Workflows also contribute to better governance and compliance. By providing a clear, auditable record of all workflow definitions and changes over time, Argo supports audit trails, version history analysis, and compliance verification. This is particularly valuable in regulated industries where operational transparency and traceability are mandatory.

Integration capabilities, including APIs and event hooks, further extend the scope of Argo Workflows, connecting it with a variety of tools and platforms. This interoperability ensures that Argo can serve as a foundational component within broader enterprise ecosystems, engaging with CI/CD tools, logging and monitoring services, external databases, and data lakes. By enabling such connections, Argo enhances overall system architecture, offering flexibility and choice in technology decisions while meeting diverse operational policies and integration needs.

In summary, the benefits of Argo Workflows are multifaceted, addressing critical requirements in modern, dynamic environments. Its Kubernetes-native approach aligns it closely with the cloud-native ethos, delivering benefits in resource efficiency, scalability, and automation. Through its elegant, declarative configuration and advanced capabilities, Argo Workflows empowers teams to manage complex tasks seamlessly, enhancing productivity and accelerating the pace of innovation. The flexibility and robustness of its design make it a compelling choice for organizations seeking efficient, scalable, and agile workflow orchestration for cloud-native applications and beyond.

1.5 Comparing Traditional Workflow Tools with Argo

The evolution of workflow orchestration tools has marked a significant shift from traditional, monolithic solutions to modern, containerized, and cloud-native paradigms like Argo Workflows. Understanding the distinctions between traditional workflow automation tools and Argo Workflows is essential for appreciating the benefits Argo brings to modern infrastructure. This section provides a detailed comparative analysis, highlighting the strengths and weaknesses of each approach and demonstrating why Argo Workflows offers compelling advantages in cloud-native environments.

Traditional workflow automation tools, such as Apache Airflow, Jenkins, and Luigi, have long been the backbone of task scheduling and orchestration. These tools were designed to automate and streamline complex tasks and data pipelines, often within the confines of static, on-premise infrastructure. They have been instrumental in handling large-scale data processing tasks, ETL pipelines, and continuous integration and deployment (CI/CD) processes.

Apache Airflow, for instance, is a widely used platform for programmatically authoring, scheduling, and monitoring workflows. It provides flexibility through Python-based DAGs, enabling users to define task dependencies and automate scripts. Airflow excels at orchestrating batch processing tasks, with a strong community supporting its extensive plugin system.

On the other hand, Jenkins is predominantly used for CI/CD automation, providing numerous plugins to integrate with different development infrastructure components. Jenkins is particularly known for its powerful pipeline-as-code feature, which allows users to define build and deployment processes using domain-specific language.

Despite their strengths, traditional workflow tools have several limitations in the face of modern, cloud-native applications:

- Infrastructure Dependency: Traditional tools often require dedicated infrastructure, which can lead to inefficiencies in resource utilization and scaling limitations. Scaling these applications typically involves provisioning additional hardware or virtual machines, which is not inherently dynamic or efficient.

- Complex Management: Configuring and managing these tools can be complex, requiring specialized knowledge and integration overhead. Managing dependencies and ensuring reliability in stateful, distributed environments can present significant challenges.

- Limited Flexibility in Dynamic Environments: These tools can struggle with the demands for dynamic scaling and resilience required by modern applications, leading to potential shortcomings in handling peak loads or orchestrating microservices-based architectures.

Argo Workflows, as a Kubernetes-native solution, addresses these challenges by inherently aligning with the cloud-native paradigm. The advantages it offers over traditional tools include:

- Kubernetes-Native Operations: As part of the Kubernetes ecosystem, Argo Workflows leverages the full power of Kubernetes for task scheduling, scaling, and resource management. This ensures that workflows can naturally scale with application demands, providing inherent resilience and reliability. Pods can

1.5. COMPARING TRADITIONAL WORKFLOW TOOLS WITH ARGO

be provisioned dynamically, driven by Kubernetes' orchestration logic, ensuring optimal resource utilization.

- Declarative Configuration: Traditional tools often have procedural configuration environments that can be complex to manage. Argo Workflows employs a declarative approach using YAML manifests, simplifying the complexity involved in defining workflows. This model aligns with Infrastructure as Code (IaC) principles, facilitating versioning, auditing, and maintenance.

```
apiVersion: argoproj.io/v1alpha1
kind: Workflow
metadata:
  generateName: simple-workflow-
spec:
  entrypoint: main
  templates:
  - name: main
    steps:
    - - name: step1
        template: myscript

  - name: myscript
    script:
      image: python:3.7
      command: ["python"]
      source: |
        print("Hello from Argo Workflows!")
```

- Elastic Scalability: Unlike traditional tools, which may require manual adjustments for scaling, Argo Workflows benefits from the elastic scalability inherent to Kubernetes. This elasticity ensures that workflows can handle changes in load without requiring manual intervention, thereby supporting the efficient handling of both spikes and nadirs in demand.

- Simplicity: Argo Workflows is designed to be easy to use, with an intuitive interface and clear logging and error-tracking features. Traditional tools may require extensive configuration and integration effort, whereas the seamless integration of Argo Workflow with Kubernetes simplifies deployment and monitoring.

- Microservices and Container Support: In stark contrast to traditional monolithic architectures, Argo Workflows' design is microservice-oriented, and it seamlessly orchestrates containerized tasks using Docker containers. This model aligns with modern software design methodologies and deployment strategies, supporting agility and scalability across distributed systems.

- Automated Management: Features such as cron-based scheduling, event-driven workflows, and retry policies allow Argo Workflows to manage recurring tasks and handle failures transparently. This enhances the automation of multi-step processes and reduces the need for manual oversight or intervention.

```
apiVersion: argoproj.io/v1alpha1
kind: Workflow
metadata:
  generateName: retry-workflow-
spec:
  entrypoint: retry-example
  templates:
  - name: retry-example
    retryStrategy:
      limit: 3
    container:
      image: alpine
      command: ["sh", "-c"]
      args: ["exit 1"]
```

- Cloud-Native Paradigm: Argo Workflows is fully aligned with cloud-native principles, allowing organizations to adopt hybrid and multi-cloud strategies without being tethered to particular infrastructure or platforms. This accelerates digital transformation initiatives and supports cloud-first directives.

- Community and Ecosystem: Argo Workflows benefits from a vibrant open-source community and ecosystem, driving innovation and rapid iteration. This community-driven model ensures a steady flow of enhancements, support, and integrations with other cloud-native tools like Prometheus for monitoring, Jaeger for tracing, and Istio for service mesh capabilities.

While traditional tools have carved out indispensable roles in many organizations, particularly for legacy applications, Argo Workflows provides a forward-looking architecture that meets the demands of present-day development and operations environments. The key differences between the two paradigms underscore a shift towards more dynamic, resilient, and cloud-native infrastructure practices that modernize application delivery.

This comparison ultimately highlights the capacity of Argo Workflows to support organizations in adopting cloud-native practices and leveraging Kubernetes' robust architecture. As businesses continue to migrate and modernize their infrastructure to take full advantage of microservices and containerization, Argo Workflows provides a strategic advantage, empowering them to orchestrate complex workflows with efficiency, scalability, and resilience in mind. This brings an indispensable transformation to enterprise technology strategies, driving future-ready operations across diverse industries.

1.6 Industry Adoption and Use Cases

Argo Workflows has witnessed significant adoption across various industries, reflecting its versatility and effectiveness as a workflow orchestration tool in cloud-native environments. Its integration into different sectors highlights both its adaptability and the breadth of use cases it supports. This section explores the industry's embrace of Argo Workflows and delves into specific applications that illustrate its transformative impact.

- **1. Financial Services and Fintech**

    In the financial sector, Argo Workflows is employed to automate complex data pipelines and enhance the efficiency of financial transaction processing. Financial institutions often deal with vast amounts of data that require processing for activities such as fraud detection, risk modeling, and compliance checks. Argo Workflows can orchestrate these processes by running parallel tasks, optimizing data throughput, and reducing latency.

- **Use Case Example: Fraud Detection Pipeline**

    Large banks and fintech companies use Argo Workflows to manage fraud detection systems. Here's a simplified version illustrating a typical fraud detection pipeline:

    ```
    apiVersion: argoproj.io/v1alpha1
    kind: Workflow
    ```

```yaml
metadata:
  generateName: fraud-detection-
spec:
  entrypoint: detect-fraud
  templates:
  - name: detect-fraud
    steps:
    - - name: data-ingestion
        template: mysql-ingest
    - - name: data-preprocessing
        template: data-preprocess
    - - name: model-predict
        template: fraud-model
    - - name: alert-trigger
        template: send-alert

  - name: mysql-ingest
    container:
      image: mysql
      command: ["mysql", "-u", "user", "-p", "database", "-e", "SQL
        QUERY"]

  - name: data-preprocess
    container:
      image: data-prep-image
      command: ["data-prep-script.sh"]

  - name: fraud-model
    container:
      image: predict-image
      command: ["predict-script.sh"]

  - name: send-alert
    container:
      image: alert-image
      command: ["alert-script.sh"]
```

In this workflow, Argo coordinates tasks from data ingestion to alert generation, optimizing each step of the pipeline for speed and accuracy.

- **2. Biotechnology and Healthcare**

The biotechnology and healthcare industries leverage Argo Workflows for applications ranging from genome sequencing to clinical data analysis. The power and scalability offered by Argo are crucial for handling large datasets inherent in these fields.

- **Use Case Example: Genome Sequencing**

Genome sequencing involves analyzing extensive genomic datasets, a process that can be simplified and accelerated by

1.6. INDUSTRY ADOPTION AND USE CASES

orchestrating tasks using Argo Workflows. Specific tasks such as data alignment, variant calling, and results annotation can run in parallel, significantly reducing time to insight.

```yaml
apiVersion: argoproj.io/v1alpha1
kind: Workflow
metadata:
  generateName: genome-sequencing-
spec:
  entrypoint: sequence
  templates:
  - name: sequence
    steps:
    - - name: align-sequences
        template: align
    - - name: call-variants
        template: variant-calling
    - - name: annotate-results
        template: annotation

  - name: align
    container:
      image: align-image
      command: ["align-script.sh"]

  - name: variant-calling
    container:
      image: variant-image
      command: ["variant-script.sh"]

  - name: annotation
    container:
      image: annotation-image
      command: ["annotation-script.sh"]
```

Argo Workflows helps streamline the computational pipeline for genome sequencing, ensuring results are obtained rapidly and accurately.

- **3. Media and Entertainment**

  In the media and entertainment industry, Argo Workflows is used for tasks such as video processing, transcoding, and rendering. The ability to handle high-volume tasks with reliability makes Argo a favored tool for large-scale content production and distribution.

- **Use Case Example: Video Transcoding Pipeline**

  Streaming services and animation studios use Argo Workflows to automate the video transcoding process, converting content into multiple formats for distribution across various platforms.

```yaml
apiVersion: argoproj.io/v1alpha1
kind: Workflow
metadata:
  generateName: video-transcode-
spec:
  entrypoint: transcode
  templates:
  - name: transcode
    steps:
    - - name: extract-frames
        template: extract
    - - name: transcode-mp4
        template: mp4
    - - name: transcode-webm
        template: webm

  - name: extract
    container:
      image: vidtools
      command: ["frame-extract.sh"]

  - name: mp4
    container:
      image: vidtools
      command: ["transcoder", "mp4"]

  - name: webm
    container:
      image: vidtools
      command: ["transcoder", "webm"]
```

This workflow enables efficient transcoding by distributing tasks across multiple worker pods, ensuring quick turnaround for large volumes of video content.

- **4. Retail and E-commerce**

The retail and e-commerce sectors use Argo Workflows for data-driven decision-making processes, including price optimization, demand forecasting, and customer segmentation. Automation of these processes is vital for improving response times and enhancing service quality.

- **Use Case Example: Demand Forecasting Pipeline**

Retailers automate demand forecasting by orchestrating data aggregation, model training, and result generation as separate steps in a workflow.

```yaml
apiVersion: argoproj.io/v1alpha1
kind: Workflow
```

1.6. INDUSTRY ADOPTION AND USE CASES

```
metadata:
  generateName: demand-forecasting-
spec:
  entrypoint: forecast
  templates:
  - name: forecast
    steps:
    - - name: aggregate-sales-data
        template: sales-aggregation
    - - name: train-forecast-model
        template: model-training
    - - name: generate-forecast
        template: forecast-generation

  - name: sales-aggregation
    container:
      image: data-analytics
      command: ["aggregate-sales.sh"]

  - name: model-training
    container:
      image: ml-tools
      command: ["train-forecast.sh"]

  - name: forecast-generation
    container:
      image: ml-tools
      command: ["generate-forecast.sh"]
```

By breaking the forecast process into modular steps, this workflow allows for efficient scaling and adaptation to changing data patterns.

- **5. Telecommunication**

  The telecommunications industry uses Argo Workflows for network monitoring, incident response automation, and resource optimization tasks. Argo's ability to trigger workflows based on certain conditions or events makes it ideal for real-time monitoring and response.

- **Use Case Example: Network Fault Detection and Response**

  Telecommunication companies automate the detection and resolution of network faults using Argo Workflows. When a network anomaly is detected, a workflow triggers a sequence of monitoring and remediation actions.

```
apiVersion: argoproj.io/v1alpha1
kind: Workflow
```

```yaml
metadata:
  generateName: network-remediation-
spec:
  entrypoint: remediate
  templates:
  - name: remediate
    steps:
    - - name: analyze-network-logs
        template: log-analysis
    - - name: diagnose-issue
        template: diagnose
    - - name: apply-fix
        template: fix

  - name: log-analysis
    container:
      image: log-analyzer
      command: ["analyze-logs.sh"]

  - name: diagnose
    container:
      image: diagnosis-tool
      command: ["diagnose-issue.sh"]

  - name: fix
    container:
      image: remediation-tool
      command: ["apply-fix.sh"]
```

This pipeline ensures that network issues are rapidly identified and addressed, minimizing downtime and service interruptions.

- **Conclusion**

Throughout these use cases, Argo Workflows provides organizations with the tools necessary to streamline complex, resource-intensive processes, optimize workflows for efficiency and speed, and ensure reliable operation across diverse infrastructure environments. Its integration into varied industries underscores its versatility and adaptability, making it an indispensable component in the evolving landscape of cloud-native operations. Each application highlights Argo's strength in enhancing automation and providing scalable, reliable solutions that empower businesses to innovate and compete in the digital age.

Chapter 2

Setting Up Your Environment: Kubernetes and Argo

This chapter provides a step-by-step guide to establishing a robust environment for running Kubernetes and Argo Workflows, crucial for executing automated workflows. Starting with the installation of Kubernetes locally and on cloud platforms, it ensures readers can seamlessly deploy clusters suited to their needs. The chapter further introduces the essential command-line tool, kubectl, for managing Kubernetes resources effectively. A detailed process for installing and configuring Argo Workflows follows, enabling readers to leverage its full capabilities. Additionally, the chapter covers the Argo CLI, enhancing user interaction with workflows, and culminates with methods for verifying the environment setup, addressing potential configuration issues.

2.1 Installing Kubernetes Locally

The process of setting up a local Kubernetes environment serves as the foundational step for developers and administrators aiming to experiment with or deploy applications within containerized infrastructures. This section elucidates the installation of a local Kubernetes cluster using popular tools such as Minikube and Kind. Each tool provides unique benefits, catering to various use cases and preferences. By understanding the installation and setup procedures, readers will equip themselves with the essential groundwork needed for deploying Kubernetes applications, specifically preparing for subsequent Argo Workflows deployment.

Minikube and Kind enable users to run Kubernetes clusters locally within a single node. Minikube leverages virtualization software to create a single-node Kubernetes cluster on a personal workstation, while Kind (short for Kubernetes IN Docker) runs Kubernetes clusters in Docker containers, eliminating the need for additional virtual machines.

Minikube Installation

Minikube is a popular choice for local Kubernetes development because it simplifies the setup process by orchestrating the creation of clusters on various operating systems, including Windows, macOS, and Linux. The following steps detail Minikube installation and configuration:

1. **Pre-requisites:**

    - Ensure virtualization is enabled in BIOS settings.
    - Install a compatible hypervisor such as VirtualBox or Hyper-V.

2. **Install Minikube:**

    ```
    # On Linux
    curl -LO https://storage.googleapis.com/minikube/releases/latest/minikube-linux-amd64
    sudo install minikube-linux-amd64 /usr/local/bin/minikube

    # On macOS
    ```

```
brew install minikube
# On Windows
choco install minikube
```

3. **Start Minikube:**

```
minikube start --driver=virtualbox
```

This command will initialize a Kubernetes cluster using Virtualbox as the hypervisor. Adjust the driver option if you are using a different virtualization tool.

4. **Verify Installation:**

```
kubectl version --client
kubectl get nodes
```

The output should show a single node ready within the cluster.

Kind Installation

Kind is particularly favored for testing Kubernetes clusters in Continuous Integration (CI) pipelines due to its lightweight nature and compatibility with existing Docker installations, bypassing the need for standalone virtual machines.

1. **Install Kind:**

```
GO111MODULE="on" go get sigs.k8s.io/kind@v0.17.0
```

Ensure you have Go installed and the workspace set up correctly.

2. **Create a Kubernetes Cluster using Kind:**

```
kind create cluster
```

This command will orchestrate the setup of a cluster comprised of Kubernetes nodes running within Docker containers.

3. **Verify Installation:**

```
kubectl get nodes
kind get clusters
```

As with Minikube, you should see a ready node displayed.

Both Minikube and Kind streamline the Kubernetes setup, enabling rapid iterative testing and application experimentation. Below, we further delve into a comparative analysis, evaluating their functionalities while elucidating configuration tips.

Comparative and Configuration Insights

Minikube and Kind each have features appealing to distinct aspects of local Kubernetes execution:

- **Resource Management:** Minikube often provides robust resource management through hypervisor options, allowing users to specify the CPU and memory allocations. These settings can be defined during cluster creation using flags such as –cpus and –memory.

```
minikube start --cpus=4 --memory=8192mb
```

  This level of granularity may diminish on systems where Docker does not efficiently allocate virtual resources.

- **Networking:** Kind excels in simulating production-like networking behaviors, leveraging Docker's built-in network capabilities. This is particularly beneficial for testing multi-cluster or multi-node architectures.

- **Multi-node Clusters:** Minikube traditionally operates within single-node topologies, whereas Kind supports multi-node configurations which can represent real-world production environments more effectively.

```
kind create cluster --config=multi-node-config.yaml
```

  In this scenario, you define your own cluster configurations within a YAML file, enabling scalable orchestrations within Docker containers.

While installing these local environments is generally straightforward, several common issues may arise. Troubleshooting insights are invaluable:

- Ensure hypervisors are operational for Minikube setups.

- Assess Docker daemon status and configurations when deploying Kind clusters.
- Verify Docker resource allocations comply with Kind's minimal requirements for creating efficient cluster operations.
- Utilize Minikube's built-in debugging tools with commands such as minikube logs to trace errors.

Understanding these installation steps and configurations situates readers advantageously for orchestrating Kubernetes clusters ready for Argo Workflow deployments. Leveraging the simplicity and operational power of Minikube and Kind will lay the groundwork for performing complex containerized workflows within localized development ecosystems.

2.2 Deploying Kubernetes in the Cloud

The proliferation of cloud computing has rendered it a highly favored milieu for deploying Kubernetes clusters due to its scalability, resilience, and reduced maintenance overhead. This section delineates the procedures for deploying Kubernetes clusters across major cloud platforms: Amazon Web Services (AWS), Google Cloud Platform (GCP), and Microsoft Azure. Focus is placed on leveraging each provider's integrated Kubernetes services—AWS Elastic Kubernetes Service (EKS), Google Kubernetes Engine (GKE), and Azure Kubernetes Service (AKS)—to foster robust, scalable, and secure containerized environments for real-world applications.

AWS Elastic Kubernetes Service (EKS)

AWS EKS provides an immensely scalable and convenient service for running Kubernetes applications, eliminating the necessity for manual cluster management. Herein are critical steps for configuring a Kubernetes cluster on AWS:

1. **Configure AWS CLI:**
```
aws configure
```

Provide your AWS access key, secret access key, region, and output format to authenticate and configure your CLI session.

2. **Create an IAM role for EKS:**

```
aws iam create-role --role-name eks-service-role --assume-role-policy-document
    file://eks-trust-policy.json
```

Attach the necessary policies to this role, such as AmazonEKSClusterPolicy.

3. **Create an EKS Cluster:**

```
aws eks create-cluster --name myEksCluster --role-arn arn:aws:iam::<
    ACCOUNT_ID>:role/eks-service-role --resources-vpc-config subnetIds=<
    SUBNET_IDS>,securityGroupIds=<SECURITY_GROUP_IDS>
```

Await for the status to change to ACTIVE.

4. **Configure kubectl for EKS:**

```
aws eks update-kubeconfig --name myEksCluster
```

This updates the kubeconfig file with your new cluster details.

5. **Launch Worker Nodes:** Utilize the AWS Management Console or AWS CLI to provision worker nodes, ensuring they have suitable connectivity with the EKS cluster.

These steps enable setting up a robust Kubernetes cluster on AWS quickly. By centralizing management in the cloud, organizations effectively reduce operational costs and enhancement of security measures.

Google Kubernetes Engine (GKE)

Google Kubernetes Engine is among the most user-friendly solutions, tightly integrated with Google Cloud's suite of services, granting easy interoperability with BigQuery, Pub/Sub, and other offerings. Here's a detailed guide for deploying a GKE cluster:

1. **Install and Authenticate with gcloud CLI:**

```
gcloud init
gcloud auth login
```

2.2. DEPLOYING KUBERNETES IN THE CLOUD

Select your desired project and authenticate to gain command-line access to Google Cloud Platform.

2. **Enable the GKE API:**

```
gcloud services enable container.googleapis.com
```

This API is requisite for deploying and operating Kubernetes clusters on GCP.

3. **Create a GKE Cluster:**

```
gcloud container clusters create my-gke-cluster --zone us-central1-a
```

Customize node numbers, machine types, and network configurations as per requirements using available flags.

4. **Get Authentication Credentials:**

```
gcloud container clusters get-credentials my-gke-cluster --zone us-central1-a
```

This command adjusts the kubectl context to interact with your new GKE cluster.

5. **Deploy Applications:** Express Kubernetes manifests apply to deploy containerized applications onto the GKE cluster, leveraging GCP's scalable infrastructure.

GKE, through deep integration with GCP services and through facilitated scalability, presents itself as an ideal choice for enterprises leveraging cloud-native applications.

Azure Kubernetes Service (AKS)

Azure Kubernetes Service empowers developers to deploy and manage Kubernetes clusters with notable ease of management and integration with Azure's cloud services, such as Azure Active Directory, for enhanced security configurations. Follow these detailed installation steps:

1. **Install Azure CLI and Log In:**

```
az login
```

Authenticate using your Azure credentials to initialize the session.

2. **Register the AKS Provider:**

```
az provider register --namespace Microsoft.ContainerService
```

3. **Create a Resource Group:**

```
az group create --name myResourceGroup --location eastus
```

4. **Create the AKS Cluster:**

```
az aks create --resource-group myResourceGroup --name myAKSCluster --node-count 3 --enable-addons monitoring --generate-ssh-keys
```

The command provisions an AKS cluster while generating SSH keys for secure node access.

5. **Configure kubectl to use the AKS Cluster:**

```
az aks get-credentials --resource-group myResourceGroup --name myAKSCluster
```

This aligns the kubectl tool with your Kubernetes cluster, ensuring full operational control.

Leveraging AKS within Azure not only ensures smooth Kubernetes cluster management but provides an extensive array of built-in services for container intelligence, database management, and networking tools, thus aligning with Microsoft's robust ecosystem.

Comparative Analysis of Cloud Platforms

While every platform offers the fundamental capabilities necessary for Kubernetes cluster deployments, nuanced differences highlight specific strategic advantages:

- **Performance and Scalability:** AWS EKS often edges out in areas requiring high availability and extensive scaling due to its mature infrastructure. GKE, however, is optimally tuned for rapid scaling backed by Google's global infrastructure.

- **Ease of Use and Integration:** Azure and Google provide seamless service integrations, enhancing developer productivity. GKE, with its Auto-Pilot mode, manages clusters autonomously, reducing administrative overhead.

- **Security and Compliance:** Azure excels with its robust security features integrating Azure Active Directory, thereby providing seamless identity solutions. AWS illustrates superior compliance capabilities across a broader array of certifications.

- **Cost-Efficiency:** While pricing strategies vary, users often opt for the platform that aligns best with existing service requirements, enterprise deals, and development tools.

Each cloud optimized Kubernetes service not only streamlines deployments but also fosters innovation through an array of integral services. Aligning these services with strategic organizational goals guarantees an optimized containerized application infrastructure.

In essence, embracing cloud platforms for Kubernetes deployments represents a strategic shift towards operational efficiency, optimized resource allocation, and enhanced application performance. The conclusion will naturally see readers harness these insights in practice, preparing a formidable structure for subsequent configurations like those introduced in Argo Workflows and beyond.

2.3 Getting Started with kubectl

The Kubernetes command-line tool, kubectl, serves as the primary interface for interacting with Kubernetes clusters. It provides comprehensive capabilities for deploying applications, inspecting and managing cluster resources, and executing various operational tasks. Mastery of kubectl is critical to achieving proficient management and orchestration of Kubernetes deployments. This section introduces the installation, basic commands, and advanced usage patterns of kubectl, thus equipping users with the fundamental skills required for efficient Kubernetes management.

Installing kubectl

Before interacting with Kubernetes clusters, installing kubectl on the local workstation is essential. The following steps outline the installation process across different operating systems:

1. **Linux:**

   ```
   curl -LO "https://dl.k8s.io/release/$(curl -L -s https://dl.k8s.io/release/stable.txt)/bin/linux/amd64/kubectl"
   chmod +x kubectl
   sudo mv kubectl /usr/local/bin/
   ```

   This script downloads the latest stable release, adds execute permissions, and relocates kubectl to the system's executable path.

2. **macOS:**

   ```
   brew install kubectl
   ```

   Using Homebrew simplifies the installation process and ensures Kubernetes' kubectl is installed alongside other dependencies.

3. **Windows:**

   ```
   choco install kubernetes-cli
   ```

   The Chocolatey package manager facilitates seamless installation on Windows systems.

4. **Verification:**

   ```
   kubectl version --client
   ```

   Ensures that kubectl is installed correctly and displays the client version.

By following these processes, users prepare their environments to issue commands to Kubernetes clusters.

Basic kubectl Commands

kubectl commands follow a structure that includes the keyword kubectl, followed by an action, resource type, and usually a resource name or selector flag. Understanding and frequently using these commands form the backbone of Kubernetes cluster management:

2.3. GETTING STARTED WITH KUBECTL

- **Configuration Management:**

```
kubectl config view
kubectl config use-context <context-name>
```

These commands allow for viewing and switching between different Kubernetes configuration contexts, enabling management of multiple clusters from a single client.

- **Resource Management:**

```
kubectl get nodes
kubectl get pods --all-namespaces
kubectl describe pod <pod-name>
```

Retrieving descriptive information about nodes and pods is crucial for monitoring cluster states. Describing a pod yields comprehensive information about its configuration and runtime state, exposing data necessary for debugging.

- **Deployments:**

```
kubectl apply -f <deployment-file.yaml>
kubectl scale deployment <deployment-name> --replicas=<number>
```

Deployments administer pod management under specified replication rules, ensuring desired state and scaling requirements are continually met.

- **Log and Debug Commands:**

```
kubectl logs <pod-name>
kubectl exec -it <pod-name> -- /bin/bash
```

These commands enable viewing application logs and executing shell commands interactively within pod contexts for real-time troubleshooting and monitoring.

Each of the above commands serves distinct purposes that foster effective resource management and troubleshooting within Kubernetes ecosystems.

Advanced Usage Patterns and Scripting

Advanced users of kubectl often adopt scripting capabilities and command chaining to enhance task automation and execution efficiency.

45

- **Bash Alias Setup:** Frequent users create aliases for common command sequences.

  ```
  alias k='kubectl'
  alias kgp='kubectl get pods'
  ```

  This setup reduces repetitive typing and expedites command execution.

- **Scripting for Automation:** Bash scripts provide powerful automation.

  ```
  #!/bin/bash
  # Check the status of pods in all namespaces and save it to a file
  kubectl get pods --all-namespaces -o wide > pod-status.txt
  ```

  Automating these actions simplifies repetitive tasks and promotes operational consistency across deployments.

- **Data Transformation with JSON Path Queries:**

  ```
  kubectl get pod -o=jsonpath='{.items[*].metadata.name}'
  ```

  JSON Path queries facilitate data extraction from resource specifications, useful for scripting and data analytics.

- **Custom Resource Definitions (CRDs):** Manage custom resource types native to Kubernetes extensions.

  ```
  kubectl apply -f crd-definition.yaml
  kubectl get <custom-resource>
  ```

  Defining and interacting with CRDs extends Kubernetes' capabilities, tailoring them for domains beyond conventional offerings.

The richness of kubectl commands and scripting adaptability empowers users to craft tailored Kubernetes interactions, enhancing productivity and operational reliability.

kubectl Contexts and Namespaces

Understanding and managing contexts and namespaces ensures precise resource targeting and avoids conflicts between environments deployed on shared clusters:

- **Context Management:**

```
kubectl config current-context
kubectl config set-context <context-name> --namespace=<namespace-name>
```

Altering contexts and namespaces sets default operational environments, reducing the need to specify them for every command iteration.

- **Namespace Utilization:**

```
kubectl create namespace <namespace-name>
kubectl config view --minify | grep namespace:
```

Namespaces partition resources, clusters, or teams, enhancing isolation and resource management across multi-team or microservice architectures.

Namespaces play critical roles in resource separation, strategic resource deployment, and team operations efficiency.

Interoperability with Kubernetes Extensions

The modular architecture of kubectl allows integration with additional plugins, extending its functionality beyond core commands.

- **kubectl Plugins:**

```
kubectl krew install <plugin-name>
```

Kubectl Krew facilitates plugin management, providing an ecosystem to obtain and manage plugins effortlessly, advancing kubectl's feature set significantly.

- **Integration with Helm:** Helm acts as a Kubernetes package manager and deploying charts alongside kubectl.

```
helm repo add stable https://charts.helm.sh/stable
helm install my-release stable/<chart>
```

Leveraging Helm standardizes application deployment, configuration, and upgrades.

Extensions and plugins incorporated through kubectl enhance Kubernetes' flexibility, adaptability, and user experience, ensuring a tailored fit across various operational paradigms.

The prowess offered by kubectl, when coupled with such frameworks, solidifies it as an indispensable tool in the Kubernetes ecosystem, a toolkit assuring efficient control, deployment, and management of resources with authoritative precision. Understanding and leveraging this command-line interface maximizes the potential yield from Kubernetes clusters, representing a cornerstone for modern cloud-native and DevOps-aligned practices.

2.4 Installing and Configuring Argo Workflows

Argo Workflows is a powerful Kubernetes-native workflow orchestration engine designed to streamline the management of jobs and tasks in complex, containerized environments. Leveraging Kubernetes' inherent scalability, Argo Workflows enables the creation and management of Directed Acyclic Graphs (DAGs) which define workflows and their dependencies. This section provides comprehensive instructions for installing Argo Workflows on a Kubernetes cluster and configuring it for reliable and efficient task orchestration.

Prerequisites for Installing Argo Workflows

Before proceeding with the installation of Argo Workflows, ensure the following prerequisites are met:

- An operational Kubernetes cluster, either on a local setup using Minikube/Kind or a cloud provider such as AWS EKS, GKE, or Azure AKS.

- kubectl configured to interact with your Kubernetes cluster.

- (Optional) Helm package manager, for simplified installation and upgrade processes.

Confirm the readiness of your Kubernetes cluster with:

```
kubectl cluster-info
kubectl get nodes
```

2.4. INSTALLING AND CONFIGURING ARGO WORKFLOWS

Upon satisfying these prerequisites, proceed with the installation steps.

Installing Argo Workflows

Argo Workflows can be installed using the default Kubernetes manifests or via the Helm package manager. Below, we detail these approaches, focusing on their applicable contexts:

Installing with Kubernetes Manifests:

1. **Clone the Argo Workflows repository:**

   ```
   git clone https://github.com/argoproj/argo-workflows.git
   cd argo-workflows/manifests
   ```

   This command fetches the Argo Workflows GitHub repository and navigates to the directory containing the application manifests.

2. **Apply installation manifests:**

   ```
   kubectl create namespace argo
   kubectl apply -n argo -f namespace-install.yaml
   ```

   Install Argo Workflows into a dedicated namespace to maintain separation from other workloads. The manifests deploy the necessary components: server, workflow controller, and dependent resources.

Installing with Helm:

1. **Add the Argo Helm repository and update:**

   ```
   helm repo add argo https://argoproj.github.io/argo-helm
   helm repo update
   ```

2. **Install Argo Workflows using Helm:**

   ```
   helm install argo argo/argo-workflows --namespace argo --create-namespace
   ```

   Utilizes Helm charts to deploy Argo Workflows, facilitating easy updates and maintenance as new releases are published.

Both methods deploy Argo Workflows and offer comparable outcomes, with Helm typically being preferred for environments where multiple deployment cycles and updates are expected.

Configuring Argo Workflows

Initial configurations tailor Argo Workflows to specific needs and improve operational integrity. Configurations are primarily handled via ConfigMap, which can be adjusted post-deployment.

1. **Access and Modify ConfigMap:**

   ```
   kubectl edit configmap workflow-controller-configmap -n argo
   ```

   This command opens the default configuration file. Modifications may include altering conciliator methods, rate limits, parallelism levels, retry strategies, and resource configurations.

2. **Configure Persistence:** Linking workflows to persistent data storage can be crucial for many applications. Use the ConfigMap to store artifact repository configurations (e.g., MinIO, S3), promoting seamless interaction between workflows and long-term data storage.

   ```
   data:
     config: |
       artifactRepository:
         s3:
           bucket: my-bucket
           endpoint: s3.amazonaws.com
           accessKeySecret:
             key: awsAccessKey
             name: my-s3-credentials
           secretKeySecret:
             key: awsSecretKey
             name: my-s3-credentials
   ```

   This configuration ensures that output artifacts from your workflows are systematically stored and retrievable.

3. **Set Resource Limits:** To safeguard the cluster's resource availability and prevent service disruptions, impose resource limits on the workflow-controller. Configure memory and CPU usage within this section of the ConfigMap.

   ```
   data:
     resources:
   ```

2.4. INSTALLING AND CONFIGURING ARGO WORKFLOWS

```
limits:
  cpu: "1"
  memory: "1Gi"
requests:
  cpu: "500m"
  memory: "512Mi"
```

Promptly apply the new configuration once adjustments are complete. Enhancements and customizations bespoke to workflow demands streamline execution and optimize resource utilization.

Verifying Argo Workflows Installation

Validation of your installation ensures the operability and readiness of Argo Workflows for task orchestration. Perform the following checks:

- **Confirm Deployments:**

```
kubectl get pods -n argo
kubectl get svc -n argo
```

Verify that the Argo Workflows controller and related services are in the "Running" state.

- **Access the Argo UI:**

```
kubectl -n argo port-forward deployment/argo-server 2746:2746
```

Access the web interface by navigating to http://localhost:2746 in your browser. The UI provides an intuitive interface for managing workflows, viewing status, and accessing logs.

Executing Sample Workflows

Get started by executing a sample workflow to understand the interaction dynamics within Argo Workflows:

1. **Submit a Hello World Workflow:**

```
kubectl -n argo create -f https://raw.githubusercontent.com/argoproj/argo-workflows/v3.1.5/examples/hello-world.yaml
```

This simple workflow demonstrates a minimal execution consisting of steps processed in the expected order.

2. **Monitor Workflow Execution:**

```
kubectl -n argo get workflows
```

Monitor the states of submitted workflows, ensuring dictionary representations of defined DAGs reflect expected processing sequences.

3. **Inspect Workflow Logs:**

```
argo logs <workflow-name> -n argo
```

Enables live monitoring of output or error streams captured during the execution of specific nodes within the workflow.

These interactions serve as initial demonstrations for exploring Argo Workflows capabilities.

Troubleshooting and Best Practices

Address common configuration and runtime issues to ensure smooth operations:

- **Pod Failures:** Investigate Kubernetes events and pod logs for failed pods with commands such as:
  ```
  kubectl describe pod <pod-name> -n argo
  kubectl logs <pod-name> -n argo
  ```

- **Networking Configurations:** Assess cluster networking configurations if the Argo UI or artifact repositories become unreachable due to misconfigured network policies.

- **Backup and Recovery:** Implement regular backups of crucial configuration and data repositories, ensuring business continuity and the ability to restore operations in the event of critical failures.

When integrated effectively, Argo Workflows becomes a pivotal tool in orchestrating sophisticated, scalable workflows that interface efficiently with Kubernetes resources. This functionality supports the creation of modern cloud-native applications, facilitating fine-grained control over automated tasks and processes with minimal human intervention. With operational deployments complete, advance towards strategic utilization and optimization of Argo's extensive workflow orchestration capabilities within your enterprise or project environments, ensuring robustness and reliability in operational tasks.

2.5 Exploring the Argo CLI

The Argo Command-Line Interface (CLI) is an indispensable tool for effectively managing and interacting with Argo Workflows within Kubernetes environments. Designed for efficiency, the Argo CLI functions as a robust interaction point, enabling users to submit, inspect, and manage workflows seamlessly from the terminal. It offers a suite of commands that cater to streamlined process automation and enhanced management capabilities, enriching the operational experience of orchestrating Kubernetes workflows. This section provides a detailed exploration of the Argo CLI, including installation, command usage patterns, and practical applications within real-world contexts.

Installing the Argo CLI

To utilize the Argo CLI, it must first be installed on a workstation. Installation steps vary by operating system, and the following instructions cover the most common platforms:

1. **Linux and macOS:**

```
# Download the latest release
curl -sLO https://github.com/argoproj/argo-workflows/releases/download/v3
    .1.8/argo-linux-amd64
# Make the binary executable
chmod +x argo-linux-amd64
# Move it to a directory included in your PATH
sudo mv argo-linux-amd64 /usr/local/bin/argo
```

This downloads the Argo binary to your system, setting it up for execution.

2. **Windows:**

```
# Download the latest release EXE
curl -sLO https://github.com/argoproj/argo-workflows/releases/download/v3
    .1.8/argo-windows-amd64.exe
```

```
# Move the executable to a folder in your system PATH
move argo-windows-amd64.exe C:\path\to\directory\argo.exe
```

Ensure the installation path is included in the system environment variables for easy access.

3. **Verification:**

```
argo version
```

Confirm that the Argo CLI is correctly installed by checking the installed version, ensuring it matches the expected release.

These installations configure the Argo CLI for operational readiness, allowing users to leverage its functionalities further.

Fundamental Argo CLI Commands

The Argo CLI operates through a series of commands structured for intuitive access to workflow management functionalities, encompassing creation, inspection, and control. Below is a comprehensive list of fundamental commands every user should grasp:

- **Submitting Workflows:** The submit command dispatches workflow specifications to the Kubernetes cluster for execution:

```
argo submit example-workflow.yaml
```

This command sends your workflow YAML file to the cluster, prompting its execution per defined specifications.

- **Listing Workflows:** To gain an overview of active and completed workflows, use:

```
argo list
```

Outputs display metadata and statuses for workflows, aiding in swift identification and operational insight.

- **Inspecting Workflow Details:** Delve into specifics with:

```
argo get <workflow-name>
```

Workflow logs and metadata dissection within this command assist debugging and comprehensive monitoring of workflow processes.

- **Terminating or Deleting Workflows:** Discard or halt workflows through:
```
argo delete <workflow-name>
argo terminate <workflow-name>
```
These commands respectively remove workflow artifacts or cease workflow execution, preserving logs for post-execution analysis.

- **Viewing Workflow Logs:** Access specific outputs from workflow execution:
```
argo logs <workflow-name>
```
Facilitates run-time debugging and log review, capturing output from active and terminal workflow phases.

- **Resubmitting Workflows:** In cases where workflows require re-execution or parameter modifications, use:
```
argo resubmit <workflow-name> --parameter key=value
```
Adapt workflows dynamically by altering input parameters and re-triggering the workflow chain, crucial for iterative testing and validations.

These commands form the core of day-to-day interactions with workflows, promoting fluid management and streamlined operational directives within Kubernetes clusters leveraging Argo Workflows.

Advanced Command Usage and Workflow Management

Advanced usage of Argo CLI embraces scenarios where complexities exceed standard operations. Script embeddings, templating, and interactions with conditional statements elevate workflow management practices:

- **Workflow Templates:** Utilize workflow templates to parametrize and replicate workflows without redundancy:

```
argo template create workflow-template.yaml
argo submit --from workflowtemplate/workflow-template-name
```

Workflow templates establish reusable patterns, integrating parameters that adjust between executions, thus optimizing code reuse and reducing error margins.

- **Cron Workflows:** Automate regular workflow executions using cron syntax:

```
argo cron create schedule.yaml
argo cron list
```

Cron workflows ensure periodic execution, automating repeated tasks reliably, akin to standard operating scheduling.

- **Multi-cluster Submissions:** Interacting across multiple clusters:

```
argo submit --server <cluster-url> -n <namespace> workflow.yaml
```

This setup allows executing workflows on specifically defined or multiple Kubernetes clusters, aligning distributed systems for cohesive operations.

- **Access Control and Role-Based Management:** Integrate Argo CLI with Kubernetes Role-Based Access Control (RBAC):

```
kubectl create rolebinding argo-role-binding --role=argo-role --user=<user>
```

Secure access constraints define operating boundaries and permissions, ensuring workflow actions align with organization security policies.

- **Workflow Archiving and Historical Data:** Record archives for accessibility:

```
argo archive list
argo archive get <workflow-name>
```

Workflow archiving stores vital execution data for posterior analysis, ensuring strategic insights for process improvement are available.

2.5. EXPLORING THE ARGO CLI

These intricate engagements widen workflow oversight and bolster robustness, fitting extensive operational schemes demanding critical thought and real-time adaptability in workflow orchestration.

Integrating Argo CLI within DevOps Pipelines

Argo Workflows and CLI integration within DevOps highlights the flexibility and efficiency possible through containerized automation:

- **Continuous Integration/Continuous Deployment (CI/CD):** Incorporate workflow operations within CI/CD systems like Jenkins or GitLab:

```
# Example: Trigger workflow within a Jenkins pipeline
sh "argo submit ci-pipeline-workflow.yaml"
```

Use the Argo CLI as a command builder to align task definitions with development pipelines, flawing seamless integration.

- **Notification and Alerting Systems:** Emit notifications linked to workflow states:

```
# Example: Slack Integration
argo logs <workflow-name> | slack-notify
```

Implement alert systems outfitted with log extracts or status changes, enhancing awareness and response times to arising issues.

- **Automated Testing and Validation:** Incorporate testing directives within workflow specs:

```
argo submit --test workflow-test.yaml
```

Pre-submit comprehensive test validations guarantee configurations align before broader application, preemptively addressing potential deploy failures.

Inlining Argo CLI with DevOps methodologies capitalizes on automated capabilities, constructing reliable, audit-ready deployments fostering efficiency and precision in development.

Troubleshooting Argo CLI

Address common Argo CLI operational hiccups through a structured approach:

- **Network Connectivity:** Ensure kubectl and Argo CLI share cluster access and network configurations. Use kubectl proxy when needed to simplify local executions.

- **Workflow Failures:** Extract deeper insights from workflow failures by direct pod log inspection, cross-referencing output against expected benchmarks:

```
kubectl logs -n argo <pod-name>
```

- **Version Compatibility:** Maintain CLI versions and manifests synced with Argo Workflows installed objects. Check compatibility matrices when integrating newer features or components.

- **Error Messages:** Direct consultations of Argo's documented error directories and community forums emphasize continuous learning and prompt user interactions, aiding rapid issue resolution.

These strategies promote operational transparency, tackling complexities through improved insights and methodical interventions. Amid mastering Argo CLI, users equip themselves with potent tools extending beyond mere workflow administration, fashioning an empowered approach aligning modern container management efficiencies with streamlined, automated process reformation. Intertwining functionality with practical execution exemplifies advanced readiness and commitment toward process optimization and resilience in the landscape of Kubernetes orchestrated triggers.

2.6 Verifying Your Setup

Ensuring that Kubernetes and Argo Workflows are correctly installed and fully operational is a pivotal step in establishing a reliable platform for automated process orchestration and management. Verification involves a meticulous series of checks across multiple layers of the infrastructure, examining cluster readiness, resource availability, configuration integrity, and workflow functionality. This section systematically delineates the verification processes, detailing diagnostic methodologies and offering strategies for troubleshooting common issues encountered during setup validation.

Kubernetes Cluster Verification

A functional Kubernetes infrastructure is foundational to the operational efficacy of any deployed application or service. Ensuring that the Kubernetes cluster is correctly configured involves the following comprehensive checks:

- **Cluster Information:** Begin by verifying the Kubernetes master and node statuses:
  ```
  kubectl cluster-info
  kubectl get nodes
  ```
  Confirm that all nodes are in the "Ready" state, indicating active and healthy participation in the cluster.

- **Pod Status Consistency:** Inspect the status of all pods within the Kubernetes environment:
  ```
  kubectl get pods --all-namespaces
  ```
  Evaluate their conditions, ensuring that essential system pods such as kube-apiserver, kube-controller-manager, and kube-scheduler are running smoothly.

- **Service Accessibility:** Validate that core services can be accessed and responded correctly:
  ```
  kubectl get services
  curl <service-endpoint>
  ```
  Use appropriate networking tools to ping and test the connectivity to service endpoints, verifying external accessibility and internal communication pathways.

- **Storage Validation:** Kubernetes should have persistent storage provisions confirmed:

```
kubectl get pv
kubectl get pvc
```

Make sure the Persistent Volumes (PVs) and Persistent Volume Claims (PVCs) align with the expected capacity and binding statuses.

Thoroughly verifying these elements ensures that the Kubernetes environment provides a robust backbone for running complex workflows.

Argo Workflows Verification

Post-installation verification of Argo Workflows guarantees operational compatibility and readiness to execute tasks as intended:

- **Deployment Status Check:** Verify that the Argo Workflows components are optimally deployed:

```
kubectl get pods -n argo
```

  Inspect the application-specific pods like the workflow controller and server for their operational status. All component pods should exhibit a running state without showing any restarts that could signify potential errors.

- **Argo Server Accessibility:** Confirm the Argo Workflows server is accessible and responsive:

```
kubectl -n argo port-forward deployment/argo-server 2746:2746
```

  Access the server through http://localhost:2746 to explore the UI, ensuring it presents the workflow overview dashboard correctly.

- **Configuration Review:** Cross-examine the configuration to ensure correctness:

```
kubectl edit configmap workflow-controller-configmap -n argo
```

  Validate that all configuration parameters, such as artifact repositories and default workflows retention policies, align with operational expectations.

- **Executing a Sample Workflow:** Submit and monitor the execution of a test workflow:

2.6. VERIFYING YOUR SETUP

```
argo submit --watch https://raw.githubusercontent.com/argoproj/argo-
    workflows/v3.1.5/examples/hello-world.yaml
```

By carefully observing the logs and outputs, confirm the workflow stages executed as expected, marking successful job processing and completion.

Each of these verification steps ascertains the reliability and integrity of the Argo Workflows setup within a Kubernetes environment.

Common Issues and Troubleshooting

Proactive identification and resolution of common problems is crucial to maintaining a healthy operational environment. Herein are examples of frequent issues and strategies to address them:

- **Network-Related Issues:** Network misconfigurations lead to service unreachability. Utilize:

```
kubectl describe service <service-name>
traceroute <service-endpoint>
```

  Trace network routes and examine events within service descriptions for discrepancies or errors potentially blocking traffic.

- **Authorization Failures:** Misaligned Role-Based Access Control (RBAC) configurations often manifest during authorization attempts:

```
kubectl describe rolebinding <role-binding-name>
kubectl auth can-i <verb> <resource> --namespace=<namespace>
```

  Verify RBAC components to confirm user permissions match roles and intended APIs without complete privilege escalation.

- **Pod CrashLoopBackOff:** This status indicates pod containers continuously fail to start. Extract logs for underlying causes:

```
kubectl logs <pod-name>
kubectl describe pod <pod-name>
```

  Address issues related to container initialization, Docker images, incorrect environment variables, or insufficient resource allocations.

- **Unexpected Service Stoppages:** Service stoppages can occur when resource quotas are exceeded:

```
kubectl describe resourcequota
kubectl describe namespace <namespace>
```

Adjust quotas to adequately meet your resource needs, economic for high-traffic services.

- **DNS Errors:** DNS resolution failures disrupt service discovery:

```
kubectl exec <dns-tools-pod> -- nslookup <service-name>
```

Implement DNS tools pods for real-time query diagnostics, facilitating the pinning down of resolution issues affecting service names or pods.

These methodologies address common stumbling blocks, reinforcing system stability and ensuring a seamless operational process flow.

Best Practices for Continuous Verification

To maintain a verified setup over time, the adoption of best practices is necessary:

- **Automated Health Checks:** Implement continuous health check services within your Kubernetes environment:

```
# Example: Kubernetes health check command in a cron job for periodic checks
kubectl get nodes | grep -v -E "Ready|NAME"
```

Automated scripts scheduled through cron jobs or equivalent systems continually assess node and service baselines, promoting an immediate reaction to deviations.

- **Logging and Monitoring:** Integrated logging and monitoring solutions such as Prometheus and Grafana provide observability:

```
# Install Prometheus using Helm (as an example)
helm install prometheus stable/prometheus
```

Active monitoring detects and visualizes metrics, recognizing anomalies and pinpointing performance bottlenecks in real time.

2.6. VERIFYING YOUR SETUP

- **Configuration Management and Audits:** Establish regular configuration audits to confirm that policies, RBAC roles, and Argo components retain their defined states:

  ```
  kubectl get configmap <configmap-name> -o yaml | diff - revision.yaml
  ```

  Repositories storing current configurations benchmark against active status, tracing unauthorized changes or erosion in settings integrity.

- **Scheduled Backups:** Protect data through frequent backup schedules and recovery plans:

  ```
  # Example: Backup persistent volumes with restic
  restic backup /data/pv-backup
  ```

  Utilize backup tools such as Velero for Kubernetes environments, providing recovery pathways for persistent data and workflow state restoration.

- **Educational and Documentation Efforts:** Continually fortify team education on the usage of Kubernetes and Argo Workflows:

  ```
  # Facilitate training with documented runbooks
  bash /training-scripts/universal-setup-guide.sh
  ```

  Create accessible runbooks and host workshops to instill best practices for managing and verifying system setups among development operations personnel.

Aggregate these practices with robust verification steps to maintain an environment where Kubernetes and Argo Workflows operate efficiently within defined resource allocations, fostering an ecosystem of resilience, scalability, and continuous reliability. Verification methodology, when implemented strategically, underscores successful operational processes and mitigates the risks associated with system downtimes or failures, solidifying a foundation for comprehensive process automation and orchestration.

Chapter 3

Understanding Argo Workflow Concepts

This chapter delves into the core concepts of Argo Workflows, providing a comprehensive overview of its architecture and essential terminology such as templates, tasks, and steps. Understanding these components is critical for effectively designing and executing workflows. Readers will explore the use of parameters and artifacts for data management within workflows, along with techniques for implementing conditional execution and loops to handle complex logic. The chapter also covers event-driven workflows and the Argo UI, which facilitates workflow visualization and management. By mastering these foundational concepts, readers will be well-equipped to harness the full potential of Argo Workflows in orchestrating Kubernetes-native processes.

3.1 Basic Workflow Terminology

In Argo Workflows, the concepts of templates, tasks, and steps form the foundation upon which complex workflows are built. Understanding these terminologies establishes a common language for effectively utilizing Argo Workflows, which orchestrate complex computation pipelines within Kubernetes.

Argo Workflows is a Kubernetes-native workflow engine, where the abstraction of workflows allows for parallel and sequential execution of tasks, facilitating scalable and reproducible data processing pipelines. Each workflow is essentially a Directed Acyclic Graph (DAG), where nodes represent steps or tasks, and edges define dependencies.

- **Templates:** Templates in Argo Workflows serve as the blueprint for defining the tasks or operations that need to be executed. A template encapsulates the logic for a single task and can be reused multiple times within a workflow. Templates can be of different types; the most common are:

    - **Container Templates:** These specify a container image to run as a part of the workflow task. Definition typically includes the image, command, and arguments.

    - **Script Templates:** Used to run inline scripts without needing a complete container definition. This encapsulates the script code and choices of interpreter.

    - **Resource Templates:** Allow for creation or modification of Kubernetes resources directly from within the workflow.

    - **Steps and DAG Templates:** Control flow logic is specified using these templates. While 'steps' define a sequential flow of tasks, 'DAG' templates define tasks with complex dependency graphs.

Each workflow typically consists of one or more templates. Importantly, templates ensure modularity, as they define reusable logic which can be easily referenced or overridden in different workflow contexts.

```
templates:
- name: my-task
  container:
    image: python:3.8
    command: ["python"]
    args: ["-c", "print('Hello World')"]
```

This YAML snippet specifically defines a template named my-task using a Python container that executes a simple print statement.

- **Tasks and Steps:** Tasks represent the execution of defined templates within workflows. A task is an instantiation of a template with provided parameters and other runtime configurations. Tasks are typically encapsulated either as part of 'steps' within a step-based template or as nodes in a DAG structure.

    Steps demonstrate a linear workflow execution. Each step in a step-based workflow executes in sequence, and the succeeding step is contingent upon the successful completion of its predecessor.

```
apiVersion: argoproj.io/v1alpha1
kind: Workflow
metadata:
  generateName: example-steps-
spec:
  entrypoint: steps-example
  templates:
  - name: steps-example
    steps:
    - - name: hello
        template: my-task
    - - name: bye
        template: my-task
```

In this example, steps-example comprises two tasks: hello and bye. Each task references the my-task template. Execution is sequential from hello to bye.

A DAG-based workflow allows for more complex dependencies between tasks, as tasks can be executed in parallel. This is defined through nodes and edges representing tasks and dependencies, respectively.

```
apiVersion: argoproj.io/v1alpha1
kind: Workflow
metadata:
  generateName: example-dag-
spec:
  entrypoint: dag-example
  templates:
  - name: dag-example
    dag:
      tasks:
      - name: task1
        template: my-task
```

```
    - name: task2
      dependencies: [task1]
      template: my-task
    - name: task3
      dependencies: [task1]
      template: my-task
```

In the dag-example, task1 is executed first, followed by parallel execution of task2 and task3, both of which depend on the completion of task1. This parallel execution capability is one of the significant benefits of DAGs in workflows, enabling efficient pipeline processing.

- **Steps and Workflow Execution Plan:** Each step within the workflow is configured to execute in a specific manner according to dependency resolution, resource availability, and user-defined parameters. The orchestrator resolves these dependencies, creating an execution plan for the workflow, scheduling tasks as per their readiness and resource allocation.

```
Task "hello" is ready for execution
Task "hello" executed successfully
Task "bye" is now ready for execution
Task "bye" executed successfully
```

This execution trace shows how the workflow controller processes tasks based on the readiness determined by user-defined dependencies.

- **Fault Tolerance:** In Kubernetes environments, network failures, node crashes, or pod evictions can occur. To address the need for reliability, Argo Workflows provide features such as retries and timeouts that can be specified within the workflow. This ensures robustness and guarantees task execution in case of transient faults.

```
templates:
- name: retry-task
  retryStrategy:
    limit: 3
    retryPolicy: "Always"
  container:
    image: busybox
    command: ["sh", "-c", "exit 1"]
```

3.1. BASIC WORKFLOW TERMINOLOGY

The retry-task template is configured to retry up to three times, implementing an Always retry policy upon failure, demonstrating Argo's ability to handle task failures gracefully.

- **Workflow Specification:** The workflow specification involves YAML configuration, where the workflow's structure and behavior are defined, including entrypoints, template listings, volume mounts, environment variables, and service accounts. Workflows need to follow Kubernetes resource definitions, so they are versioned with 'apiVersion', designated a 'kind', and associated metadata to identify the workflow resources within a Kubernetes environment.

An entrypoint is a primary template that initiates execution, and optional features like tolerations, node selectors, and affinity rules can also be specified for advanced configuration scenarios.

```
apiVersion: argoproj.io/v1alpha1
kind: Workflow
metadata:
  generateName: complex-workflow-
spec:
  entrypoint: main
  templates:
  - name: main
    dag:
      tasks:
      - name: A
        template: task-template
      - name: B
        dependencies: [A]
        template: task-template
      - name: C
        dependencies: [B]
        template: task-template
  - name: task-template
    container:
      image: alpine
      command: ["/bin/sh", "-c"]
      args: ["echo \"Running task\""]
```

In this YAML file, the workflow is defined under the complex-workflow prefix, building a sequence of interdependent tasks extending from A to C using a task-template that utilizes an Alpine Linux container to execute a simple shell command.

- **Leveraging Reusable Components:** The use of templates as reusable components optimizes workflow management by providing a mechanism for code reuse. These templates can be parameterized to alter execution specifics, thereby enhancing the flexibility of workflow design and maintenance. Parameters allow for dynamic assignment of values, improving adaptability across different execution scenarios.

```
templates:
- name: parameterized-task
  inputs:
    parameters:
    - name: msg
  container:
    image: alpine
    command: ["/bin/sh", "-c"]
    args: ["echo {{inputs.parameters.msg}}"]
```

Here, the parameterized-task template specifies an input parameter, enabling customized execution; effectively demonstrating how dynamic values can be incorporated into template execution.

- **Significance of Terminology:** Mastering basic Argo Workflow terminology—comprehending templates, tasks, steps, and how they interact—is vital for engineering and managing effective workflows. It establishes a solid conceptual framework necessary for constructing scalable, reliable, and efficient workflow systems, enabling practical orchestration of complex computation pipelines central to data-driven applications. Through understanding these foundational elements, users can leverage the full capabilities of Argo Workflows, ensuring seamlessly orchestrated Kubernetes-native processes.

3.2 Argo Workflow Architecture

The architecture of Argo Workflows is a quintessential example of how cloud-native and containerized applications are deployed and managed within the Kubernetes ecosystem. Argo Workflows is a robust, Kubernetes-native workflow engine designed to orchestrate complex job orchestration and metering. Understanding its architecture reveals

3.2. ARGO WORKFLOW ARCHITECTURE

how it seamlessly integrates with Kubernetes to facilitate scalable and efficient workflow management.

Argo Workflows capitalize on Kubernetes' capabilities to ensure high availability, resilience, and scalability. The core components of Argo Workflow Architecture consist of the Workflow Controller, Workflow Executor, Workflow Custom Resource Definitions (CRDs), Persistence Layer, and optional User Interfaces.

- **Workflow Controller:** The Workflow Controller is the primary orchestrator within the Argo Workflow architecture. It functions as a Kubernetes controller responsible for lifecycle management of workflows. The controller watches for 'Workflow' objects created in the Kubernetes cluster and manages their execution.

  The Workflow Controller handles task scheduling, driven by the Kubernetes scheduler, ensuring that compute resources are optimally used. It scales workflows by leveraging Kubernetes resources such as pods, and orchestrates task dependencies based on the specified DAG structure or sequential steps.

  ```
  kubectl create namespace argo
  kubectl apply -n argo -f https://raw.githubusercontent.com/argoproj/argo-
      workflows/stable/manifests/install.yaml
  ```

  This command sequence deploys the Workflow Controller into an 'argo' namespace within a Kubernetes cluster using pre-defined configuration manifests.

- **Workflow Executor:** The Workflow Executor is a sidecar or init container responsible for executing the individual steps of a workflow within a Kubernetes pod. Each task of a workflow is assigned an executor which manages the interaction with the Kubernetes API, executing container commands, streaming logs, and handling outputs.

  The choice of executor ('pns', 'k8sapi', 'emissary', etc.) can influence performance optimizations, such as the pns executor which uses the pod namespace mode to isolate processes without privileged mode, bolstering security.

  ```
  templates:
  - name: example-task
  ```

```
container:
  image: busybox
  command: ["/bin/sh", "-c", "echo hello world"]
executor:
  type: emissary
```

In this example, the executor type is specified within the workflow template, selecting the emissary executor for executing the container commands.

- **Workflow CRDs:** Custom Resource Definitions (CRDs) are Kubernetes extensibility mechanisms that enable users to introduce custom resources to their clusters. In Argo, the Workflow CRD defines the abstract model of workflows. These resources leverage the Kubernetes API for lifecycle management.

The Workflow CRD allows users to submit workflows described in a YAML manifest as Kubernetes custom resources. The workflow YAML defines templates, inputs, outputs, and the execution logic, transforming applications interactions into manageable Kubernetes resources.

```
apiVersion: argoproj.io/v1alpha1
kind: Workflow
metadata:
  generateName: hello-world-
spec:
  entrypoint: main
  templates:
  - name: main
    container:
      image: busybox
      command: ["echo", "hello world"]
```

This YAML snippet shows a minimal example of a Workflow CRD deployed to a Kubernetes cluster, encapsulating a simple 'hello world' command.

Persistence Layer

Argo Workflows can optionally integrate with a persistence layer—such as MinIO, AWS S3, or a database—to store workflow metadata, logs, and artifacts persistently. Persistence enhances recoverability and facilitates analysis of past workflow execution.

When enabled, the persistence layer allows for resumption of workflows, efficient query of execution data, and a consolidated log manage-

3.2. ARGO WORKFLOW ARCHITECTURE

ment system. Interactions with the persistence layer are incorporated via configuration in 'ConfigMap' or the use of parameters in workflow templates.

```
persistence:
  archive: true
  nodeStatusOffload: true
  connectionPool:
    maxIdleConns: 10
    maxOpenConns: 30
  postgresql:
    host: postgres.example.com
    port: 5432
    database: argo
    userNameSecret:
      name: argo-postgresql
      key: username
    passwordSecret:
      name: argo-postgresql
      key: password
```

The persistence configuration in this example enables PostgreSQL for offloading node status and workflow archiving, thereby ensuring a robust mechanism for workflow state retention.

User Interfaces

Argo provides a web-based User Interface (UI) to view and manage workflows. Users can visualize workflow progression, inspect logs, and interact with running workflows. The UI considerably simplifies debugging and operational monitoring.

The Argo UI is typically served as a Kubernetes service and can be accessed through port-forwarding or ingress configurations.

```
kubectl -n argo port-forward deployment/argo-server 2746:2746
```

Executing this command creates a secure tunnel to the Argo UI, allowing examination of workflows through a web browser at 'http://localhost:2746'.

Handling Scalability and Load

Argo Workflow's architecture inherently balances the designed requirements between scalability and task load management. The robust Kubernetes scheduler ensures that resource allocation is efficiently performed across multiple nodes, optimizing for distributed task execution.

A critical aspect of scalability in Argo Workflows involves horizontal scalability, achieved by deploying multiple controller instances with leader election enabled. This approach supports distribution of workflow control load, mitigating performance bottlenecks during peak operation periods.

Cluster Autoscaler configurations can dynamically scale Kubernetes worker nodes up or down based on workflow demands, placing the correct resource allocation emphasis per user-defined limits and thrusts.

Access Control and Security

Argo Workflows employ Role-Based Access Control (RBAC) of Kubernetes to enforce security policies across different cluster roles and permissions. Each task, pod, or workflow execution needs pertinent permissions to interact with the Kubernetes API and other cluster resources.

Users can define service accounts with appropriate roles to execute workflows securely, ensuring that RBAC policies adhere to the principle of least privilege. Additionally, leveraging Kubernetes secrets for storing sensitive information, such as API keys, enhances security.

```
apiVersion: rbac.authorization.k8s.io/v1
kind: Role
metadata:
  namespace: argo
  name: workflow-role
rules:
- apiGroups: ["argoproj.io"]
  resources: ["workflows"]
  verbs: ["get", "list", "watch", "create", "update", "patch", "delete"]
```

The example defines a role workflow-role with appropriate permissions on the workflow resources, allowing operations required for the lifecycle management of workflows.

Extending Argo Workflows

Argo Workflows provide multiple extension points, including custom templates, scripting, and third-party integrations. Extending workflows to interact with external services can leverage Webhook notifications, automated alerts, and custom metrics to adapt workflow behavior dynamically.

Argo Events is an Argo project that enhances workflows with event-

3.2. ARGO WORKFLOW ARCHITECTURE

driven capabilities, enabling conditional execution triggered by workflows, messages, or external stimuli.

Integration with Continuous Integration/Continuous Deployment (CI/CD) pipelines allows for seamless development and production workflow deployment. Templating and scripting options provide additional flexibility in customizing workflow parameters and behaviors.

Resilience in Failure Handling

Under contingent conditions, robust failure handling guarantees workflow reliability within Argo. Built-in support for managing task retries establishes a mechanism to mitigate transient errors using exponential backoff or customized retry policies, extending the robustness horizon of workflows.

```
templates:
- name: fault-tolerant-task
  container:
    image: node:14
    command: ["node", "-e", "process.exit(1)"]
  retryStrategy:
    limit: 3
    backoff:
      duration: "5"
      factor: 2
```

The template fault-tolerant-task demonstrates a retry strategy integrated with exponential backoff, accommodating field failures by gradually increasing retry intervals.

The Argo Workflow Architecture's composition illustrates the design logic aligned with Kubernetes paradigm—flexibility, extensibility, and resilience—offering a foundation for orchestrating sophisticated operational workflows essential in automating and streamlining cloud-native, data-intensive tasks. Its effective combination of workflow engagement components, robust failure recovery strategies, and extensible third-party integration frameworks presents a comprehensive toolkit for orchestrated process excellence in Kubernetes.

3.3 Defining Templates and Tasks

Templates and tasks are the quintessential building blocks of Argo Workflows, facilitating the definition and execution of complex workflows within Kubernetes. Defining these components effectively is paramount to leveraging Argo's capabilities in orchestrating scalable, robust, and efficient workflows. This section provides a comprehensive analysis of defining templates and tasks, delving into their syntax, structure, and implementation strategies.

Templates: Core Constructs

In Argo Workflows, a template is a reusable blueprint that defines a task or a series of tasks. Templates encapsulate the logic necessary for executing a task and can be parameterized to increase flexibility and reuse. The primary types of templates include:

Container Templates:

Container templates specify a container image, the command to run, and the associated arguments. They facilitate the execution of discrete tasks or applications within isolated environments, defined by the desired container.

```
templates:
- name: download-data
  container:
    image: alpine
    command: ["/bin/sh", "-c"]
    args: ["wget -q https://example.com/data.csv -O /tmp/data.csv"]
```

This example illustrates a container template download-data that utilizes the Alpine Linux image to download a file using the wget command. The operating environment, command definitions, and execution context are laid out explicitly within the template structure.

Script Templates:

Script templates allow inline scripting with specified interpreters, facilitating simple tasks without the overhead of image management.

```
templates:
- name: process-data
  script:
    image: python:3.8
    command: [python]
```

3.3. DEFINING TEMPLATES AND TASKS

```
source: |
  import pandas as pd
  df = pd.read_csv('/tmp/data.csv')
  df['processed'] = True
  df.to_csv('/tmp/data_processed.csv', index=False)
```

Here, a process-data script template utilizes Python to perform data processing. Inline Python script execution is configured within the template, integrating data ingestion and manipulation using Pandas, with the results written back to a CSV file.

Resource Templates:

Resource templates extend the Kubernetes object mechanisms within workflows, enabling creation, modification, or deletion of resources and serving as a bridge between workflows and the Kubernetes API.

```
templates:
- name: create-service
  resource:
    action: create
    manifest: |
      apiVersion: v1
      kind: Service
      metadata:
        name: my-test-service
      spec:
        selector:
          app: MyApp
        ports:
        - protocol: TCP
          port: 80
          targetPort: 9376
```

This example resource template creates a Kubernetes Service, illustrating the declarative configuration structure that facilitates direct manipulation of Kubernetes resources.

Steps and DAG Templates:

The steps and dag templates define the execution topology of workflows:

- Steps: Enforce sequential execution.

- DAGs: Define parallel execution paths and dependencies between tasks.

```
templates:
- name: sequential-processing
  steps:
  - - name: step-one
      template: download-data
  - - name: step-two
      template: process-data
```

This sequential-processing step template arranges two tasks, download-data and process-data, executing them sequentially, with each step depending on the prior step's successful completion.

Tasks: Instance of Execution

Tasks are instantiations of templates within a workflow. They bring templates to life by providing the necessary parameters and directly influencing the workflow's execution flow. Each task corresponds to a container, script, or resource template with specified execution specifics.

Tasks can be defined within workflows using specific parameters that modify the behavior of template instantiation. The interplay between tasks and templates is pivotal in customizing workflows.

```
templates:
- name: data-analysis
  inputs:
    parameters:
    - name: analysis-type
  container:
    image: data-analysis:latest
    command: ["analyze"]
    args: ["{{inputs.parameters.analysis-type}}", "/tmp/data_processed.csv"]
```

The data-analysis template leverages parameters to define analysis-type, ensuring that the specified analysis type is executed over processed data at runtime.

Template Parameterization

Parameterization is a powerful feature in Argo Workflows that provides the flexibility needed for dynamic runtime configurations. Parameters in templates allow user input or programmatic determination of values, granting adaptability over static workflows.

Parameters can be simple variables or complex data structures such as Artifacts. Artifacts represent complex data objects, supporting inputs and outputs for file and directory management between tasks.

3.3. DEFINING TEMPLATES AND TASKS

```
templates:
- name: artifact-manipulation
  inputs:
    artifacts:
    - name: input-data
      path: /tmp/input/data.csv
  script:
    image: debian:latest
    command: ["/bin/bash"]
    source: |
      head -n 10 {{inputs.artifacts.input-data}}
```

Here, the artifact-manipulation template consumes an input-data artifact specified as an input, performing a head operation on the file to display the first ten rows.

Dynamic Templates with Parameterization

Simple Parameters:

The simplest form of parameters includes integer, string, or Boolean values passed into tasks, determining runtime execution specifics.

```
templates:
- name: simple-param-example
  inputs:
    parameters:
    - name: timeout
  script:
    image: ubuntu
    command: ["/bin/bash"]
    source: |
      echo "Task execution timeout is set to {{inputs.parameters.timeout}}"
```

In this script-template, simple-param-example, the parameter timeout dynamically dictates execution behavior by being injected into the script body.

Utilizing Global Outputs:

Workflows can derive values from previous tasks as inputs for subsequent tasks using global outputs, facilitating continuation-passing style programming.

```
templates:
- name: task-one
  script:
    image: alpine
    command: ["/bin/sh", "-c"]
    source: |
      echo `date +%Y-%m-%d` > /tmp/date.out
```

79

CHAPTER 3. UNDERSTANDING ARGO WORKFLOW CONCEPTS

```
    outputs:
      parameters:
      - name: current-date
        valueFrom:
          path: /tmp/date.out
- name: task-two
  script:
    image: alpine
    command: ["/bin/sh", "-c"]
    source: |
      echo "The current date is {{workflow.outputs.parameters.current-date}}"
```

This workflow illustrates the combination of task-one generating a current-date output, which is utilized by task-two for customized task execution.

Advanced Execution Patterns

Execution patterns in Argo Workflow templates directly influence workflow characteristics such as fault tolerance, retry mechanisms, concurrency checks, and suspension points.

Retry Mechanisms:

Templates allow specification of retry strategies for handling transient failures, facilitating the robust execution of tasks.

```
templates:
- name: retry-task
  container:
    image: busybox
    command: ["sh", "-c", "exit 1"]
  retryStrategy:
    limit: 5
    retryPolicy: "Always"
    backoff:
      duration: "10s"
      factor: 2
      maxDuration: "60s"
```

Within retry-task, a retry strategy is built-in to perform up to five retries with exponential backoff, enabling resilient execution under the presence of failure.

Concurrency and Parallelism:

Templates, especially DAG templates, define concurrency controls for tasks, managing workload distribution without overburdening resources.

3.4. USING PARAMETERS AND ARTIFACTS

```
templates:
- name: process-batches
  dag:
    tasks:
    - name: process-{count}
      template: process-data
      arguments:
        parameters:
        - name: batch-id
          value: "{{item}}"
      withItems: [1, 2, 3, 4, 5]
concurrency: 2
```

This DAG template illustrates a batch processing setup with a concurrency limit of 2, controlling the number of parallel executions to mitigate resource exhaustion.

Suspension and Resumable Workflows:

Suspension points allow interactive workflows to be paused and resumed through manual or conditional triggers, facilitating gatekeeping or user intervention within workflows.

```
templates:
- name: conditional-approval
  suspend:
    duration: "1h"
```

The conditional-approval template introduces a suspension of 1h, representing workloads waiting for user approval or external event synchronization.

Understanding the intricacies of defining templates and tasks enables practitioners to design workflows aligned with desired workload characteristics, utilizing parameterization and advanced execution patterns for efficiency and robustness. Mastering template creation and task instantiation fosters flexible and maintainable workflow architectures, unlocking the full potential of Argo Workflows in Kubernetes-native process orchestration.

3.4 Using Parameters and Artifacts

Within Argo Workflows, parameters and artifacts serve as pivotal elements in fostering dynamic workflow execution, enabling workflows to adapt to varying inputs and efficiently manage data exchanges between tasks. Understanding how to leverage these components is crucial for designing sophisticated workflows capable of complex data processing and task orchestration.

Parameters allow workflows to be flexible and adaptable, enabling tasks to receive and process dynamic input values at execution time. They can be defined at the workflow level or within individual templates, providing the ability to customize execution based on external inputs or previous workflow results.

Defining Parameters: Parameters are defined within the inputs field of a workflow or template specification. They can be simple types like strings, integers, or booleans, used to dictate operational behavior dynamically.

```
apiVersion: argoproj.io/v1alpha1
kind: Workflow
metadata:
  generateName: params-example-
spec:
  entrypoint: parameter-demo
  arguments:
    parameters:
    - name: greeting
      value: "Hello"
  templates:
  - name: parameter-demo
    inputs:
      parameters:
      - name: name
    container:
      image: alpine
      command: ["/bin/sh", "-c"]
      args: ["echo {{inputs.parameters.greeting}}, {{inputs.parameters.name}}!"]
```

In this example, greeting and name are parameters used within the parameter-demo template to customize its execution logic. These parameters allow for dynamic greeting messages, where the actual output depends on the specific values passed at invocation.

Global Parameters: Global parameters are passed to a workflow through the arguments section of a workflow's spec. They enable users to specify values that should be accessible by any task within the workflow, allowing consistency and reducing redundancy.

3.4. USING PARAMETERS AND ARTIFACTS

```yaml
apiVersion: argoproj.io/v1alpha1
kind: Workflow
metadata:
  generateName: global-params-
spec:
  entrypoint: main-task
  arguments:
    parameters:
    - name: common-directory
      value: "/data"
  templates:
  - name: main-task
    container:
      image: ubuntu
      command: ["/bin/bash", "-c"]
      args: ["ls {{workflow.parameters.common-directory}}"]
```

This workflow demonstrates a common-directory global parameter accessible throughout the workflow execution. This ensures all tasks have consistent directory paths, eliminating disparities across task invocations.

Using Parameters for Conditional Logic: Parameters significantly enhance workflow adaptability by influencing conditional logic. They allow tasks to dynamically adjust their behavior based on runtime conditions.

```yaml
apiVersion: argoproj.io/v1alpha1
kind: Workflow
metadata:
  generateName: conditional-params-
spec:
  entrypoint: evaluate-condition
  templates:
  - name: evaluate-condition
    inputs:
      parameters:
      - name: condition
        value: "true"
    steps:
    - - name: task-true
        template: when-true
        when: "{{inputs.parameters.condition}} == true"
    - - name: task-false
        template: when-false
        when: "{{inputs.parameters.condition}} != true"

  - name: when-true
    container:
      image: alpine
      command: ["/bin/sh", "-c"]
      args: ["echo 'Condition is true'"]
```

```
  - name: when-false
    container:
      image: alpine
      command: ["/bin/sh", "-c"]
      args: ["echo 'Condition is false'"]
```

In this workflow, the parameter condition dictates which task to execute based on its value, showcasing how parameters can control execution paths through conditional logic.

Artifacts complement parameters by handling complex data types such as files or binary blobs. They allow users to pass data between tasks efficiently, essential for workflows involving substantial data processing or manipulation.

Artifact Configuration: Artifacts are defined under the inputs and outputs sections, associating an artifact with a storage location or path. Artifacts can interface with object storage systems like S3, GCS, or local paths within a Kubernetes cluster.

```
apiVersion: argoproj.io/v1alpha1
kind: Workflow
metadata:
  generateName: artifacts-example-
spec:
  entrypoint: artifact-demo
  templates:
  - name: artifact-demo
    inputs:
      artifacts:
      - name: input-file
        path: /tmp/input.txt
        s3:
          endpoint: s3.amazonaws.com
          bucket: my-bucket
          key: data/input.txt
    outputs:
      artifacts:
      - name: output-file
        path: /tmp/output.txt
    container:
      image: ubuntu
      command: ["/bin/sh", "-c"]
      args: ["cp {{inputs.artifacts.input-file.path}} {{outputs.artifacts.output-file.path
             }}"]
```

The artifact-demo template shows how to use S3-based artifacts for transferring an input file from a bucket and creating an output file for

3.4. USING PARAMETERS AND ARTIFACTS

subsequent tasks to leverage.

Artifact Transformation: In workflows, artifacts undergo transformation steps, where one task's output becomes another's input. This chaining is vital for complex workflows like machine learning pipelines, where one stage refines data for the next.

```
apiVersion: argoproj.io/v1alpha1
kind: Workflow
metadata:
  generateName: artifact-chaining-
spec:
  entrypoint: start
  templates:
  - name: start
    container:
      image: alpine
      command: ["/bin/sh", "-c"]
      args: ["echo 'Hello Argo!' > /tmp/message.txt"]
    outputs:
      artifacts:
      - name: initial-message
        path: /tmp/message.txt

  - name: upper-case
    inputs:
      artifacts:
      - name: input-message
        path: /tmp/input-message.txt
    outputs:
      artifacts:
      - name: transformed-message
        path: /tmp/upper-message.txt
    container:
      image: alpine
      command: ["/bin/sh", "-c"]
      args: ["tr '[:lower:]' '[:upper:]' < /tmp/input-message.txt > /tmp/upper-message.txt"]

  - name: display
    inputs:
      artifacts:
      - name: final-message
        path: /tmp/final-message.txt
    container:
      image: ubuntu
      command: ["/bin/cat"]
      args: ["/tmp/final-message.txt"]

  arguments:
    artifacts:
    - name: final-input
      from: "{{workflows.artifact.workflow-name.upper-case.outputs.artifacts.transformed-message}}"
```

CHAPTER 3. UNDERSTANDING ARGO WORKFLOW CONCEPTS

This example demonstrates artifact transformation through separate tasks: start, which generates a message, upper-case, which transforms it into uppercase, and display, which reads and displays it.

Artifact Passing between Tasks: Artifacts can be passed between tasks seamlessly using from directives, ensuring that outputs feed into subsequent task inputs, enhancing data flow within the workflow.

```
apiVersion: argoproj.io/v1alpha1
kind: Workflow
metadata:
  generateName: artifact-passing-
spec:
  entrypoint: initial-task
  templates:
  - name: initial-task
    container:
      image: python:3.8-slim
      command: ["python"]
      args: ["-c", "with open('/tmp/sample.txt', 'w') as f: f.write('Sample Data')"]
    outputs:
      artifacts:
      - name: sample-artifact
        path: /tmp/sample.txt

  - name: final-task
    inputs:
      artifacts:
      - name: incoming-artifact
        from: "{{steps.initial-task.outputs.artifacts.sample-artifact}}"
        path: /tmp/incoming.txt
    container:
      image: ubuntu
      command: ["/bin/cat"]
      args: ["/tmp/incoming.txt"]
```

artifact-passing utilizes artifacts produced by initial-task and directly inputs them into final-task, illustrating efficient and seamless artifact passing.

Argo Workflow's parameters and artifacts play vital roles in creating advanced workflows. Below are some intricate techniques and examples to enhance their utilization:

Dynamic Parameter Injection: Argo Workflows support dynamic parameter injection, where parameters can derive values from expressions or script outcomes.

3.4. USING PARAMETERS AND ARTIFACTS

```
templates:
- name: dynamic-param-task
  script:
    image: python:3.8
    command: ["python"]
    source: |
      import os
      param_value = os.getenv('DYNAMIC_PARAM', 'default')
      print(f'Received dynamic value: {param_value}')
```

Users can flexibly set environment variables to influence script parameters dynamically, promoting high runtime variability.

Constraints and Modifiers: Constraints and modifiers enable task customization according to parameter/metatag configurations, tailoring job execution specifics.

```
templates:
- name: constraint-example
  inputs:
    parameters:
    - name: task-size
      value: "medium"
  container:
    image: ubuntu
    command: ["/bin/bash", "-c"]
    args: ["echo Task size is {{inputs.parameters.task-size}}"]
```

Using parameter-defined constraints, users determine task specification explicitly, driven by runtime, parameterized values.

Automation and Orchestration with Parameters: Automation scripts can opt for CLI or API interactions for automated parameter handling and workflow orchestration.

```
argo submit myworkflow.yaml -p "task-size=large" --watch
```

This command executes workflow submission with argument-driven parameterization, fostering automation efficiencies.

Sophisticated usage of parameters and artifacts enables the seamless orchestration of data and task flows within Argo Workflows. These components play crucial roles in creating adaptable, data-driven, and scalable workflows. By mastering parameter and artifact handling, users can construct workflows that efficiently respond to dynamic inputs and deliver robust performance in processing complex data sets within Kubernetes-native environments.

3.5 Conditional Execution and Loops

Conditional execution and loops are critical features in Argo Workflows, providing the mechanisms needed to handle decision-making and iterative processes within workflows. These functionalities allow users to dynamically influence the flow of tasks based on conditions and repetitions, thus enhancing the flexibility and robustness of workflow designs.

Conditional execution involves executing tasks based on logical evaluations of parameters or workflow states. This capability enables workflows to adapt dynamically, executing different branches or tasks based on pre-defined conditions, akin to conditional logic structures found in traditional programming languages.

The when Field: The when field in Argo Workflows allows specifying a conditional expression to determine if a task should be executed. These expressions utilize 'go-template' syntax for evaluation, operating in tandem with the logic provided by input parameters.

```
apiVersion: argoproj.io/v1alpha1
kind: Workflow
metadata:
  generateName: conditional-execution-
spec:
  entrypoint: main
  templates:
  - name: main
    inputs:
      parameters:
      - name: execute-task
    steps:
    - - name: conditional-task
        template: task-to-run
        when: "{{inputs.parameters.execute-task}} == true"

  - name: task-to-run
    container:
      image: alpine
      command: ["/bin/sh", "-c"]
      args: ["echo 'Task executed successfully'"]
```

3.5. CONDITIONAL EXECUTION AND LOOPS

In this example, the task conditional-task is conducted only when the execute-task parameter equals true. This dynamic behavior highlights how the conditional expression impacts task execution.

Composite Conditions: Argo Workflows supports composite conditions using logical operators like and, or, and not. This enablement facilitates complex decision trees within workflows, converging multiple conditions into conjunctive or disjunctive evaluations.

```
...
steps:
- - name: conditional-task
    template: task-to-run
    when: "{{inputs.parameters.conditionA}} == true and {{inputs.parameters.conditionB}} == true"
...
```

By employing composite conditions, users can refine logical pathways, executing certain parts of workflows only when specific multiple conditions align.

Handling Execution Outcomes: Conditional task execution can influence subsequent workflow paths based on previous task outcomes. This interaction allows more granular control over failure handling and alternate pathway execution.

```
templates:
- name: conditional-paths
  steps:
  - - name: first-task
      template: task-a
    - - name: second-task
      template: task-b
      when: "{{steps.first-task.status}} == Succeeded"

- name: task-a
  container:
    image: busybox
    command: ["sh", "-c", "exit 0"]

- name: task-b
  container:
    image: busybox
    command: ["sh", "-c", "echo 'Follow-up task'"]
```

In this configuration, second-task executes only if first-task results in a successful status, ensuring logical progression based on task completion states.

Loops enable iterative task execution in contexts requiring repetitive processes. Loop constructs in Argo Workflows allow for iterating over a set of elements or conditions. This implementation flexibility accommodates scenarios like batch processing, data partitioning, and resource scaling.

Loops Using withItems: The withItems keyword allows for task execution within a loop by iterating over an array of values. Each iteration induces a separate instantiation of the task, adapting the input value accordingly.

```
apiVersion: argoproj.io/v1alpha1
kind: Workflow
metadata:
  generateName: looping-example-
spec:
  entrypoint: loop-template
  templates:
  - name: loop-template
    steps:
    - - name: looping-task
        template: repeatable-task
        arguments:
          parameters:
          - name: item
            value: "{{item}}"
        withItems:
        - "apple"
        - "banana"
        - "cherry"

  - name: repeatable-task
    inputs:
      parameters:
      - name: item
    container:
      image: alpine
      command: ["/bin/sh", "-c"]
      args: ["echo Processing {{inputs.parameters.item}}"]
```

This workflow loops over a list of fruits; each loop iteration assigns a different fruit value to repeatable-task, demonstrating a simple data processing loop.

Parallel and Sequential Iteration: Argo facilitates both parallel and sequential task executions in loops, accommodating various exe-

3.5. CONDITIONAL EXECUTION AND LOOPS

cution strategies for resource management optimization.

```
...
concurrencyPolicy: "Allow"
parallelism: 3
withItems:
 - "1"
 - "2"
 - "3"
 - "4"
 - "5"
...
```

By specifying a parallelism parameter, loops can run multiple instances concurrently, aligning with desired resource availability constraints.

Matrix-Style Looping: Advanced looping allows matrix-style nested iterations to conduct complex processes over multidimensional arrays, enabling high-dimensional processing workflows.

```
templates:
- name: matrix-loop-example
  steps:
  - - name: outer-loop
      template: inner-loop
      arguments:
        parameters:
        - name: outer-param
          value: "{{item}}"
      withItems:
      - "alpha"
      - "beta"

- name: inner-loop
  inputs:
    parameters:
    - name: outer-param
  steps:
  - - name: inner-step
      template: process-pair
      arguments:
        parameters:
        - name: inner-param
          value: "{{item}}"
      withItems:
      - "first"
      - "second"

- name: process-pair
  inputs:
    parameters:
    - name: outer-param
    - name: inner-param
  container:
```

```
image: ubuntu
command: ["echo"]
args: ["Processing outer {{inputs.parameters.outer-param}} and inner {{inputs.
    parameters.inner-param}}"]
```

This matrix-style looping exemplifies nested iterations, processing paired values forming a product space of given elements; delivering complex workflows tailored for data-intensive tasks.

Error management and resolution are crucial when implementing conditional logic and loops, ensuring that the workflow can gracefully deal with failures and unexpected behaviors.

Retry and Backoff Strategies: Implementing retry strategies, with options for exponential backoff, provides resilience against failure points within conditional tasks or loop iterations.

```
...
retryStrategy:
  limit: 3
  backoff:
    duration: "5s"
    factor: 2
...
```

Defining managed retry limits coupled with adaptive backoff strategies enables tasks to cope with transient issues while maintaining workflow integrity.

Conditional After Callback: Enabling "always" conditional paths facilitates cleanup or compensatory actions regardless of the preceding task's success.

```
templates:
- name: with-cleanup
  steps:
  - - name: primary-task
      template: main-operation
  - - name: cleanup-task
      template: tidy-up
      when: "{{workflow.status}} == Failed || {{workflow.status}} == Succeeded"
- name: tidy-up
  container:
    image: busybox
    command: ["sh", "-c", "echo 'Cleaning up resources'"]
```

3.5. CONDITIONAL EXECUTION AND LOOPS

In this setup, cleanup-task executes whether primary-task succeeds or fails, demonstrating a mitigation approach to unresponsive or failed tasks within workflows.

When implementing conditional execution and loops in Argo Workflows, following best practices can minimize complexity while maximizing efficacy:

Criterion Simplicity: Ensuring conditional criteria remain concise and intuitive prevents overly complex logic chains, enhancing readability and maintainability.

Iterative Capability Control: Restricting task parallelism and concurrency according to resource constraints optimizes utilization, preventing accidental overload or downtime.

Assertion Based Validation: Using assertions and variable-logging within conditional and loop evaluations provides diagnostic transparency; developers can rapidly isolate conditional fallacies through comprehensible debug information.

```
...
command: ["python"]
args: ["-c", "import logging; logging.basicConfig(level=logging.DEBUG); logging.debug
    ('{{inputs.parameters.item}} processed')"]
...
```

Incorporating logging captures real-time iteration insights aiding in verification phase, securing workflow correctness and logical adherence.

Conditional execution and loops empower Argo Workflows, transforming static process definitions into adaptable, iterative, and robust retry-capable execution plans. Harnessing conditionals enables focused control flows, while loops provide iterative data handling mechanisms essential for modern data pipelines. Understanding these fundamental elements positions practitioners to create scalable, resilient workflows capable of meeting dynamic operational needs.

3.6 Events and Signals in Argo Workflows

In the landscape of cloud-native IoT and microservices architectures, being able to respond to external events and signals is crucial for enabling intricate automation and reactive systems. Argo Workflows supports a robust event-driven architecture, allowing workflows to reactively execute in response to a plethora of events and signals. This section elucidates how workflows can integrate with event-driven systems, describe event sources and signals, and provide comprehensive examples illustrating their implementation.

Event-Driven Architecture Event-driven architecture involves the components within a system responding to events, which are state changes or signals generated due to user actions, scheduled dispatches, or other triggers. For cloud-native applications deployed on Kubernetes, integrating workflows with event-driven capabilities streamlines real-time processing and enhances automation.

Argo Workflows relies on Argo Events, a sister project that delivers event-driven and cloud-native integration for workflows, providing connectors for numerous event sources.

Setting Up Argo Events: Argo Events consist of sensors and gateways, where gateways listen for incoming events, and sensors trigger workflows based on matched events. This structure decouples workload orchestration from event producers, enhancing scalability and modularity.

```
kubectl create namespace argo-events
kubectl apply -n argo-events -f https://github.com/argoproj/argo-events/releases/
    download/v1.4.0/install.yaml
```

This command deploys Argo Events in the designated namespace, integrating event listening and dispatching capabilities with the existing Kubernetes setup.

3.6. EVENTS AND SIGNALS IN ARGO WORKFLOWS

Event Sources Event sources determine where and how events are generated. These sources include, but are not limited to, webhook invocations, S3 object changes, message queue updates, calendar events, or periodic triggers. Each event gateway is tailored to a specific type of event stream or API, facilitating diverse event integrations for workflow triggers.

Webhooks: Webhooks are lightweight HTTP callbacks triggered by certain events on servers. Leveraging webhooks facilitates real-time event processing, initiating workflows immediately upon event detection.

```
apiVersion: argoproj.io/v1alpha1
kind: EventSource
metadata:
  name: example-webhook
spec:
  service:
    ports:
      - port: 12000
        targetPort: 12000
  webhook:
    example:
      endpoint: /hook
      method: POST
      port: 12000
```

This example defines an event source listening on port 12000, triggering an event upon receiving a POST request at the specified endpoint.

S3 Bucket Notifications: S3 event sources track object lifecycle events. When objects are created, removed, or overwritten in an S3 bucket, it can trigger corresponding workflows in Argo.

```
apiVersion: argoproj.io/v1alpha1
kind: EventSource
metadata:
  name: s3-source
spec:
  service:
    ports:
      - port: 9100
        targetPort: 9100
  s3:
    example:
      bucket: my-s3-bucket
      region: us-west-2
      events:
```

```
- s3:ObjectCreated:*
```

This configuration enables an S3 event source for object creation events in a specific bucket, using AWS region us-west-2.

Calendrical Events: Calendrical events are ideal for workflows managed by intervals or schedules. Periodic jobs can automate dataset generations, report compilations, or backups based on specified schedules.

```
apiVersion: argoproj.io/v1alpha1
kind: EventSource
metadata:
  name: calendar-timer
spec:
  schedule:
    my-schedule:
      schedule: "0 9 * * *"
      timezone: "America/Los_Angeles"
```

This cron-style schedule initiates events daily at 9 AM PST, offering temporal triggers suited for routine automation.

Signals within Argo Workflows A signal within Argo Workflows encompasses any actionable message from an event source that a sensor can interpret to execute dependent tasks or workflows. Syncing workflows with signals enables reactive processing tailored to incoming event data.

Sensors and Triggers: Sensors in Argo Events are associated with one or more event sources, matching incoming event payloads to predefined filters before triggering specific workflows or tasks.

```
apiVersion: argoproj.io/v1alpha1
kind: Sensor
metadata:
  name: webhook-sensor
spec:
  template:
    serviceAccountName: argo-events-sa
  dependencies:
    - name: webhook-gateway
      eventSourceName: example-webhook
      eventName: example
  triggers:
```

3.6. EVENTS AND SIGNALS IN ARGO WORKFLOWS

```yaml
    - template:
        name: argo-trigger
        argoWorkflow:
          group: argoproj.io
          version: v1alpha1
          namespace: argo
          source:
            resource:
              apiVersion: argoproj.io/v1alpha1
              kind: Workflow
              metadata:
                generateName: webhook-triggered-
              spec:
                entrypoint: main
                templates:
                - name: main
                  container:
                    image: busybox
                    command: ["/bin/sh", "-c"]
                    args: ["echo 'Triggered by webhook event'"]
```

This sensor configuration connects to an example-webhook gateway, listening for specific events, and invokes an associated Argo Workflow upon event matching.

Data-Driven Workflows: Sensors enable context-driven execution paths by capturing, accessing, and adapting workflows based on event data, supporting dynamic payloads and decisions.

```yaml
...
triggers:
  - template:
      name: data-driven-trigger
      argoWorkflow:
        source:
          resource:
            spec:
              arguments:
                parameters:
                - name: event-data
                  value: "{{inputs.parameters.webhook.data}}"
...
```

The workflow accesses event-generated data, demonstrating how workflows adapt to event-specific inputs, enabling data-driven actions embedded within event signals.

Practical Applications of Events and Signals Argo Workflows' event-driven foundation supports diverse applications across industry domains, catering to scenarios requiring real-time data processing, seamless integration, and intelligent reaction systems.

CI/CD Pipelines: By integrating VCS webhooks, Argo Workflows can drive automated CI/CD processes triggered by git push events, initiating builds, tests, and deployments.

```
webhook:
  handlePushEvent:
    endpoint: /webhook
    method: POST
    port: 3030
    filters:
      metadata:
        content-type: application/json
```

This configuration establishes a GitHub webhook listener for repository changes, aligning workflow triggers to continuous integration tasks.

ETL Workflows: Argo Workflows automate ETL (Extract, Transform, Load) processes from S3 events, conducting data transformations and loading structured data into analytical or storage systems.

```
...
templates:
- name: etl-process
  steps:
  - - name: extract
      template: extract-data
  - - name: transform
      template: transform-data
  - - name: load
      template: load-data
...
```

This workflow orchestrates the ETL pipeline into discrete phases prompted by S3 object state changes, facilitating seamless data synchronization.

Serverless Function Triggers: Microservices architectures gain enhancements from Argo's capability to trigger serverless functions or cloud services upon event reception, connecting workflows with cloud-native operations.

```yaml
apiVersion: argoproj.io/v1alpha1
kind: Sensor
metadata:
  name: lambda-sensor
spec:
  triggers:
    - template:
        name: lambda-trigger
        webhook:
          method: POST
          url: <AWS_LAMBDA_FUNCTION_URL>
```

This example illustrates the triggering of an AWS Lambda function through a webhook, exemplifying custom serverless integration possibilities.

Security and Best Practices Ensuring security in event-driven architectures involves stringent practices around authentication, access control, and data privacy, particularly within multi-tenant environments.

Authentication and Access: Employing secure token-based authentication when designing gateway interfaces bolsters event source credibility and integrity. Lifecycle management and rotation practices on tokens and access keys enhance security robustness.

Data Validation: When workflows respond to incoming event data, validation mechanisms must be in place, ensuring the integrity, confidentiality, and accuracy of processed data inputs, mitigating injection attacks and malformed data vulnerabilities.

Resource Quota Management: Sensible restriction of resource consumption based on quota policies deters exhausting system capacity, safeguarding operational stability amid elevated signal bursts.

Ecosystem Integration and Future Directions Events and signals within Argo Workflows serve as the linchpin between reactive control systems and complex process automation. Expanding these integrations across various platforms, APIs, and technologies heralds significant strides towards comprehensive IoT automation, intelligent orchestration, and harmonized hybrid-cloud workloads.

Through continuous development of connectors, plugins, and extensions, Argo aims to broaden its event source inclusivity, encouraging seamless ecosystem integration. Long-term prospects envision deeper AI augmentation, where machine learning intelligence fabricates predictive analytics within event-processing logics, redefining operational paradigms in software architectures and workflows.

3.7 Visualization and Management with Argo UI

In the sophisticated ecosystem of Kubernetes, Argo Workflows offers an invaluable toolset for orchestrating complex workflows. However, managing and visualizing these workflows through purely command-line interfaces can be cumbersome, especially for intricate pipelines. Argo provides a comprehensive web-based User Interface (UI) that simplifies the visualization, management, and monitoring of workflows, thereby enhancing ease of use, debugging, and operational efficiency.

Argo UI is a graphical user interface designed to interact with Argo Workflows. It provides an interactive and intuitive platform for users to monitor workflow execution, inspect workflow templates, view detailed logs, and manage ongoing and past workflow runs. The UI reduces the complexity involved in handling large-scale workflows by offering visual insights and enabling a user-friendly interaction paradigm.

Features of Argo UI: Argo UI caters to several crucial aspects of workflow management:

- **Visual Workflow Editor:** Provides a graphical representation of workflows, showcasing task flows, dependencies, and execution status.

- **Real-time Status Monitoring:** Offers live updates on the

3.7. VISUALIZATION AND MANAGEMENT WITH ARGO UI

state of workflows, including succeeded, running, and failed tasks.

- **Logging and Debugging:** Facilitates in-depth log inspection for individual tasks to aid debugging.
- **Multi-workflow Management:** Allows browsing and managing multiple workflows simultaneously, supporting complex operational requirements.
- **Access Controls and Visibility:** Integrates with Kubernetes' Role-Based Access Control (RBAC) to manage user permissions and visibility.
- **Resource Efficiency Tracking:** Enables assessment of resource usage metrics, fostering informed resource allocation and optimization.

Argo UI operates as a Kubernetes service. To set up the UI, users must ensure the Argo Workflows controller is deployed within their cluster, and the UI server is properly configured.

Deploying Argo UI: Argo UI is typically included as part of the Argo Workflows installation. Users need to ensure the services are correctly set to render the UI operational.

```
kubectl apply -n argo -f https://raw.githubusercontent.com/argoproj/argo-workflows/stable/manifests/install.yaml
```

This command effectively deploys Argo Workflows along with the UI server in the 'argo' namespace, setting the ground for intuitive workflow management through a browser interface.

Accessing the Interface: Access to the Argo UI can be gained via port-forwarding, through a configured ingress or load balancer, which allows remote access to cluster resources.

```
kubectl -n argo port-forward svc/argo-server 2746:2746
```

Once port-forwarding is established, the UI can be accessed by navigating to 'http://localhost:2746' in a web browser, offering seamless interaction with workflows and their data.

The UI is organized to visually represent workflows, allowing easy exploration and management of ongoing and completed jobs. The main components of the UI include:

Welcome Dashboard: Upon login, users are greeted by a centralized dashboard overviewing the cluster's workflows. This dashboard displays active, completed, and recent workflows, detailing their status and facilitating quick access to specific jobs.

Workflow Details: Selecting a workflow opens a detailed view, showcasing a comprehensive breakdown including:

- **Workflow Graph:** A DAG illustrating node connectivity, task dependencies, real-time statuses with intuitive color-coding for succeeded, in-progress, and failed tasks.

- **Timeline View:** A chronological layout providing execution order insights, aiding in performance analysis.

- **Input/Output Parameters:** Accessibility to injected parameters and returned outputs for each task within the workflow, supporting data verification.

- **Step Logs:** Integrated log viewer that displays detailed logs per task aiding in diagnosing workflow execution issues.

- **Execution Metrics:** Showcases runtime metrics such as pod allocation, CPU, and memory utilization, enabling resource management and debugging.

The Argo UI not only facilitates visualization of workflows but offers a host of management options to manipulate and interact with workflows dynamically. Users can perform actions such as:

Workflow Submission:

- **New Workflow Launch:** Initiate workflows directly through the UI, specifying templates, input parameters, and configuration settings.

3.7. VISUALIZATION AND MANAGEMENT WITH ARGO UI

```
apiVersion: argoproj.io/v1alpha1
kind: Workflow
metadata:
  generateName: my-workflow-
spec:
  entrypoint: main
  templates:
  - name: main
    steps:
    - - name: hello-world
        template: hello-world-step

  - name: hello-world-step
    container:
      image: busybox
      command: ["echo"]
      args: ["hello world"]
```

Submitting the above workflow via Argo UI loads the YAML manifest directly, easing quick deployments without CLI interference.

Workflow Pause and Resume:

- **Suspend/Resume Workflows:** Temporarily pause workflows during execution to address errors, debugging, or resource unavailability, resuming with retained state continuity.

Workflow Retry:

- **Retry Mechanics:** Trigger task evaluation and rerun failed execution paths directly from the UI to reconcile with transient faults or errors in earlier steps.

Workflow Abortion:

- **Terminate/Abort Running Workflows:** Powerfully stop unnecessary or erroneous workflows to conserve resources.

Logs are essential for understanding workflow task performance and debugging. Argo UI enhances logging capabilities by integrating task-level log displays directly within workflow interfaces. Users can analyze logs for:

- Verification of command executions
- Detection of discrepancies or failures
- Understanding task input/output dynamics

Enhanced with search and filtering options, Argo's UI provides direct links to log streams, enhancing the investigative process.

Efficient execution of workloads demands continual performance and resource usage monitoring. Argo UI's metrics visualization capabilities empower administrators and developers to:

- **Visualize CPU and memory footprint:** Examine exact resource consumption metrics per task, identifying hotspots or inefficiencies.
- **Analyze Task Duration:** Identify bottlenecks in workflows based on excerpted runtime analyses.
- **Optimize Resource Allocation:** Allocate cluster resources based on actual task demand, enhancing operational efficiency.

Ensuring secure access to Argo UI is crucial, especially within sensitive production environments. Role-Based Access Control (RBAC) settings define user permissions, with capabilities to:

- **Define User Roles:** Set UI access levels, securing sensitive functions to only authorized personnel.
- **Integrate identity management:** Utilize OAuth or SAML for authentication, enhancing security with Single Sign-On (SSO) facilities.

Continuous development of the Argo UI ecosystem fosters advancements in visualization, integration, and functionality frameworks:

Advanced Visualization: Future enhancements include 3D visualization expansions for sophisticated DAG representations, catering to increasingly complex workflows with multiple interdependent layers.

3.7. VISUALIZATION AND MANAGEMENT WITH ARGO UI

API and Third-party Integration: Stemming from partnerships or ecosystem extensions, direct linkage rule settings for third-party monitoring tools enrich Argo's visualization potential, fostering ecosystem-wide cohesion.

Enhanced Workflow Analytics: Integration of data science analytics within the UI transforms visual inspection into advanced predictive insights, offering real-time resource demand forecasts and analytic dashboards.

AI-Driven Decision Support: Adopting AI models to suggest workflow optimizations, error mitigation strategies, or potential enhancements trumpets future capabilities, placing Argo at the forefront of intelligent workflow orchestration.

Argo UI transcends traditional CLI-based management, providing comprehensive visualization and management apparatus for dynamic workflows. By amplifying operational insights and monitoring capabilities, it empowers organizations to administer, optimize, and advance their Kubernetes-native applications with efficiency and precision.

Chapter 4

Creating Your First Argo Workflow

This chapter guides readers through the process of creating their first Argo Workflow, providing a practical approach to building and deploying workflows on Kubernetes. It begins with preparing the necessary environment and defining a simple workflow template, detailing crucial syntax and basic elements. Readers learn how to submit their workflows using kubectl and the Argo CLI, followed by techniques for real-time monitoring of workflow execution. The chapter addresses error handling and retry logic to ensure resilience, concluding with insights on retrieving workflow outputs and iterating on workflow design to enhance functionality and performance.

4.1 Setting the Stage for Your First Workflow

Establishing a robust environment is paramount for seamless workflow execution within Kubernetes, with Argo Workflows requiring a properly configured setup to leverage its full potential. This section delves into configuring the necessary tools and setting up the environment, encompassing Kubernetes cluster creation, the installation of Argo Workflows, and essential preparatory steps.

The fundamental prerequisite involves having a Kubernetes cluster. Kubernetes, an open-source platform for managing containerized applications, serves as the backbone for Argo Workflows. A Kubernetes cluster can be established either locally or on cloud service providers such as Google Kubernetes Engine (GKE), Amazon Elastic Kubernetes Service (EKS), or Microsoft Azure Kubernetes Service (AKS). For testing and development purposes, tools like Minikube or kind (Kubernetes IN Docker) offer a convenient local environment.

```
curl -LO https://storage.googleapis.com/minikube/releases/latest/minikube-linux-
    amd64
sudo install minikube-linux-amd64 /usr/local/bin/minikube
minikube start --driver=docker
```

Upon successful Kubernetes installation, verify the cluster's functionality with the following command:

```
kubectl get nodes
```

Upon confirmation that the node is ready, you can proceed with installing Argo Workflows, leveraging its powerful orchestration capabilities. The recommended approach for installation uses kubectl, the Kubernetes command-line tool, which manages Kubernetes cluster components.

Ensure your kubectl configuration is aligned with the Kubernetes cluster context. If you are using Minikube, switch the context to Minikube:

```
kubectl config use-context minikube
```

Argo Workflows is typically installed via the application of predefined manifests. Execute the following commands to retrieve and apply configuration files for Argo Workflows swiftly:

```
kubectl create namespace argo
kubectl apply -n argo -f https://github.com/argoproj/argo-workflows/releases/
    download/v3.0.7/install.yaml
```

Verify the installation of Argo Workflows by listing services in the Argo namespace:

4.1. SETTING THE STAGE FOR YOUR FIRST WORKFLOW

```
kubectl get pods -n argo
```

The expected output should confirm the running state of essential Argo components such as workflow-controller and argo-server. These components are crucial for processing and monitoring workflows on the Kubernetes cluster.

```
NAME                                 READY  STATUS   RESTARTS  AGE
argo-server-6d9ccdccf7-8j8tw         1/1    Running  0         5m
workflow-controller-76f7f5f54-k5xgt  1/1    Running  0         5m
```

Having deployed Argo successfully, the next preparatory task involves installing the Argo CLI. The command-line interface provides additional features for managing workflows directly from the console. Installation can be executed with these commands:

```
curl -sLO https://github.com/argoproj/argo-workflows/releases/download/v3.0.7/argo-
     linux-amd64
chmod +x argo-linux-amd64
sudo mv ./argo-linux-amd64 /usr/local/bin/argo
```

Validate the installation by checking the version:

```
argo version
```

This basic setup allows for seamless interaction with both Kubernetes and Argo Workflows, where workflows are submitted, monitored, and managed effectively.

Environmental variables significantly influence workflow execution, requiring a meticulously defined configuration. Documenting environment-specific variables crucial to Kubernetes ensures that workflows remain scalable and adaptable to shifts in application requirements or infrastructure changes. It is beneficial to catalog nodes, pods, and services interacting with the Argo subsystem to maintain an optimized execution environment.

Furthermore, effective identity and access management enhance security protocols and mitigate unauthorized access. Implementing Kubernetes Role-Based Access Control (RBAC) integrates with Argo to enforce granular access policies:

```
apiVersion: rbac.authorization.k8s.io/v1
kind: Role
```

```
metadata:
  namespace: argo
  name: argo-role
rules:
- apiGroups: ["argoproj.io"]
  resources: ["workflows"]
  verbs: ["get", "list", "watch", "create", "delete"]
```

After defining roles, bind them to users or service accounts with a RoleBinding:

```
apiVersion: rbac.authorization.k8s.io/v1
kind: RoleBinding
metadata:
  name: argo-binding
  namespace: argo
subjects:
- kind: ServiceAccount
  name: default
  namespace: argo
roleRef:
  kind: Role
  name: argo-role
  apiGroup: rbac.authorization.k8s.io
```

These steps culminate in a fortified setting for Argo Workflows, positioning your infrastructure for efficacious workflow orchestration. Addressing data locality and affinity rules further optimizes the performance of distributed workloads within Kubernetes, ensuring efficient resource use and minimizing latency in communications between pods.

Networking within the Kubernetes cluster presents intricate requirements, particularly when sensitive data is transmitted. Ensuring that communication channels leverage Transport Layer Security (TLS) protocols is crucial, particularly for workflows requiring data-sensitive operations. Encrypting traffic both in transit and at rest is a recommended best practice.

Rounding out the preparatory stage is logging and monitoring infrastructure, pivotal for debugging and understanding workflow execution behavior. Kubernetes offers integration with popular logging solutions such as Fluentd, Prometheus, and Grafana, providing deep insights into real-time events. Logging captures error states and execution paths, whereas Prometheus and Grafana visualize performance metrics and historical trends.

Proper attention to infrastructure readiness before creating and executing Argo workflows enhances not only performance but also reliability and security. Scalability considerations embedded at this initial stage ensure the system's resilience and adaptability as demands evolve. The following sections will delve deeper into crafting workflow templates, running workloads, and managing lifecycle events—all operating on this meticulously configured stage.

4.2 Defining a Simple Workflow Template

Crafting a workflow template constitutes a crucial step in leveraging Argo Workflows, allowing for the orchestration of tasks across a Kubernetes cluster. This section focuses on defining a simple workflow template, illuminating the core structure, necessary components, and various syntax features vital for constructing a viable Argo Workflow.

A workflow within Argo is expressed using YAML, a human-readable data serialization standard that is both flexible and easy to use. The structure encapsulates metadata, specifying essential parameters and defining a sequence of steps representing tasks. This clear definition of tasks as directed acyclic graphs (DAGs) enhances the coordination and scheduling of containerized applications.

Start by considering the elementary components of a workflow YAML specification. Below is a rudimentary example:

```
apiVersion: argoproj.io/v1alpha1
kind: Workflow
metadata:
  generateName: hello-world-
spec:
  entrypoint: whalesay
  templates:
  - name: whalesay
    container:
      image: docker/whalesay:latest
      command: [cowsay]
      args: ["hello world"]
```

In this simple template, the 'apiVersion' and 'kind' fields identify the resource type within Kubernetes. The 'metadata' field, crucial for resource management, includes 'generateName', creating uniqueness for each workflow instance through automatic suffix addition. The 'spec' field delineates the specifics of the workflow operation.

Introducing the 'entrypoint' defines the initial template executed when the workflow commences. This template is a collection of specifications that dictate what containerized tasks to perform. Here, the workflow declares a single 'whalesay' task using the 'docker/whalesay' image, executing the 'cowsay' command.

Although this example showcases basic operations, workflows usually comprise multiple steps and can incorporate conditional executions, loops, and advanced scheduling mechanisms. Understanding task and data dependencies is integral for constructing complex workflows. Argo utilizes DAGs to enable this modeling, ensuring tasks execute based on their precursors' completion.

To model a sequence of tasks, the 'dag' template type explicitly outlines each node and its dependencies. Consider extending the basic workflow by introducing a multi-step sequence:

```
apiVersion: argoproj.io/v1alpha1
kind: Workflow
metadata:
  generateName: sequential-
spec:
  entrypoint: sequential-example
  templates:
  - name: sequential-example
    dag:
      tasks:
      - name: step-one
        template: whalesay
      - name: step-two
        template: print-date
        dependencies: [step-one]

  - name: whalesay
    container:
      image: docker/whalesay:latest
      command: [cowsay]
      args: ["Task one completed"]

  - name: print-date
    container:
      image: busybox
      command: ["date"]
```

This workflow illustrates two steps: 'step-one' and 'step-two'. The 'step-two' only executes after 'step-one', thus enforcing sequential pro-

4.2. DEFINING A SIMPLE WORKFLOW TEMPLATE

cessing. Dependencies are explicitly highlighted within the task definition. Argo's ability to manage task dependencies with DAGs naturally supports this design, enabling rich orchestration patterns.

A more advanced workflow exploits both parameter passing and artifacts, enhancing workflow interactivity and allowing tasks to share computations' results. Parameters are frequently employed for dynamic task configuration. Argo supports parameterization via the 'arguments' and 'parameters' fields:

```
apiVersion: argoproj.io/v1alpha1
kind: Workflow
metadata:
  generateName: parameterized-
spec:
  entrypoint: parameter-example
  arguments:
    parameters:
    - name: message
      value: "Hello Argo!"
  templates:
  - name: parameter-example
    inputs:
      parameters:
      - name: message
    container:
      image: alpine
      command: [echo]
      args: ["{{inputs.parameters.message}}"]
```

This parameterized workflow injects a dynamic 'message' across tasks, demonstrating customization and reusability potential in workflow design. Parameters offer the flexibility needed to adapt workflows based on input data without modifying the workflow definition drastically.

Artifacts transform workflows' inter-task communication, serving as integral components when tasks necessitate the consumption of other tasks' outputs. These outputs, materialized as artifacts, enable complex operations like data processing and analysis pipelines. The following illustrates how to manage artifacts within a workflow:

```
apiVersion: argoproj.io/v1alpha1
kind: Workflow
metadata:
  generateName: artifact-dependency-
spec:
  entrypoint: artifact-example
  templates:
  - name: artifact-example
    dag:
```

113

CHAPTER 4. CREATING YOUR FIRST ARGO WORKFLOW

```
    tasks:
    - name: produce-artifact
      template: generate-artifact
    - name: consume-artifact
      template: use-artifact
      arguments:
        artifacts:
        - name: sample-artifact
          from: "{{tasks.produce-artifact.outputs.artifacts.sample}}"
- name: generate-artifact
  outputs:
    artifacts:
    - name: sample
      path: /tmp/sample.txt
  container:
    image: busybox
    command: ["sh", "-c"]
    args: ["echo 'Argo workflow' > /tmp/sample.txt"]
- name: use-artifact
  inputs:
    artifacts:
    - name: sample-artifact
      path: /tmp/sample.txt
  container:
    image: busybox
    command: [cat]
    args: ["/tmp/sample.txt"]
```

Artifact management within Argo facilitates the output from one step becoming the input to another, preserving state and enabling sophisticated data-driven workflows. For seamless data transition across tasks, Argo supports storage backends like S3, Google Cloud Storage, and MinIO, thus providing substantial flexibility.

Conditional task execution further enriches workflow capabilities, optimizing resource usage and adhering to business logic. Armed with expression templates leveraging 'when' clauses, workflows can pivot execution paths dynamically:

```
apiVersion: argoproj.io/v1alpha1
kind: Workflow
metadata:
  generateName: conditional-
spec:
  entrypoint: conditional-example
  templates:
  - name: conditional-example
    dag:
      tasks:
      - name: true-step
        when: "{{inputs.parameters.runStep}} == true"
```

4.2. DEFINING A SIMPLE WORKFLOW TEMPLATE

```
      template: whalesay
    - name: false-step
      when: "{{inputs.parameters.runStep}} == false"
      template: print-date

 - name: whalesay
   container:
     image: docker/whalesay:latest
     command: [cowsay]
     args: ["This step only runs if true"]

 - name: print-date
   container:
     image: alpine
     command: ["date"]
```

The inclusion of 'when' clauses introduces logic operations within workflows, streamlining condition-based execution and fostering efficient resource utilization.

Structured workflow design practices ensure maintainability and scalability, qualities crucial for production-level operations. Appropriately naming templates and parameters enhances readability, helping developers and operators quickly understand workflow logic. Documentation through annotations within the 'workflow' or 'template' fields augments transparency, fostering collaborative development and workflow sharing.

Developing a workflow template encompasses a breadth of considerations, from defining data dependencies to implementing parameterization and artifact management, all designed to leverage Argo Workflow's full capabilities. As workflow complexity increases, so does the demand for robust testing strategies. Testing workflows in controlled environments ensures accurate functionality and resource utilization before deployment, mitigating potential disruptions in production.

The process of constructing a workflow template in Argo is one that benefits from iterative design and refinement. Embarking on small, testable increments assures alignment with desired outcomes while allowing space for future augmentations. Properly designed workflows, extending beyond simple sequences, integrate advanced scheduling, conditional logic, and robust error handling, ultimately driving efficient orchestration at scale across Kubernetes clusters.

4.3 Submitting Your Workflow to Kubernetes

Following the construction of a thoroughly defined workflow template, the next logical step in the lifecycle of an Argo Workflow is its submission to a Kubernetes cluster. Submission of workflows not only translates to deploying tasks for execution but also entails managing resources, monitoring execution states, and interfacing with Kubernetes and Argo components. This section dives into the intricacies of workflow submission, emphasizing command-line tools, efficient resource allocation, and submission strategies that cater to diverse requirements.

At the heart of submitting workflows lies the Kubernetes command-line tool, kubectl, and the Argo CLI. Both tools offer distinct features for submission tasks, providing administrators and developers the necessary functionality to manage and scale workflows efficiently.

- **Workflow Submission with Argo CLI:**

The Argo CLI simplifies the process of managing workflows. Utilizing direct commands, administrators submit, monitor, and control workflows with minimal configuration. Below is an example command used to submit a workflow YAML file:

```
argo submit -n argo hello-world.yaml
```

This command submits a workflow, typically described in a YAML file such as 'hello-world.yaml', to the Argo namespace within a Kubernetes cluster. The output of this action is a successfully scheduled workflow instance, visible and trackable within Argo's ecosystem.

To capture rapid feedback and monitor the progress of an active workflow, employ the following command:

```
argo watch @latest
```

The 'watch' command outputs real-time status updates, offering insight into task execution, resource utilization, and potential bottlenecks or failures that require intervention.

4.3. SUBMITTING YOUR WORKFLOW TO KUBERNETES

- **Workflow Submission Using kubectl:**

Kubernetes' native command-line interface, kubectl, provides an alternative workflow submission mechanism. By leveraging its rich set of features, users can engage cluster-level operations, submit YAML configurations, and harness advanced resource controls. The following demonstrates how to initiate a workflow using kubectl:

```
kubectl apply -f hello-world.yaml -n argo
```

This command applies the workflow configuration to the specified namespace, deploying tasks as encapsulated in the workflow template. Upon execution, workflows are subjected to Kubernetes' robust scheduling and resource orchestration functionalities.

- **Resource Allocation and Scheduling:**

Sound resource management is paramount in optimizing workflow execution within Kubernetes. Each workflow's resource needs depend on its tasks, influencing scheduling priorities, and performance. The Kubernetes scheduler evaluates workflow resource requests, provisioning them based on node availability, configured limits, and resource quotas.

Here is a snippet illustrating resource requests and limits in a template definition:

```
spec:
  templates:
  - name: resource-intensive-task
    container:
      image: resource-intensive-image
      resources:
        requests:
          memory: "512Mi"
          cpu: "0.5"
        limits:
          memory: "1Gi"
          cpu: "1"
```

The 'resources' field delineates CPU and memory specifications guiding the Kubernetes scheduler. Requests define baseline resource requirements, ensuring task execution, while limits protect against resource overconsumption, preserving cluster equilibrium.

Adjusting resource allocations supports diversified workload demands, encouraging maximum throughput, and minimizing potential cross-task contention. For workflows spanning numerous tasks, specify resource needs accurately to align with cluster capacity and optimize task parallelism through efficient resource distribution.

- **Networking and Service Integration:**

Networking and service integration form another critical layer when deploying workflows. Access to external services, databases, and APIs expands a workflow's functional breadth, necessitating conducive network policies and service configurations. Consider workflows requiring data ingestion from an external database or submission of task outputs to a web API; ensure that the network interfaces and routes are adequately configured for reliable connectivity.

Establish Kubernetes Services to expose pods with necessary configurations. Here is how to create a basic service entry to facilitate networking:

```
apiVersion: v1
kind: Service
metadata:
  name: workflow-service
spec:
  selector:
    app: my-workflow
  ports:
    - protocol: TCP
      port: 80
      targetPort: 9376
```

This service configuration enhances the accessibility of workflow pods, encompassing fixed entry points for consumption by other systems or workflows.

- **Debugging and Error Resolution:**

Identifying and resolving errors in workflow submission and execution is vital for maintaining operational stability. Leveraging logs and event details promotes effective diagnostics and remedial measures. Both Kubernetes and Argo provide comprehensive logging facilities, enriching transparency and guiding debugging processes.

4.3. SUBMITTING YOUR WORKFLOW TO KUBERNETES

Use the following to retrieve log outputs for a specific workflow pod:

```
kubectl logs <pod-name> -n argo
```

Argo's CLI also supports extracting logs from workflow nodes, simplifying the acquisition of detailed execution narratives:

```
argo logs @latest
```

Incorporating logging practices and instrumenting workflows for enhanced observability facilitates swift identification of execution anomalies. These logs often highlight root causes of failures ranging from image pull errors to scripting or deployment misconfigurations.

- **Best Practices for Workflow Submission:**

  - Namespace Segregation: Deploy workflows in dedicated namespaces, minimizing interferences and optimizing resource management through isolated contexts.

  - Version Management: Use versioning for workflow templates and application images, tracking changes, and facilitating rollback strategies during workflow modifications.

  - Resource Monitoring: Actively monitor resource usage with Kubernetes metric systems like Prometheus, detecting overprovisioning or bottlenecks, and recalibrating resource distribution.

  - Security Hardening: Integrate security controls, applying network policies, implementing service mesh technologies, and restricting pod access via Kubernetes Role-Based Access Control (RBAC).

By adhering to these best practices, the integrity and efficiency of the workflow submission process are elevated, fostering a stable and predictable execution environment.

- **Workflow Submission Scalability:**

Embracing workflow submission at scale requires sophisticated orchestration patterns and automation techniques. Use Kubernetes Operators or Helm charts to automate the deployment of complex Argo Workflows, supporting scale-out strategies that address evolving workflow volumes.

Further encoding workflows into an Infrastructure-as-Code (IaC) paradigm extends the scalability by enabling automated delivery pipelines, thus transforming workflow deployment into a repeatable, maintainable, and transparent operation.

The submission of workflows to Kubernetes involves intricate orchestration, leveraging both fundamental command-line utilities and advanced resource management strategies. Submitting workflows is a continuous cycle, with ongoing adjustments and optimizations required to maintain peak performance, resource efficiency, and security alignment. As demands and requirements evolve, the outlined strategies provide a solid foundation for deploying workflows robustly and responsively within a Kubernetes environment. This continuous improvement loop ensures the operational excellence of workflows throughout their lifecycle.

4.4 Monitoring Workflow Execution

Effective monitoring of workflow execution is indispensable for maintaining the operational integrity and performance of Argo Workflows running on Kubernetes. This section explores comprehensive monitoring strategies, delves into data collection and analysis methods, and introduces tools and techniques to oversee and manage workflow execution. Real-time monitoring facilitates swift anomaly detection, optimizes resource allocation, and aids in meeting predefined Service Level Agreements (SLAs).

- **Key Monitoring Objectives:** Monitoring seeks to accomplish several core objectives, each focusing on different aspects of workflow execution:
    - **Execution Status:** Determine the real-time state of workflows, identifying whether they are pending, running, succeeded, or failed.

- **Performance Metrics:** Track and analyze task completion times, resource usage (CPU, memory), and I/O operations to ensure efficient execution.
- **Error Detection:** Detect and diagnose operational issues or task failures promptly, minimizing potential downtime or disruptions.
- **Resource Utilization:** Monitor resource consumption trends to guide optimizations in cluster resource allocations.

- **Monitoring Tools and Technologies:** Several tools and technologies facilitate monitoring Argo Workflows within Kubernetes, each possessing unique capabilities and integrations:
  - **Argo CLI:** Provides immediate feedback and monitoring capabilities, allowing users to query workflow status, logs, and completion details through command-line interactions.
  - **Argo UI:** Web-based interface offering visual representations of workflow execution, ideal for observing real-time progress and diagnosing issues visually.
  - **Prometheus and Grafana:** Popular for deploying robust monitoring metrics, Prometheus collects data while Grafana visualizes trends and patterns across workflows.
  - **Fluentd and ELK Stack:** Support extensive logging capabilities, enabling detailed introspection of workflow operations for better audit and debugging.

- **Monitoring with Argo CLI:** The Argo CLI commands streamline the monitoring process by providing succinct execution status overviews. For instance, to retrieve the status of a specific workflow:

```
argo get <workflow-name>
```

This command outputs critical status elements such as the start and finish time of workflows, the success state of each task, and the total duration required for execution.

Real-time oversight of active workflows can be acquired via the 'watch' command:

```
argo watch <workflow-name>
```

- **Visual Monitoring with Argo UI:** The Argo UI extends monitoring through an interactive graphical dashboard, showcasing visual interpretations of workflows and their respective tasks. Upon accessing the UI, users can visually inspect workflow execution paths, click on tasks for detailed output logs, and filter workflows based on namespaces or resource characteristics.

  The Argo UI typically deploys as part of the Argo Workflows installation and can be accessed through port-forwarding to expose its service:

```
kubectl -n argo port-forward service/argo-server 2746:2746
# Access at http://localhost:2746
```

  The front-end provides holistic representations of workflow statuses, encapsulating error and success states, making it easier to steer operational decisions from a macroscopic viewpoint.

- **Prometheus and Grafana Integration:** To build sophisticated monitoring frameworks, Argo Workflows integrates seamlessly with Prometheus for metric collection and Grafana for dynamic data visualization. Prometheus scrapes custom metrics from the Kubernetes cluster, while Grafana compiles these into intuitive dashboards.

  Below illustrates enabling metrics in Kubernetes using Prometheus:

```
apiVersion: monitoring.coreos.com/v1
kind: ServiceMonitor
metadata:
  name: argo-metrics
  labels:
    release: prometheus
spec:
  selector:
    matchLabels:
      app: argo
  namespaceSelector:
    matchNames:
    - argo
  endpoints:
  - port: metrics
    path: /metrics
```

Prometheus automates the collection of metrics exposed in '/metrics' path, enabling continuous insights on execution performance. Meanwhile, Grafana imports these metrics and portrays visual metrics such as CPU load, memory usage, workflow runtimes, and throughput over time.

- **Advanced Log Management using Fluentd and ELK Stack:** The ELK (Elasticsearch, Logstash, Kibana) stack, alongside Fluentd, reinforces workflow execution with sophisticated logging capabilities. Fluentd aggregates and forwards logs from sources like Kubernetes pods into Elasticsearch, where Logstash processes them. Kibana presents these logs in coherent patterns, supporting root cause analysis.

For Fluentd setup, fluent configuration defines log routing:

```
<source>
  @type tail
  path /var/log/argo/*.log
  pos_file /var/log/td-agent/argo.log.pos
  tag kube.argo.*
  format none
</source>

<match kubernetes.**>
  @type elasticsearch
  host elasticsearch.logging.svc.local
</match>
```

This setup efficiently orchestrates log ingestion into Elasticsearch, generating rich logs repositories available for querying and visualization in Kibana.

- **Proactive Issue Resolution:** Embedded monitoring enables proactive issue detection and resolution. Define alerts in Prometheus to trigger notifications upon meeting specific thresholds, such as task failures or excessive resource usage:

```
groups:
- name: argoAlerts
  rules:
  - alert: WorkflowFailure
    expr: argo_workflow_status{status="failed"} > 0
    for: 1m
    labels:
      severity: critical
    annotations:
      summary: "Workflow {{ $labels.name }} is failing"
```

Alert rules facilitate prompt notifications by email, Slack, or other platforms using Prometheus Alertmanager, enhancing responsiveness to workflow execution problems.

- **Optimizing Resource Management:** Utilizing monitoring insights for resource management ensures workflows operate within optimal parameters. Constant data feed facilitates informed decision-making, such as scaling resources up or down based on historical and real-time data insights. Analyze performance graphs to fine-tune workflow templates—adjusting resource requests, concurrency limits, and task dependencies to bolster efficiency.

- **Conclusion: Comprehensive Workflow Monitoring:** Workflow monitoring in Kubernetes with Argo Workflows is a multi-faceted domain requiring the integration of real-time data analysis, sophisticated logging, and performance insights. By utilizing the CLI and UI tools, integrating with Prometheus and Grafana, and harnessing the ELK stack alongside Fluentd, teams significantly improve their ability to manage, diagnose, and fine-tune workflow operations.

   Successful monitoring lays the foundation for resilience and efficiency, ensuring workflows accomplish intended objectives without adversities. Through vigilant monitoring, workflows seamlessly fulfill operational demands, supported by a framework that anticipates needs and responds adaptively to environmental conditions. This results in a robust, trustworthy, and scalable workflow environment that continuously drives productivity and innovation.

4.5 Handling Errors and Retries

The execution of workflows in Kubernetes using Argo Workflows can encounter various errors, stemming from both logical issues within task definitions and environmental inconsistencies in the Kubernetes cluster or external dependencies. Proper error handling and retry

4.5. HANDLING ERRORS AND RETRIES

mechanisms are vital to ensuring resilience, reliability, and the capability to recover from transient faults. This section dissects strategies for addressing errors, implementing retries, configuring error handling policies, and integrating advanced debugging techniques to maintain operational robustness.

Understanding Workflow Errors

Errors within workflows can typically be categorized into:

- **Task-level Errors:** Arising from syntax errors, misconfigurations, runtime exceptions, or resource constraints within individual tasks.

- **Dependency Failures:** Caused by external dependencies, such as network latencies, unavailable services, or API rate limits, leading to execution impediments.

- **System-level Errors:** Cluster-related issues like node failures, insufficient resources, or Kubernetes misconfigurations affecting workflow execution stability.

Error Handling in Argo Workflows

Argo Workflows offers built-in mechanisms to define how errors are managed by tasks or entire workflows:

- **Fail-fast:** Workflows immediately terminate upon encountering errors.

- **Continue-on-error:** Overrides failure cases, enabling execution of successive steps regardless of preceding errors.

- **Retry Policies:** Define systematic retries for transient errors, increasing resiliency and reducing the likelihood of complete workflow failure.

Here is a workflow template showcasing fail-fast behavior:

```
apiVersion: argoproj.io/v1alpha1
kind: Workflow
metadata:
  generateName: fail-fast-
```

```
spec:
  entrypoint: example
  templates:
  - name: example
    steps:
    - - name: fail-step
        template: fail-task
    - - name: succeeding-step
        template: success-task

  - name: fail-task
    container:
      image: alpine
      command: [sh, -c]
      args: ["exit 1"]

  - name: success-task
    container:
      image: alpine
      command: [echo]
      args: ["This step will not run"]
```

Implementing Retry Logic

Retries are employed to recover from non-critical errors, often caused by intermittent network issues or temporarily unavailable resources. Argo Workflows provides a built-in retry mechanism through the 'retryStrategy' field, configurable with several parameters including 'limit', 'backoff', and retry strategies.

Below is an example outlining retry strategy:

```
apiVersion: argoproj.io/v1alpha1
kind: Workflow
metadata:
  generateName: retry-example-
spec:
  entrypoint: retry-task
  templates:
  - name: retry-task
    retryStrategy:
      limit: 3
      backoff:
        duration: "5s"
        factor: 2
        maxDuration: "30s"
    container:
      image: alpine
      command: [sh, -c]
      args: ["if [ $(($RANDOM%2)) -eq 0 ]; then exit 1; else echo Success; fi"]
```

Limit specifies the maximum retry attempts, while the **backoff** policy adds delays between retries, beginning at 'duration', multiplying

4.5. HANDLING ERRORS AND RETRIES

by 'factor', until 'maxDuration'. This exponential backoff minimizes load on external resources and enhances resilience against transient conditions.

Configuring Error Policies

Customize how workflows handle errors through granular error policies, deciding whether to skip errors or continue regardless of task results. The 'continueOn' field assists by specifying the continuation condition based on 'failed', 'error', and 'timeout' states:

```
apiVersion: argoproj.io/v1alpha1
kind: Workflow
metadata:
  generateName: continue-on-error-
spec:
  entrypoint: continue-on-error-example
  templates:
  - name: continue-on-error-example
    steps:
    - - name: first-step
        template: possible-fail
    - - name: second-step
        template: always-run
        continueOn:
          failed: true

  - name: possible-fail
    container:
      image: alpine
      command: [sh, -c]
      args: ["exit 1"]

  - name: always-run
    container:
      image: alpine
      command: [echo]
      args: ["This step runs despite previous failure"]
```

The workflow above forces subsequent execution, demonstrating how critical steps continue following recoverable (or non-critical) errors.

Advanced Debugging Techniques

While error handling strategies mitigate sudden drops in operation due to transient conditions, debugging remains pivotal in uncovering systematic errors. Effective debugging locates root causes through detailed insights gathered from log analysis and runtime environments.

Log Analysis: Logs are primary debugging tools, capturing execution traces, environment states, exceptions, and other vital debugging information. Retrieve logs using:

```
kubectl logs <pod-name> -n argo
```

For focused debugging, Argo CLI returns step-specific log content:

```
argo logs @latest
```

Pod Annotations and Labels: Annotated workflow steps grant engineers a lens into specific execution facets. Labels and annotations assign additional metadata relevant for search, filtering, and tracing scope.

Debugging with Breakpoints: Employing breakpoints in scripts acts as a checkpoint, pausing execution, allowing inspection, and alterations to verify hypotheses or assumptions. Although less common for production systems, breakpoints can assist development and testing phases.

Leveraging Observability for Reliability

Enhanced observability allows for predictive and proactive issue identification, expediting troubleshooting and reducing mean time to recovery (MTTR). Prometheus and Grafana aggregate metrics, encouraging insights into real-time workflow health, while alerting frameworks (e.g., Alertmanager) notify operators of emerging incidents.

Integrating Testing into Workflow Lifecycle

Testing workflow components in simulated environments beforehand prevents unmonitored errors from propagating. Employ unit test frameworks to ensure task scripts execute independently, infrastructure as code (IaC) tools to test deployment and resource management scenarios, and canary deployments to verify workflow behavior without full-scale deployment risks.

Mocking services also isolates external dependencies, thus standardizing test scenarios and reducing interference from service volatility in testing phases.

Best Practices for Error Handling and Retries

- **Understand Error Types:** Differentiate between transient and persistent errors, tailoring retry policies and error handling mechanisms to their nature.

- **Avoid Retry Storms:** Implement backoff strategies to avoid overwhelming systems with excessive repeated requests, ensuring network resource economy.

- **Design for Failure:** Architect workflows anticipating potential failures, considering idempotency in tasks to ensure repeated executions yield identical results.

- **Comprehensive Logging:** Instrument tasks for enhanced observability, coupling log data with contextual parameters and dynamic levels based on task criticality.

- **Thorough Testing:** Prioritize comprehensive testing throughout the lifecycle, encompassing unit tests, regression tests, and integration tests, aligning with CI/CD pipelines to enforce validation and verification before production deployments.

Error handling and retry configurations in Argo Workflows form a cornerstone for resilient operations. Skillfully addressing the multifaceted nature of errors, incorporating robust retry mechanisms, and deploying enhanced debugging techniques foster reliable, effective workflow systems. As workflows evolve, maintaining vigilance in error management ensures the sustained fulfillment of operational objectives, strategic goals, and service quality commitments. This proactive approach yields enduring benefits, catalyzing sustainable performance and continuous improvement across the workflow architecture's breadth.

4.6 Exploring Workflow Status and Outputs

Once an Argo Workflow is submitted and executed within a Kubernetes cluster, understanding its status and analyzing its outputs become critical for evaluation, troubleshooting, and optimizing workflow performance. Workflow status provides a comprehensive view of execution states, while outputs convey crucial data generated by tasks. This section delves into interpreting workflow status, extracting outputs, and utilizing this information to derive insights and improvements.

Understanding Workflow Status The status of a workflow represents its current state within the execution lifecycle, reflecting whether it is in initial processing, actively running, successfully completed, or unexpectedly failed. Key status stages include:

- **Pending:** Signifies that the workflow is queued for execution but has not yet begun due to resource availability or scheduling conditions.

- **Running:** Indicates that one or more tasks within the workflow are actively executing in the cluster.

- **Succeeded:** Denotes successful completion, where all tasks have finished execution without encountering errors.

- **Failed:** Reveals that one or more tasks have failed, preventing the workflow from completing successfully.

Argo Workflows offers tools and interfaces to query and track these statuses, providing clear visibility into the current state of workflows.

Accessing Workflow Status Using Argo CLI The Argo CLI presents a straightforward approach to examining workflow status directly from the command line. To obtain summary information, use the following command:

```
argo get <workflow-name>
```

This command outputs detailed status data, including start and end times, individual task statuses, metrics, artifact information, and more, affording users a holistic view of workflow activity.

For instance, you might retrieve output similar to:

```
Name:             example-hello-world
Namespace:          argo
ServiceAccount:     default
Status:           Running
Conditions:
 Completed         False
Phase             Running
Started At        2023-05-01 10:00:00 +0000 UTC
```

130

4.6. EXPLORING WORKFLOW STATUS AND OUTPUTS

Monitoring Execution with Argo UI The Argo UI augments status insights with visual representations. Access workflows graphically, where color-coded nodes demonstrate real-time status, graphically linking task dependencies, and execution timelines.

By accessing the Argo UI, monitor active workflows with high engagement, benefiting from visual cues and dynamic interaction capabilities to diagnose and verify states:

- **Green Nodes:** Illustrate successfully completed tasks.
- **Yellow Nodes:** Represent tasks currently processing.
- **Red Nodes:** Highlight failures requiring attention.

Extracting Workflow Outputs Workflow outputs offer meaningful data resulting from task execution, such as logs, computed results, and artifacts. Extracting these outputs facilitates greater understanding and augments report generation, auditing, and post-processing.

Outputs can be grouped into:

- **Logs:** Capturing both informative and error messages logged during task execution.
- **Artifacts:** Files generated or transformed by tasks, potentially used by subsequent tasks or external systems.
- **Parameters:** Variable data produced during workflow, shared among tasks through parameter passing.

Accessing Logs Logs represent a narrative of execution, captured at each point in the task lifecycle. They provide direct insights into task operations and should be meticulously reviewed.

View logs using Kubernetes 'kubectl' or Argo CLI:

```
kubectl logs <pod-name> -n argo
```

```
argo logs @latest
```

These logs convey critical data for debugging, performance tuning, and understanding interaction dynamics with external systems.

Managing Artifacts Tasks often generate artifacts, which can be results files, logs, or interim data products. Artifacts are vital for holistic workflow comprehension, pinpointing both successes and work-in-progress data.

Workflows define artifact paths within templates:

```
outputs:
  artifacts:
  - name: sample-artifact
    path: /output/sample.txt
```

Artifact stores, such as S3, GCS, or MinIO, often manage larger outputs, enabling retention, sharing, and post-execution processing.

Leveraging Parameters Parameters facilitate efficient data flow, sharing intermediate results across tasks without redundant computation, encapsulating specific configuration or execution results.

Example of passing parameters between tasks:

```
apiVersion: argoproj.io/v1alpha1
kind: Workflow
metadata:
  generateName: param-example-
spec:
  entrypoint: main
  templates:
  - name: main
    steps:
    - - name: generate-parameters
        template: param-generator
    - - name: use-parameters
        template: param-user
        arguments:
          parameters:
          - name: generated
            value: "{{steps.generate-parameters.outputs.parameters.result}}"

  - name: param-generator
    script:
      image: python:3.9
      command: [python]
      source: |
        print("example_output")
        import os
        os.system('echo "result={{escape parameters.result}}" > /tmp/output.zip')

  - name: param-user
    script:
      image: python:3.9
      command: [python]
```

4.6. EXPLORING WORKFLOW STATUS AND OUTPUTS

```
source: |
  import os
  os.system('echo "{{inputs.parameters.generated}}" > /tmp/generated_output.
      txt')
```

Understanding and leveraging outputs provide meaningful insights that reflect workflow efficacy, optimization opportunities, and actionable intelligence for ongoing adaptation and improvement.

Analyzing Workflow Performance Beyond acknowledging statuses and extracting outputs, scrutinizing workflow performance is imperative. Areas for focus include:

- **Task Efficiency:** Analyze time, resource utilization, and throughput for individual tasks.

- **Resource Management:** Balance requests and limits against actual usage, ensuring optimal resource allocation without excessive contention or waste.

- **Execution Bottlenecks:** Identify points of delay or errors, seeking improvements or optimizations such as parallelization.

Best Practices for Exploring Status and Outputs Efficient exploration of workflow status and outputs should include:

- **Data Centralization:** Store outputs in centralized, accessible systems like cloud storage backends, providing easy analysis and collaborative review.

- **Regular Audit and Analysis:** Continually review logs and outputs to ensure conformance to expectations, catching deviations that suggest optimization opportunities or unanticipated behaviors.

- **Automated Reporting:** Use automated systems to generate status reports or summaries, enhancing visibility across teams and streamlining decision-making processes.

- **Consistent Metrics Gathering:** Collect key metrics representative of workflow execution, resource consumption, and task success rate, aligning with business KPIs.

By thoroughly exploring workflow statuses and outputs, organizations derive actionable insights that transform operational efficiency and elevate strategic planning, aligning execution outcomes with broader business objectives and service excellence goals. Comprehensive understanding of these insights offers the potential for not only fixing performance issues but also unlocking value increases through closer alignment of resource transitions and workforce agility to the evolving demands of technology-driven ecosystems.

4.7 Iterating and Improving Your Workflow

The lifecycle of a workflow within the context of Argo Workflows on Kubernetes does not terminate with its successful execution. Iteration and continuous improvement are crucial steps that follow initial deployment, ensuring workflows remain efficient, adaptable, and aligned with evolving requirements. Iteration involves refining workflows based on performance analytics, emerging demands, technological advancements, and operational feedback. This section provides an extensive overview of strategies, methodologies, and best practices for iterating and enhancing workflows, fostering enhanced performance and adaptability.

The Importance of Iteration

Iterating on workflows ensures they maintain optimal performance and scalability against evolving business and technical landscapes. As workloads mature, initial design choices can become suboptimal, necessitating iterations. A committed improvement approach translates into:

- **Enhanced Efficiency**: Refined workflows reduce execution time, cost, and resource overhead.

4.7. ITERATING AND IMPROVING YOUR WORKFLOW

- **Robustness and Resilience**: Improved error handling and recovery mechanisms bolster reliability.
- **Scalability and Flexibility**: Scalable workflows that adapt to increased volume or complexity without degradation.
- **Innovation Enablement**: New features or advanced capabilities augment functionality and support business objectives.

Basic Workflow Iteration Cycle

The iteration cycle for workflows can be distilled into several key activities:

- **Assessment and Analysis**: Evaluate current workflow performance using metrics and operational feedback.
- **Identification of Bottlenecks and Pain Points**: Scrutinize redundant processes, overused resources, and critical delays.
- **Implementation of Improvements**: Develop enhancements, streamline processes, and reduce complexity.
- **Testing and Validation**: Certify that changes meet desired outcomes without introducing issues.
- **Deployment and Monitoring**: Re-deploy workflows with improvements, continuously monitor and gather feedback.

Assessment and Analysis

Use workflow metrics, logs, and user feedback to assess system performance and workflow efficiency. Critical areas for analysis include:

- **Resource Utilization**: Monitor CPU, memory, I/O, and network usage.
- **Execution Time**: Analyze which tasks or steps consume excessive time.

- **Error and Failure Rates**: Review logs for recurring issues or failures.
- **Scalability Metrics**: Evaluate workflows under varying load conditions and their adaptability.

Armed with this data, identify the areas necessitating improvements or optimizations.

Identifying Bottlenecks

Bottlenecks impede workflow execution by delaying progress or consuming unnecessary resources. Typical bottlenecks include:

- **Inefficient Task Sequencing**: Poorly ordered tasks introduce avoidable waits or increase dependencies.
- **Resource Constraints**: Insufficient allocation of CPU, memory, or bandwidth at node, pod, or task levels.
- **External Dependencies**: Dependencies on external systems, databases, or services sometimes exceed capacity, causing hold-ups.

Optimize data pipelines and use parallel execution patterns where order-preservation is unnecessary, effectively leveraging Kubernetes' inherent scaling capabilities.

Implementing Improvements

Iterating on workflows involves implementing improvements, from reducing unnecessary complexity to adopting modern computational paradigms. Concrete steps include:

- **Parameter Optimization**: Fine-tune algorithm parameters influencing performance.
- **Parallelization**: Transform sequential tasks into parallel executables where logicalness allows.

4.7. ITERATING AND IMPROVING YOUR WORKFLOW

- **Caching and Precomputation**: Implement caching to save computation results for reuse, reducing on-demand calculation time.
- **Advanced Error Handling**: Introduce robust retry strategies and alternative execution paths for heightened resilience.
- **Resource Allocation Tuning**: Adjust resource requests and limits for efficient resource provisioning.

Here's how parallelization is introduced in workflow with a 'DAG' template:

```
apiVersion: argoproj.io/v1alpha1
kind: Workflow
metadata:
  generateName: parallel-example-
spec:
  entrypoint: parallel-dag
  templates:
  - name: parallel-dag
    dag:
      tasks:
      - name: task-a
        template: simple-task
      - name: task-b
        template: simple-task
      - name: task-c
        template: simple-task
        dependencies: [task-a, task-b]

  - name: simple-task
    container:
      image: alpine
      command: [sh, -c]
      args: ["echo 'Executing Task'"]
```

Testing and Validation

Thorough testing and validation are essential steps post-implementation to avoid unintended consequences:

- **Unit Testing**: Use unit tests to verify specific task behaviors and script logic.
- **Integration Testing**: Ensure cohesive, integrated behavior across workflow components, especially when interfaces or task

interactions have changed.

- **Load Testing**: Simulate varied loads to assess scalability, speaking to the workflow's endurance under pressure.

- **Regression Testing**: Guard against functional regressions, ensuring new changes don't perturb previous results.

Utilize automated testing pipelines to seamlessly integrate this continuous testing regime, benefiting from swift feedback and streamlined development cycles.

Deployment and Monitoring

After successful validation, deploy the improved workflow. Implement monitoring tools to gather execution data using meaningful metrics, facilitating ongoing insight and iteration:

- **Kubernetes Metrics**: Observe pod-level metrics emphasizing resource consumption and task-related performance.

- **Prometheus and Grafana Dashboards**: Leverage these to produce visual insights and track performance over time.

- **Log Aggregation**: Use logging systems to collect and analyze voluminous log data, revealing insights into operational continuity and persistent errors.

Monitoring additionally ensures workflows continue to meet operational expectations post-deployment, validating real-world execution hypotheses.

Continuous Improvement and Best Practices

Workflows should be seen as evolving entities with iteration spurring continuous enhancement. Adopting best practices throughout this process helps maintain clarity and motivation:

- **Incremental Changes**: Introduce small, testable changes over sweeping reforms, allowing focused measurement and adjustment.

- **Collaboration**: Foster collaboration across teams to bring diverse perspectives, ideas, and solutions to workflow management.

- **Documentation**: Maintain thorough documentation of changes, enhancements, and rationale for iterative steps ensuring team alignment and facilitating onboarding.

- **Version Control**: Utilize tools like Git for tracking changes, facilitating reversal of unintended consequences, and promoting organized development.

- **Feedback Loops**: Establish mechanisms for ongoing feedback from users and stakeholders, aligning workflows with operational realities and business priorities.

Regularly revisiting workflows with the lens of improvement and innovation enables systems to remain strategically aligned to evolving requirements. Existing limitations transform into refinements and adaptations, leveraging collective learning and skill growth across teams.

Iterating and improving workflows in Kubernetes using Argo Workflows presents an opportunity for meaningful optimizations. When approached as an ongoing journey, workflow iteration promises robust, scalable, and responsive systems capable of weaving into organizational and operational objectives seamlessly. Through careful assessment, systematic implementation, rigorous testing, and insightful deployment, workflows evolve to support and drive toward overarching success metrics, supporting strategic growth and operations harmony within technology-driven environments.

Chapter 5

Managing Data Pipelines with Argo

This chapter examines the management of data pipelines using Argo Workflows, focusing on designing effective workflows tailored for data-focused tasks. Readers will explore strategies for managing data flow using parameters and artifacts, ensuring seamless data transfer between pipeline components. The chapter provides insights into scheduling data pipelines, automating ETL processes, and integrating data validation to maintain data quality. Additionally, it discusses methods for connecting workflows to external data sources within Kubernetes, enabling comprehensive and dynamic data processing pipelines that leverage the full capabilities of Argo Workflows.

5.1 Understanding Data Pipelines

The concept of data pipelines pertains to the automation of data-driven workflows, where data is transported, transformed, and loaded in a streamlined manner across systems. Data pipelines serve as the backbone for data processing in contemporary analytics and big data environments, enabling cohesive data management and fostering efficient insight derivation.

A data pipeline consists of a series of processes that data undergoes, ranging from collection at its source to eventual processing, storage, and analysis. Within such a pipeline, several components work in unison to maintain the integrity, quality, and usability of the data. These components include data ingestion, processing, storage mechanisms, transformation logic, and eventual analysis frameworks.

The initial component of a data pipeline is the data ingestion phase, where raw data is collected from various sources. These sources can be transactional systems, sensors, applications, or even social media. The data can arrive in multiple forms such as JSON, XML, text, or complex hierarchical formats. Data ingestion tools and protocols, such as Kafka, Flume, or traditional extract methods, are employed to acquire this data in a structured manner, ensuring minimal latency and maintaining data fidelity.

Data processing entails cleansing, organizing, and enriching the data to meet the analytical requirements. During this phase, incomplete or noisy data is processed using algorithmic techniques to filter, interpolate, or deduplicate entries. In scientific terms, data noise refers to irrelevant or random information that a data collection process includes, which may distort the integrity of the data projections or insights.

Once data is processed, it must be stored efficiently. Storage solutions range from relational databases, such as PostgreSQL or MySQL, to cloud storage services like AWS S3, and distributed systems like Hadoop Distributed File System (HDFS). Each storage system is selected based on the volume, velocity, variety, and veracity of the ingested data. The choice of storage influences the performance and scalability of the data pipeline; hence, its importance cannot be understated.

Data transformation is a critical operation within a data pipeline. It involves modifying data schemas, aggregating disparate data points, or performing complex joins to produce data sets readily usable by analytical tools. Transformation logic, often realized through SQL queries, Spark transformations, or even Python scripts within Jupyter notebooks, enables the conversion of raw data into structured datasets suitable for consumption.

5.1. UNDERSTANDING DATA PIPELINES

Subsequently, these datasets are made available for analysis. Analytical frameworks such as Apache Hive, Apache Drill, or machine learning libraries like TensorFlow leverage the transformed data to derive insights or predictive models. Data pipelines facilitate this eventuality by ensuring that data processed at each preceding stage is accurate, timely, and relevant.

An example of a typical data pipeline might include a sequence where log data from web servers is ingested using Apache Kafka, processed in real-time using Apache Flink, stored in HDFS, and finally analysed using Hadoop MapReduce jobs. The precision of each step ensures the accuracy of outputs and drives decision-making processes based on these analytics.

```
import pandas as pd

# Load raw data into DataFrame
raw_data = pd.read_csv('web_server_logs.csv')

# Filter out irrelevant data and handle missing values
processed_data = raw_data.dropna(subset=['user_id', 'access_time'])
processed_data = processed_data[processed_data['response_code'] == 200]

# Aggregate data by user session
user_sessions = processed_data.groupby('session_id').agg({
    'access_time': ['min', 'max'],
    'bytes_transferred': 'sum'
})

# Save processed data for further analysis
user_sessions.to_csv('processed_sessions.csv')
```

The code example highlights a data transformation operation using Python's pandas library. Initially, raw web server logs are loaded and processed to remove irrelevant (non-200 HTTP response codes) or incomplete data (missing user IDs or access times). Subsequently, the dataset is aggregated by user session, calculating metrics such as session duration and total bytes transferred. The processed dataset is then stored for future analysis.

Data pipeline design must consider the interdependency and sequence of tasks. Task orchestration involves scheduling and sequencing tasks, handling dependencies, and ensuring mechanisms for recovery in case of node failures or data inconsistencies. Orchestration tools like Apache Airflow, Luigi, or commercial solutions like AWS Data Pipeline provide robust frameworks for managing these complexities, ensuring each task executes in the correct sequence and mild discrepancies are handled autonomously.

For effective implementation, it is crucial to set up robust monitoring and logging mechanisms. These utilities track pipeline performance, detect anomalies such as data delays or processing errors, and facilitate swift troubleshooting without operational downtimes. Observability is typically accomplished using monitoring solutions such as Prometheus coupled with Grafana dashboards, rendering real-time analytical metrics and insights into pipeline performance.

Data pipelines must be constructed with adaptability in mind, ensuring they can evolve with shifting business requirements or technological advancements. Modularity is a paradigm suggesting that individual components within a data pipeline should be independently replaceable or upgradable without disrupting the entire pipeline. Modularity fosters resilience and accelerates the innovation cycle within organizations.

Security and governance of data pipelines are other paramount considerations. Compliance with data protection laws, such as GDPR, mandates that organizations exercise stringent access control, encryption, and auditing across their data pipelines. Techniques such as role-based access control, encryption in transit and at rest, and audit logging for access attempts are crucial practices for safeguarding sensitive data.

The application of machine learning within pipelines automates intelligent decisioning based on historical patterns detected within the data. Machine learning models can be integrated naturally into data pipelines, handling tasks such as anomaly detection in real-time streams or personalizing user content recommendations based on user behavior.

One illustrative example involves using a pipeline to automate the predictive maintenance of industrial machinery. Here, sensor data from machines is ingested and processed in real-time to monitor performance metrics like temperature, vibration, or pressure. Machine learning algorithms are applied to this data to predict potential failures before they occur, facilitating preemptive maintenance actions and substantially reducing downtime.

```python
from sklearn.externals import joblib
import numpy as np

# Load pre-trained anomaly detection model
model = joblib.load('anomaly_detection_model.pkl')

# Assume sensor_data is a DataFrame with latest machine metrics
sensor_data = pd.DataFrame({
    'temperature': [75.4, 74.9, 76.7],
    'vibration': [0.02, 0.04, 0.01],
    'pressure': [120.0, 119.9, 121.1]
})

# Feature extraction and prediction
features = sensor_data.values
anomalies = model.predict(features)

# Log anomalies for review and alert necessary personnel
for index, anomaly in enumerate(anomalies):
    if anomaly == 1:
        print(f"Anomaly detected at index {index}, metrics: {sensor_data.iloc[index].to_dict()}")
```

In the given Python script, a machine learning model pre-trained to detect anomalies in machine metrics is utilized within a data pipeline. Sensor data coming from industrial equipment is processed, extracting necessary features, which are subsequently fed into the model. Detected anomalies are logged for human review, allowing any necessary maintenance actions to be pursued promptly.

Overall, understanding the mechanics and components of data pipelines furnishes the capability to design and implement robust, efficient systems that enable the effective management of data throughout its lifecycle. These systems are indispensable for modern organizations operating at the cutting edge of data-driven insights and continuous innovation in response to evolving technological and market landscapes.

5.2 Designing Workflows for Data Pipelines

Designing workflows for data pipelines encompasses the strategic configuration of tasks and processes to efficiently handle data movement, transformation, and storage while ensuring system robustness and scalability. Argo Workflows, a Kubernetes-native workflow orchestration framework, is particularly suited for crafting such pipelines due to its flexibility, scalability, and integration capabilities.

At the core of designing workflows for data pipelines is task management. Each task in a data pipeline represents a distinct processing step, encapsulating specific logic to be executed. These range from data extraction and cleansing to complex machine learning model training and deployment. A workflow orchestrates these tasks, defining their sequence, dependencies, and conditions for execution.

When designing workflows for data pipelines using Argo, one begins by defining the Directed Acyclic Graph (DAG) structure that specifies the sequencing and interdependencies of tasks. In a DAG, each node represents an individual task, while directed edges define task execution order based upon dependencies.

Argo Workflows utilize YAML format to define such DAGs, allowing users to configure containers for executing specific task operations within the Kubernetes environment. Each workflow is articulated through templates that encapsulate the specifications, dependencies, and data artifacts required for task completion.

Below is an example of a simple Argo Workflow YAML file that defines a basic pipeline with three sequential tasks: data ingestion, transformation, and loading:

```
apiVersion: argoproj.io/v1alpha1
kind: Workflow
metadata:
  generateName: simple-data-pipeline-
spec:
  entrypoint: data-pipeline-flow
  templates:
  - name: data-pipeline-flow
    dag:
      tasks:
      - name: ingest-data
        template: ingest
      - name: transform-data
        template: transform
        dependencies: [ingest-data]
      - name: load-data
        template: load
        dependencies: [transform-data]

  - name: ingest
    container:
      image: python:3.8
```

5.2. DESIGNING WORKFLOWS FOR DATA PIPELINES

```
    command: ["python", "-c"]
    args: ["import time; time.sleep(1); print('Data Ingested')"]

- name: transform
  container:
    image: python:3.8
    command: ["python", "-c"]
    args: ["import time; time.sleep(1); print('Data Transformed')"]

- name: load
  container:
    image: python:3.8
    command: ["python", "-c"]
    args: ["import time; time.sleep(1); print('Data Loaded')"]
```

In this example, the workflow includes three main phases. The ingest-data task runs first without dependencies, performing data ingestion operations. Following completion, transform-data is triggered, using the ingested data for transformation processing. Finally, upon successful transformation, the load-data task runs to load the data into a target system.

In complex pipelines, tasks often exhibit a wide array of dependencies and data-sharing requirements. Argo facilitates such needs by allowing file and volume sharing between tasks, the use of parameters between nodes, and leveraging artifacts. Artifacts are parameterized paths to files located at specified storage levels, offering a mechanism to manage intermediate data generated during pipeline execution.

Next, the design phase must accommodate error-handling and recovery. This entails specifying error strategies for task failures. Employing retries, backoff policies, or alternative task paths can mitigate failure impacts. Argo Workflows supports these features through its robust error-handling configurations:

```
apiVersion: argoproj.io/v1alpha1
kind: Workflow
metadata:
  generateName: error-handling-pipeline-
spec:
  entrypoint: error-processing-flow
  templates:
  - name: error-processing-flow
    dag:
      tasks:
      - name: task-with-retry
        template: task
        # Retry logic
        retryStrategy:
          limit: 3
```

```
        backoff:
          duration: "10s"
          factor: 2
          maxDuration: "1m"
  - name: task
    container:
      image: alpine
      command: ["/bin/sh", "-c"]
      args: ["exit 1"]
```

The retryStrategy section within the task-with-retry task provides a means to specify retry attempts with geometric delay increments until maximum attempts or timeout is reached.

Parallelism is another crucial aspect when designing workflows, exceptionally useful to optimize resource utilization and reduce data processing latency. Argo allows tasks to run concurrently by specifying parallel task execution paths in the DAG. The benefits of parallelism are particularly evident in operations that process independent data segments or execute machine learning model training across multiple parameter sets.

The example below details an Argo Workflow configuration implementing parallel tasks:

```
apiVersion: argoproj.io/v1alpha1
kind: Workflow
metadata:
  generateName: parallel-processing-pipeline-
spec:
  entrypoint: parallel-data-flow
  templates:
  - name: parallel-data-flow
    dag:
      tasks:
      - name: parallel-task-1
        template: execute-task
      - name: parallel-task-2
        template: execute-task

  - name: execute-task
    container:
      image: python:3.8
      command: ["python", "-c"]
      args: ["print('Executing task in parallel')"]
```

In this workflow, parallel-task-1 and parallel-task-2 run concurrently, exploiting the available computational nodes within the Kubernetes environment.

5.2. DESIGNING WORKFLOWS FOR DATA PIPELINES

Advanced data pipelining needs extend to embedding conditional task executions, supporting dynamic decision-making during pipeline runtime. This involves directing each task path dependent on the processed data or external parameters, effectively allowing adaptive workflows. Argo supports conditionals directly, using standard control mechanisms like when clauses integrated within DAG task definitions.

```
apiVersion: argoproj.io/v1alpha1
kind: Workflow
metadata:
  generateName: conditional-pipeline-
spec:
  entrypoint: conditional-data-flow
  templates:
  - name: conditional-data-flow
    dag:
      tasks:
      - name: generate-number
        template: random-number
      - name: process-even
        template: process-task
        when: "{{tasks.generate-number.outputs.result}} \% 2 == 0"
      - name: process-odd
        template: process-task
        when: "{{tasks.generate-number.outputs.result}} \% 2 != 0"

  - name: random-number
    container:
      image: python:3.8
      command: ["python", "-c"]
      args: ["import random; print(random.randint(0, 100))"]

  - name: process-task
    container:
      image: python:3.8
      command: ["python", "-c"]
      args: ["print('Processing task based on condition')"]
```

This example demonstrates the workflow's ability to conditionally diverge paths based on the generated number, leveraging dynamic decision-making in task execution.

In addition to task structuring, computational resource allocation and management are pivotal in Argo-based pipeline design, ensuring task workload congruency with resource capabilities. It is critical to specify appropriate CPU and memory requests and limits, precluding resource contention and maximizing pipeline throughput.

```
apiVersion: argoproj.io/v1alpha1
kind: Workflow
metadata:
  generateName: resource-managed-pipeline-
```

```
spec:
  entrypoint: resource-intensive-task
  templates:
  - name: resource-intensive-task
    container:
      image: image-intensive-task
      resources:
        requests:
          memory: "128Mi"
          cpu: "500m"
        limits:
          memory: "512Mi"
          cpu: "1000m"
      command: ["./data_processing_script"]
```

In this resource-managed pipeline, specific compute capacities are requested, aligning task needs with cluster resources to harness optimal performance.

Designing workflows for data pipelines necessitates a thorough understanding of Argo's capabilities, including the management of task orchestrations and dependencies, accurate resource estimations, the integration of parallel processing and error-handling strategies, and leveraging advanced branching and conditional logic. These principles form the foundation of constructing robust, scalable pipelines capable of adapting swiftly to evolving data processing requirements, positioning organizations to derive optimized value from their data assets.

5.3 Managing Data Flow with Parameters and Artifacts

Effective management of data flow is central to the design and execution of data pipelines. In Argo Workflows, data flow between different components of a pipeline is managed using parameters and artifacts. Parameters and artifacts facilitate the transfer of essential data by ensuring that individual tasks can communicate efficiently while retaining the contextual detail necessary for cohesive execution across the pipeline.

Parameters in Argo Workflows allow for the passage of small, superficial pieces of data such as strings, numbers, or boolean values between tasks. They serve as placeholders for values that can be filled

5.3. MANAGING DATA FLOW WITH PARAMETERS AND ARTIFACTS

at runtime, providing the needed flexibility in configuring task execution based on the specific requirements. Parameters enhance pipeline dynamism by enabling runtime customization, where different executions of a workflow can operate with varying configurations without modifying the workflow definition itself.

Below is a foundational example illustrating how parameters are used in an Argo Workflow:

```
apiVersion: argoproj.io/v1alpha1
kind: Workflow
metadata:
  generateName: parameter-example-
spec:
  entrypoint: parameter-sample
  arguments:
    parameters:
    - name: example-greeting
      value: "Hello, Argo!"
  templates:
  - name: parameter-sample
    inputs:
      parameters:
      - name: example-greeting
    container:
      image: python:3.8
      command: ["python", "-c"]
      args: ["print('{{inputs.parameters.example-greeting}}')"]
```

In this example, the workflow uses a parameter named 'example-greeting' with a default value of "Hello, Argo!". The parameter is passed to a container executing a Python script that prints the greeting. This demonstrates how parameters can be leveraged to pass simple data between workflow components and achieve runtime adaptability.

On the other hand, artifacts facilitate the transfer of larger, structured data sets across task boundaries within a pipeline. Artifacts encompass file-based data or binary objects, often used for sharing intermediary results like processed datasets, logs, or binary model files. Artifacts are capable of handling broader data scenarios than parameters due to their support for file storage and retrieval capabilities.

Artifacts usage in Argo Workflows involves declaring their locations and retrieval methods, usually stored in remote object storage systems such as AWS S3, Google Cloud Storage, or MinIO. An example of leveraging artifacts in an Argo Workflow can be seen below:

```
apiVersion: argoproj.io/v1alpha1
```

```yaml
kind: Workflow
metadata:
  generateName: artifact-example-
spec:
  entrypoint: artifact-sample
  templates:
  - name: artifact-sample
    outputs:
      artifacts:
      - name: example-data
        path: /data/example-output.txt
    container:
      image: python:3.8
      command: ["python", "-c"]
      args: ["with open('/data/example-output.txt', 'w') as f: f.write('This is an artifact
        .')"]

  - name: consume-artifact
    inputs:
      artifacts:
      - name: example-data
        path: /data/example-input.txt
    container:
      image: python:3.8
      command: ["python", "-c"]
      args: ["with open('/data/example-input.txt', 'r') as f: print(f.read())"]
```

In this workflow, two tasks are managed using artifacts. The first task outputs a file named 'example-output.txt' as an artifact. The second task, 'consume-artifact', takes the file as input, opening it to read and print its contents. This showcases artifact utility in managing file dependencies.

Integrating both parameters and artifacts into Argo Workflows necessitates a comprehensive understanding of their characteristics, ensuring they are adapted appropriately based on the data size and intended use case. Parameters are ideal for lightweight data exchanges and control flags, whereas artifacts are better suited for transferring significant data payloads that may require persistence beyond task runtime.

Tasks within an Argo Workflow carry specific requirements in terms of data dependencies, which must be clearly delineated for seamless data transitions. Dependencies can be explicit (directly specified between tasks) or implicit (inferred from shared data artifacts or parameters). Argo supports both modes, providing flexibility in defining complex, interdependent workflows that reflect real-world processing logic.

An efficient data flow management strategy necessitates stringent attention to both temporal and spatial data locality. Temporal data local-

5.3. MANAGING DATA FLOW WITH PARAMETERS AND ARTIFACTS

ity addresses the order and timing with which data transitions occur, ensuring that data is available as needed during dependent task execution. Spatial data locality, conversely, ensures that transferred data maintains sufficient proximity to consuming tasks, mitigating latency issues and maximizing throughput.

The 'workspaces' feature in Argo allows for efficient handling of data flow, particularly crucial when dealing with Workflow-level artifacts shared across tasks. Workspaces offer a capacity similar to that of volumes in Kubernetes: they provide centralized storage access points for multiple tasks within a workflow, facilitating shared data use and transient data storage.

```
apiVersion: argoproj.io/v1alpha1
kind: Workflow
metadata:
  generateName: workspace-example-
spec:
  entrypoint: workspace-sample
  volumeClaimTemplates:
  - metadata:
      name: shared-data
    spec:
      accessModes: ["ReadWriteOnce"]
      resources:
        requests:
          storage: 1Gi
  templates:
  - name: workspace-sample
    steps:
    - - name: produce-file
        template: produce-task
    - - name: consume-file
        template: consume-task

  - name: produce-task
    script:
      image: alpine
      volumeMounts:
      - name: shared-data
        mountPath: /workspace
      command: [sh]
      source: |
        echo "Shared data" > /workspace/shared-data.txt

  - name: consume-task
    script:
      image: alpine
      volumeMounts:
      - name: shared-data
        mountPath: /workspace
      command: [sh]
      source: |
```

```
cat /workspace/shared-data.txt
```

In this implementation, using a volume claim template named 'shared-data', both 'produce-task' and 'consume-task' access the workspace at '/workspace' for writing and reading a file, respectively. It highlights workspaces' capability in centralizing artifact management without duplicating storage declarations across tasks.

Optimizing data flow with parameters and artifacts requires a robust understanding of the file system interfaces and data serialization formats utilized. Formats such as JSON, Avro, Parquet, or CSV provide serialization options relevant in varied contexts, balancing human readability, schema enforcement, and processing efficiency.

A subtle understanding and leveraging of the workflow environment, operational constraints, and data characteristics are needed to design data flows effectively. Balancing across these dimensions ensures that workflows are efficiently modular, remain maintainable and flexible, reduce computational overhead, enable parallelism, and seamlessly adapt to organizational needs.

While Argo Workflows offers substantial tooling for data flow management, designing workflows also entails careful orchestration of schedules and trigger points. Temporal scheduling of workflows using cron jobs or Pub/Sub mechanisms can synchronize tasks with external systems, adapting data ingestion and processing rates to the temporal requirements of data sources or consumption expectations.

```
apiVersion: argoproj.io/v1alpha1
kind: CronWorkflow
metadata:
  generateName: scheduled-pipeline-
spec:
  schedule: "0 6 * * *"
  concurrencyPolicy: "Allow"
  startingDeadlineSeconds: 60
  workflowSpec:
    entrypoint: scheduled-task
    templates:
    - name: scheduled-task
      container:
        image: python:3.8
        command: ["python", "-c"]
        args: ["print('Scheduled Workflow Run')"]
```

In this cron-defined workflow, processes are initiated according to a

5.4. SCHEDULING DATA PIPELINES

defined schedule, coordinating with broader operational timelines for systematic data ingestion and processing within determined intervals.

Overall, managing data flow through parameters and artifacts ensures smooth operation across a data pipeline, fitting the specific expressive needs of pipeline tasks and data characteristics. Whether employing parameters for fine-tuning operational subtleties or artifacts for substantial data transitions, the capacity to manage contents efficiently within workflows is pivotal for dynamic, scalable, and resilient data pipeline design.

5.4 Scheduling Data Pipelines

The ability to schedule data pipelines is an integral component of effective workflow management, facilitating the timely execution of data processing tasks to ensure continuous data flow and meeting the analytical needs of organizations. In the context of Argo Workflows, scheduling is accomplished through the use of cron workflows, a powerful mechanism that leverages cron expressions to define the timing of workflow executions.

Cron workflows enable the automation of routine data processing tasks, ensuring that pipelines can run at predefined intervals. This automates data ingestion, processing, and loading without human intervention, enhancing operational efficiency and reliability of data-driven operations. The predictable execution of data workflows supports business intelligence, reporting, ETL (Extract, Transform, Load) operations, and other repetitive tasks.

The essence of scheduling data pipelines lies within the powerful syntax of cron expressions. A cron expression represents a schedule in a time-based job scheduler, typically defining minute, hour, day of the month, month, day of the week, and year fields. This granular control allows workflows to run at almost any conceivable interval, from every few minutes to once a year.

To illustrate the mechanism of cron scheduling, consider this basic Argo Cron Workflow:

```
apiVersion: argoproj.io/v1alpha1
kind: CronWorkflow
```

```
metadata:
  generateName: cron-workflow-example-
spec:
  schedule: "0 * * * *" # Executes once every hour, on the hour
  concurrencyPolicy: "Allow"
  workflowSpec:
    entrypoint: hourly-task
    templates:
    - name: hourly-task
      container:
        image: python:3.8
        command: ["python", "-c"]
        args: ["print('Hourly Workflow Execution')"]
```

This example demonstrates the implementation of an Argo Cron Workflow where the specified schedule "0 * * * *" ensures task execution every hour. The 'concurrencyPolicy' set to "Allow" ensures that multiple instances of the workflow can run concurrently if a scheduled run does not complete before the next trigger.

Argo Cron Workflows support three concurrency policies:

- **Allow**: Multiple instances of the workflow may overlap if new instances are triggered before the prior instance completes.

- **Forbid**: New workflow instances will not start if a prior instance is still running at the scheduled start time.

- **Replace**: A new instance replaces any currently executing instances of the workflow.

Selecting the appropriate concurrency policy is crucial and should align with an organization's performance, data accuracy, and resource management objectives. For systems requiring strict sequential processing and data integrity, "Forbid" may be the most suitable choice.

Complex scheduling requirements may arise requiring workflows that align with business hours or specific non-uniform periods. Argo Cron Workflows, unlike traditional cron implementations that only allow specifying time constraints, enable integration with custom triggering mechanisms, adapting to more sophisticated scheduling needs via external signals or API calls.

Consider a scenario where pipeline execution must adapt to dynamic intervals triggered by business events or external conditions. Argo sup-

5.4. SCHEDULING DATA PIPELINES

ports custom triggering logic using Kubernetes Events, leveraging its flexible architecture to respond to non-time-based conditions.

Implementing event-based scheduling, often alongside cron scheduling, involves creating Kubernetes resources that can emit events to trigger new workflow instances. Event-based scheduling's edge lies in its capability to enable immediate response to changes in state or specific conditions known at runtime. Such workloads can be particularly beneficial in volatile, data-intensive environments where immediate processing is required upon data arrival or status change.

Distributed systems enhance the scale and reliability of scheduled data pipelines; however, they introduce complexity through asynchronous task execution and coordination. Within Argo Workflows, leveraging native Kubernetes constructs, each instance of a workflow executes within a dedicated pod, ensuring isolation, resource management, and scalability.

In an enterprise context, the reliable scheduling of data pipelines extends to considerations surrounding observability and monitoring. Comprehensive logging and metrics should be available for each workflow execution, tracking performance, resource allocation, and fault diagnostics. Tools such as Prometheus, Grafana, and Elasticsearch may be integrated with Argo, facilitating real-time monitoring, diagnostics, and alerting.

The use of standardized interfaces, such as JSON or gRPC, to convey completed task data between systems ensures agility in response to scheduling challenges without necessitating structural changes to the pipeline. Workflow logs provide traceability, maintaining accountability for each scheduled instance and aiding compliance with data governance standards.

Security considerations in scheduled executions, particularly with sensitive data in distributed systems, necessitate careful attention. Role-based access control, isolated processing environments, and secure data transmission protocols help in safeguarding data while maintaining seamless pipelined operations. Workflow manifest files should be versioned to prevent unauthorized access or alterations, crucially important in the pipeline lifecycle management.

Below is an expansive configuration illustrating the integration of an

Argo Cron Workflow with external logging and monitoring systems:

```
apiVersion: argoproj.io/v1alpha1
kind: CronWorkflow
metadata:
  generateName: monitored-cron-workflow-
spec:
  schedule: "*/30 * * * *"  # Executes every 30 minutes
  concurrencyPolicy: "Replace"
  workflowSpec:
    entrypoint: monitored-task
    templates:
    - name: monitored-task
      container:
        image: my-logging-enabled-image
        command: ["python", "-c"]
        args: ["import logging; logging.basicConfig(level=logging.INFO); logging.info('
          Workflow execution with monitoring')"]
        resources:
          limits:
            cpu: "1000m"
            memory: "512Mi"
```

The 'monitored-task', set to run every 30 minutes using the "Replace" policy, efficiently operates within resource constraints. Integration with logging frameworks permits third-party systems like logging.handlers.SysLogHandler to capture workflow activities across instances.

Furthermore, the scalability of scheduled data pipelines allows addressing significant computational demand fluctuations across different corporate departments or business units autonomously. Both cloud-based (AWS, GCP, Azure) and private Kubernetes clusters can potentially host multiple Argo Workflows, balancing workload distribution effectively across shared infrastructures.

Argo Workflows' support for scheduling combined with its deep Kubernetes integration offers versatile, reliable solutions for orchestrating complex pipeline tasks. Ultimately, harnessing real-time analytics, machine learning processes, or massive ETL workloads within streamlined, automatically triggered data pipelines fosters operational excellence, timely decision making, and the harnessing of emerging opportunities amidst shifting digital landscapes.

5.5 Implementing ETL Processes

The ETL (Extract, Transform, Load) process is a critical component in data engineering, facilitating the movement of data from source systems to a unified data repository where it is transformed and stored for analytical purposes. Implementing ETL processes using Argo Workflows harnesses the capabilities of Kubernetes to orchestrate complex data operations efficiently and at scale.

ETL processes classically involve three primary steps:

- **Extract**: Data is collected from various source systems, which may include databases, APIs, flat files, or streaming platforms. The extraction phase must ensure data consistency and accuracy by fetching the latest records without overlap or loss.

- **Transform**: After extraction, raw data is transformed into a more usable format. This may involve cleaning, deduplication, aggregation, enrichment, or even applying business logic to make the data more relevant for analytical tasks or operations.

- **Load**: The transformed data is then loaded into a target system, typically a data warehouse or data lake, where it can be accessed for reporting and analysis. The loading process must be done with efficiency and integrity, ensuring that all transformed data is available for immediate consumption.

Designing ETL processes in Argo Workflows involves creating task sequences or orchestrated pipelines that systematically carry out these operations. With Argo's native support for containerized tasks and Kubernetes' scalability, complex ETL workflows can be effectively streamlined, allowing processing to adapt dynamically to data volumes and operational demands.

Below is a conceptual Argo Workflow configuration implementing a simple ETL pipeline:

```
apiVersion: argoproj.io/v1alpha1
kind: Workflow
metadata:
  generateName: etl-example-
spec:
```

```
entrypoint: etl-flow
templates:
- name: etl-flow
  steps:
  - - name: extract-data
      template: extract
  - - name: transform-data
      template: transform
  - - name: load-data
      template: load

- name: extract
  container:
    image: my-db-connector
    command: ["python", "/scripts/extract.py"]
- name: transform
  container:
    image: python:3.8
    command: ["python", "/scripts/transform.py"]
- name: load
  container:
    image: my-data-storage-client
    command: ["python", "/scripts/load.py"]
```

In this workflow, the ETL sequence is defined with three sequential template steps: extract-data, transform-data, and load-data, each referencing a distinct container image equipped with custom scripts that carry out the respective tasks.

Extraction (extract-data)

The extract phase involves connecting to diverse data sources to retrieve raw data. The data extraction strategy must consider the data source's nature (e.g., database, flat file, API) and the data size. Efficiency during extraction can be achieved by employing incremental extraction techniques, fetching only new or changed records. Here, pagination and filtering mechanisms can also be applied if dealing with paginated APIs or database partitions.

```
import psycopg2
import json

# Connection parameters to PostgreSQL database
params = {
    'dbname': 'example_db',
    'user': 'db_user',
    'password': 'secure_password',
    'host': '127.0.0.1',
    'port': '5432'
}
```

5.5. IMPLEMENTING ETL PROCESSES

```python
# Establish connection
conn = psycopg2.connect(**params)
cursor = conn.cursor()

# Define query for incremental data extraction
query = """
SELECT * FROM sales_data
WHERE last_updated > (current_timestamp - interval '1 day')
"""

# Execute query
cursor.execute(query)
rows = cursor.fetchall()

# Extract to JSON
sales_data = [{'id': row[0], 'amount': row[1], 'timestamp': row[2]} for row in rows]

# Save as JSON file
with open('/data/extracted_sales_data.json', 'w') as f:
    json.dump(sales_data, f)

# Close connections
cursor.close()
conn.close()
```

In this Python script, the data extraction connects to a PostgreSQL database to incrementally fetch records from the sales_data table based on a timestamp.

Transformation (transform-data)

Transformation involves applying a series of operations to prepare data for loading. These operations might include filtering out unwanted data, aggregating values, performing computations, or enforcing schema changes. Argo's scalable environment allows potentially intensive transformation tasks to be distributed or executed in parallel when dealing with large datasets.

```python
import pandas as pd
import json

# Load extracted data
with open('/data/extracted_sales_data.json', 'r') as f:
    sales_data = json.load(f)

# Convert to DataFrame for complex transformations
df = pd.DataFrame(sales_data)

# Filter records where the amount is greater than 100
df = df[df['amount'] > 100]

# Group by date and aggregate amounts
```

```
aggregated = df.groupby(df['timestamp'].str[:10]).agg({'amount': 'sum'}).reset_index()

# Save transformed data
aggregated.to_json('/data/transformed_sales_data.json', orient='records')
```

This script reads the extracted JSON data, processes it using the pandas library to filter and aggregate sales amounts by date, and outputs the result to a new JSON file.

Loading (load-data)

Loading involves ingesting the processed data into the destination system, which could include data warehouses like Amazon Redshift, Google BigQuery, or Snowflake. The loading strategy may require ensuring data consistency and minimizing downtime, such as performing batch loads during low-peak periods or employing atomic load operations through transaction control.

```
import boto3
import json

# AWS S3 connection setup
s3 = boto3.client('s3')

# Read transformed data
with open('/data/transformed_sales_data.json', 'r') as f:
    transformed_data = json.load(f)

# Upload to a specific S3 bucket
s3.put_object(
    Bucket='example-bucket',
    Key='sales_data/transformed_sales_data.json',
    Body=json.dumps(transformed_data),
    ContentType='application/json'
)
```

In this snippet, transformed data is loaded into an AWS S3 bucket, serving as either the data's final resting place or intermediary storage before ingestion into an analytical platform.

Optimizing ETL Processes

An optimized ETL implementation within Argo must take into account the pipeline's performance requirements, scalability constraints, and error-handling mechanisms. For larger datasets or complex transformations, parallel task execution utilizing Argo's native scheduling and resource management (e.g., using sidecar or volumes) can greatly enhance throughput and responsiveness.

5.5. IMPLEMENTING ETL PROCESSES

ETL jobs must incorporate robust error management to halt further operations upon encountering critical data issues, with retries, logging, and alert mechanisms in place. Argo supports task retry strategies to handle transient errors gracefully via retryStrategy declarations within task templates.

```
- name: fetch-data
  template: extract
  retryStrategy:
    limit: 3
    backoff:
      duration: "5s"
      factor: 2
```

Observability of ETL processes should be augmented with logging frameworks, including real-time monitoring solutions (e.g., Prometheus or Grafana), providing insights into task performance metrics and timely alerts on long runtime instances or failures.

Several pipelines may necessitate real-time or streaming ETL evolution due to concurrent data shifts. Implementing such processes within an Argo Workflow can exploit Kubernetes' ability to trigger workflows based on real-time data ingestion, detecting and responding rapidly to incoming data with stream processing tools like Apache Flink or Kafka Streams.

With Argo's seamless integration with CI/CD frameworks, ETL workflows can also support continuous integration cycles, automatically applying needed updates or new data models into production pipelines with minimal delay, ensuring that analytical frameworks receive the most accurate and timely data possible.

Implementing ETL processes in Argo Workflows empowers organizations to maintain consistent, scalable, and efficient data pipelines. The modularization and separation of concerns facilitated by individual steps in Argo enhance maintainability, allowing incremental changes without the need for full pipeline redeployments and ultimately delivering high-quality, actionable data outputs for strategic decision-making.

5.6 Data Validation and Quality Checks

Ensuring the integrity and quality of data is paramount in any data processing pipeline. The inclusion of data validation and quality checks solidifies the reliability of analysis results and bolsters confidence in data-driven decision making. Within the context of Argo Workflows, incorporating data validation and quality checks involves embedding systematic validation tasks into the broader workflow, leveraging its orchestration capabilities to handle complex pipeline requirements efficiently.

Data validation involves the verification of data against predefined rules or standards, ensuring that incoming or processed data adheres to required formats, known constraints, or expected values. Quality checks encompass broader measures designed to evaluate the accuracy, completeness, consistency, and integrity of data as it moves through each processing stage.

Defining Data Validation Rules

To implement effective data validation, it is crucial first to define validation rules tailored to the specific dataset and business requirements. These rules could span various checks such as:

- **Schema Validation**: Ensures that data structures conform to expected schemas, encompassing field names, data types, and non-null constraints.

- **Range Checks**: Validate the numerical values by ensuring they are within specified ranges.

- **Regex Pattern Checks**: Validate that string fields match expected patterns, such as specific email formats or IDs.

- **Cross-field Validation**: Ensure that related fields have logically consistent values, like start dates preceding end dates.

- **Uniqueness Checks**: Verify that there are no unintended duplicate records within datasets.

Annotating each rule with precision is crucial to safeguard data integrity and cast a wide net over possible QA scenarios that the data

5.6. DATA VALIDATION AND QUALITY CHECKS

may encounter in the pipeline flow.

Incorporating Data Validation into Argo Workflows

To integrate validation in Argo Workflows, a dedicated validation step is typically inserted early in the process, between data extraction and transformation. Should validation checks fail, the workflow should halt or redirect to error-handling routines, such as notifications or corrective actions.

Below is an Argo Workflow detailing a simplified validation step:

```
apiVersion: argoproj.io/v1alpha1
kind: Workflow
metadata:
  generateName: data-validation-workflow-
spec:
  entrypoint: validation-etl-flow
  templates:
  - name: validation-etl-flow
    steps:
    - - name: extract-data
        template: extract
    - - name: validate-data
        template: validate
    - - name: transform-data
        template: transform
        when: "{{tasks.validate-data.outputs.parameters.validation-status}} == true"

  - name: extract
    container:
      image: my-db-batch-image
      command: ["python", "/scripts/extract.py"]

  - name: validate
    container:
      image: python:3.8
      command: ["python", "/scripts/validate.py"]
    outputs:
      parameters:
      - name: validation-status
        valueFrom:
          path: /outputs/validation-status.txt

  - name: transform
    container:
      image: python:3.8
      command: ["python", "/scripts/transform.py"]
```

In this example, the 'validate-data' step runs a Python script to apply checks on extracted data. The 'validation-status' parameter determines whether to proceed with subsequent transformations based on the validation outcome.

Python Script for Data Validation

The corresponding Python validation logic may be structured using a library like pandas for versatility in handling various data checks:

```python
import pandas as pd

# Load extracted dataset
df = pd.read_csv('/data/extracted_data.csv')

# Apply validation rules
# Check for missing values
if df.isnull().any().any():
    validation_status = 'false'
else:
    # Range check: Validate 'amount' within range
    if (df['amount'] < 0).any() or (df['amount'] > 10000).any():
        validation_status = 'false'
    else:
        # String format validation via regex
        df['email'].apply(lambda x: re.match(r'[^@]+@[^@]+\.[^@]+', str(x)))
        validation_status = 'true'

# Write validation status for conditional workflow continuation
with open('/outputs/validation-status.txt', 'w') as f:
    f.write(validation_status)
```

This script enforces several basic validation checks, including null detection, range checks, and string pattern validation using regular expressions, outputting the results for use in conditional Argo logic.

Implementing Quality Checks

Beyond individual field-wise validation gleaned in preliminary validations, comprehensive quality checks should be systematically embedded within pipelines to address broader data integrity measures.

A typical example of a quality check is ensuring completeness, where datasets are assessed for sufficient data rows and columns to meet analytical needs. These checks might include evaluating data consistency—ensuring that related datasets are in alignment or transparency regarding data lineage by auditing possible data deviations from the expected path.

Argo Workflows can orchestrate quality checks by splitting dataset processing across parallel paths designed to calculate and verify quality metrics.

```yaml
apiVersion: argoproj.io/v1alpha1
kind: Workflow
metadata:
```

5.6. DATA VALIDATION AND QUALITY CHECKS

```
    generateName: data-quality-workflow-
spec:
  entrypoint: quality-etl-flow
  templates:
  - name: quality-etl-flow
    steps:
    - - name: extract-raw-data
        template: extract
    - - name: verify-quality-checks
        template: quality-check
    - - name: commit-transform
        template: transform
        when: "{{tasks.verify-quality-checks.outputs.parameters.quality-status}} == true
"

  - name: extract
    container:
      image: connector-image
      command: ["python", "/scripts/extract_data.py"]

  - name: quality-check
    container:
      image: python:3.8
      command: ["python", "/scripts/quality_check.py"]
    outputs:
      parameters:
      - name: quality-status
        valueFrom:
          path: /outputs/quality-status.json

  - name: transform
    container:
      image: python:3.8
      command: ["python", "/scripts/transform_data.py"]
```

This workflow introduces a 'verify-quality-checks' step that evaluates the dataset's quality against defined criteria before proceeding to the transformation stage.

Python Script for Data Quality Checks

```
import pandas as pd

# Load data for quality check
df = pd.read_csv('/data/raw_data.csv')

# Execute quality checks
# Completeness: Ensure expected row count
expected_rows = 1000
if len(df) != expected_rows:
    quality_status = 'false'
else:
    # Consistency: Column value consistency check
    if not df['status'].isin(['active', 'inactive']).all():
        quality_status = 'false'
    else:
```

```
    # If all checks pass
    quality_status = 'true'
# Output result
status_output = '{"quality-status": "' + quality_status + '"}'
with open('/outputs/quality-status.json', 'w') as f:
    f.write(status_output)
```

The quality_check.py script enforces data completeness and value consistency checks. It subsequently controls execution flow ensuring data that fails integrity checks is not propagated downstream incorrectly.

Advanced Integration with Verification Frameworks

In complex scenarios, comprehensive validation frameworks such as Great Expectations or deequ can be used to script detailed validation/quality requirements that integrate with Argo tasks. These frameworks inject data validation into cooperative workflows by interfacing with test suites to ensure real-time compliance with organizational data quality standards.

Continuous Integration of Data Validation and Quality Metrics

Implementing continuous data validation involves embedding real-time checks using streaming platforms or feedback loops within the ETL process. Integrating validations as part of continuous integration workflows ensures that deployed changes in templates or schema evolutions remain validated continuously against baseline scenarios to minimize disruptions in data outputs.

Conclusion

Data validation and quality checks being pivotal in maintaining high-quality, reliable data pipelines directly impact the accuracy and dependability of downstream processes. Structuring versatile and robust validation checks into Argo Workflows—tailored to business context and data characteristics—ensures that the integrity is preserved across transformations, offering error-resilient, data-driven insights that empower organizational efficiencies. Crafting quality-check-rich infrastructures in Argo provides a backbone for maintaining trust in generated analytics and can act as safeguards against data drifts, ultimately steering data strategies towards greater accomplishments.

5.7 Integrating External Data Sources

The integration of external data sources into a data pipeline expands the horizon of information accessible for analysis and decision-making. Leveraging data from diverse entities, such as third-party APIs, cloud storage solutions, or external databases, enables organizations to augment internal data assets, enrich analytics, and drive nuanced insights. Within Argo Workflows, integrating external data sources is facilitated by its Kubernetes-native capabilities, offering seamless, scalable, and flexible solutions.

At the heart of integrating external data sources is the capacity to handle different data retrieval mechanisms and formats, considering the unique characteristics and protocols required for each source. Depending on the source, integration might involve RESTful API calls, secure database connections, streaming data ingestion, or transfer of data artifacts from cloud services.

- **Leveraging RESTful APIs**

REST APIs are a common interface for accessing external data, offering structured endpoints for retrieving or posting data. Integrating APIs into an Argo Workflow involves configuring tasks to perform HTTP requests, handling authentication, and processing responses. Built-in tools within containers, like curl or the requests library in Python, can efficiently handle these operations, ensuring data retrieval aligns with the pipeline's orchestration.

```
apiVersion: argoproj.io/v1alpha1
kind: Workflow
metadata:
  generateName: api-integration-
spec:
  entrypoint: call-api
  templates:
  - name: call-api
    container:
      image: curlimages/curl:7.73.0
      command: ["sh", "-c"]
      args: ["curl -X GET 'https://api.example.com/data' -H 'Authorization: Bearer $TOKEN' -o /data/api_data.json"]
```

In this workflow, the call-api task uses curl to retrieve data from an API and store the response JSON locally. This approach leverages environment variables for authentication and configuration, maintaining security and flexibility.

- **Python-based API Integration Example**

```python
import requests
import os
import json

# Set API endpoint and authentication
api_endpoint = "https://api.example.com/data"
headers = {
    'Authorization': f"Bearer {os.getenv('API_TOKEN')}"
}

# Perform GET request
response = requests.get(api_endpoint, headers=headers)

if response.status_code == 200:
    data = response.json()
    with open('/data/api_data.json', 'w') as f:
        json.dump(data, f)
else:
    print("Failed to retrieve data", response.status_code)
```

Here, the requests library facilitates API interaction handled within an Argo container, thanks to environment variable API_TOKEN.

- **Database Connections**

For accessing external databases, the workflow can establish secure connections with databases such as MySQL, PostgreSQL, or MongoDB, performing CRUD operations directly within designated task templates. Database connections necessitate secure handling of credentials and optimal query management to retrieve and process data efficiently.

Consider Argo's integration with a PostgreSQL database:

```yaml
apiVersion: argoproj.io/v1alpha1
kind: Workflow
metadata:
  generateName: db-integration-
spec:
  entrypoint: query-database
  templates:
  - name: query-database
    container:
      image: postgres:13-alpine
```

5.7. INTEGRATING EXTERNAL DATA SOURCES

```
command: ["sh", "-c"]
args: [
  "psql -h $DB_HOST -U $DB_USER -d $DB_NAME -c 'COPY (SELECT *
    FROM example_table) TO /data/output.csv WITH CSV HEADER'"
]
```

This task capitalizes on a PostgreSQL database client `psql` to extract data as a CSV file, defining host and authentication details through environment variables.

- **Cloud Storage Solutions**

Integrating data from cloud storage, such as AWS S3, GCP Storage, or Azure Blob Storage, involves accessing and managing large volumes of data spread across distributed cloud resources. Argo Workflows facilitate these connections through object storage interfaces, often employing service-specific CLI tools within containerized tasks.

```
apiVersion: argoproj.io/v1alpha1
kind: Workflow
metadata:
  generateName: s3-integration-
spec:
  entrypoint: download-from-s3
  templates:
  - name: download-from-s3
    container:
      image: amazon/aws-cli:latest
      command: ["sh", "-c"]
      args: ["aws s3 cp s3://my-bucket/input_data.csv /data/input_data.csv"]
```

In this workflow, the AWS CLI is used to retrieve data files stored in an S3 bucket. Credentials and permissions are handled via appropriate IAM roles and Kubernetes Secrets, ensuring secure and compliant access.

- **Streaming Data Sources**

For real-time data scenarios, integrating streaming platforms such as Kafka or AWS Kinesis enables the Argo Workflow to ingest flowing records into the pipeline. These systems capture high-frequency data and ensure robust distribution to consumers within the Argo ecosystem for immediate processing or enrichment.

Argo Workflows can trigger streaming consumers using containerized connectors:

CHAPTER 5. MANAGING DATA PIPELINES WITH ARGO

```
apiVersion: argoproj.io/v1alpha1
kind: Workflow
metadata:
  generateName: kafka-consumer-
spec:
  entrypoint: consume-kafka
  templates:
  - name: consume-kafka
    container:
      image: docker.io/confluentinc/cp-kafka:latest
      command: ["sh", "-c"]
      args: ["kafka-console-consumer --bootstrap-server my-kafka-cluster:9092 --topic
            my-topic --from-beginning"]
```

This configuration listens to a Kafka topic called "my-topic," processing records incoming via the specified bootstrap server throughout the workflow.

- **Authentication and Security**

The integration of external data sources necessitates robust authentication and protection of credentials. Approaches include using API keys, OAuth tokens, IP whitelisting, or mutual TLS for accessing APIs, databases, or storage endpoints. Argo Workflows augment security by utilizing Kubernetes Secrets or ConfigMaps to securely inject credentials at runtime:

```
apiVersion: v1
kind: Secret
metadata:
  name: api-credentials
data:
  token: <base64-encoded-token>

---

apiVersion: argoproj.io/v1alpha1
kind: Workflow
metadata:
  generateName: external-data-integration-
spec:
  entrypoint: secure-access
  templates:
  - name: secure-access
    container:
      image: my-api-client-image
      command: ["python", "/scripts/access_external.py"]
      env:
      - name: API_TOKEN
        valueFrom:
          secretKeyRef:
```

5.7. INTEGRATING EXTERNAL DATA SOURCES

```
name: api-credentials
key: token
```

In this example, sensitive credentials are managed through Kubernetes Secrets, ensuring they remain secure while accessible to workflow tasks at execution time.

- **Challenges and Best Practices**

Integrating external data sources presents challenges including handling diverse data formats, managing network latency, orchestrating fault tolerance, and ensuring compliance with data sovereignty regulations. Best practices include:

- **Data Enrichment**: Combine external data with internal data sources to offer more comprehensive insights.

- **Latency Optimization**: Position data transfer nodes close to data sources to minimize latency for optimized retrieval.

- **Error Handling**: Implement robust error handling for API timeouts, rate limits, network issues, or unexpected data formats, with retries or compensating mechanisms.

Adopting a modular approach within Argo Workflows enables separation of concerns, adhering to microservices architectures for seamless scalability, maintainability, and enhanced clarity of task responsibilities.

Integrating external data sources using Argo Workflows enriches data pipelines with scalable and adaptable orchestration power. It ensures organizations leverage a full spectrum of data assets, fostering strategic agility and empowering robust data-driven outcomes amidst complex and evolving data environments.

Chapter 6

Advanced Workflow Features and Patterns

This chapter explores the advanced features and patterns available in Argo Workflows, offering readers the tools to design sophisticated and efficient workflows. It covers dynamic workflow generation, allowing workflows to adapt in real-time using templates and parameterization. Parallel task execution is discussed to optimize for speed and resource efficiency. Common Directed Acyclic Graph (DAG) patterns and the use of workflow templates are examined to promote modular and scalable solutions. The chapter also delves into advanced retry strategies, error handling, and workflow resumability, ensuring robust execution. Additionally, it addresses synchronization techniques, providing comprehensive strategies for managing complex task dependencies. Run failed with status: expired

6.1 Parallel Task Execution

In the context of workflow systems, parallel task execution represents a critical paradigm to optimize computational resources and speed up the processing of workflows. Through effective parallelization, tasks within a workflow can be executed simultaneously, thus minimizing runtime and maximizing efficiency. Parallel task execution leverages the inherent concurrency of processes, which allows systems to better utilize the available CPU cores and other computing resources.

Parallelism is achieved by defining tasks that can be executed concurrently within the constraints of task dependencies. This requires understanding the task graph of a workflow, identifying independent nodes, and deploying these tasks across multiple execution units such as CPU cores, threads, or cluster nodes.

- The primary prerequisite for parallel task execution is the determination of task dependencies. Only tasks that do not have dependencies on one another can be executed in parallel. Dependency-driven task scheduling forms a core principle in systems that support directed acyclic graphs (DAGs).

- Consider a workflow defined in a DAG form where nodes represent tasks and directed edges signify dependencies. If tasks A and B are on different paths that converge into task C, A and B can be executed in parallel as long as they are not dependent on one another. Execution of C requires both A and B to complete.

```
dag = {
    'A': [],
    'B': [],
    'C': ['A', 'B']
}
# On executing, A and B can run in parallel, followed by C.
```

Several concurrency models are employed in parallel task execution. These models are chosen based on the specific application requirements and the underlying computing architecture, including shared-memory, distributed processing, and hybrid models.

- In shared-memory systems, multiple threads can execute tasks and access shared resources. This facilitates rapid communication between tasks but demands sophisticated synchronization to avoid write conflicts. Languages like C++ and Java provide

6.1. PARALLEL TASK EXECUTION

threading libraries to exploit shared-memory parallelism efficiently.

```
#include <thread>
#include <vector>

void taskA() {
    // taskA implementation
}

void taskB() {
    // taskB implementation
}

int main() {
    std::thread threadA(taskA);
    std::thread threadB(taskB);

    threadA.join();
    threadB.join();
    return 0;
}
```

- In distributed concurrency, tasks are executed on different nodes in a computing cluster. This approach can handle larger workloads and datasets that exceed the capacity of a single machine. Frameworks like Apache Spark and Hadoop facilitate distributed execution by managing task distribution across cluster nodes.

- Hybrid approaches combine shared-memory and distributed concurrency to leverage both within a heterogeneous computing environment. This can be achieved using a mix of MPI (Message Passing Interface) for distributed communication and OpenMP for node-level parallelism.

Workflow systems such as Argo Workflows explicitly support parallel task execution. By defining task templates and specifying dependencies, users can enable workflows with parallel paths.

```
{
  "apiVersion": "argoproj.io/v1alpha1",
  "kind": "Workflow",
  "metadata": {
    "generateName": "parallel-tasks-"
  },
  "spec": {
    "entrypoint": "parallel-dag",
    "templates": [
```

```
{
  "name": "parallel-dag",
  "dag": {
    "tasks": [
      {
        "name": "task-a",
        "template": "task-a-template"
      },
      {
        "name": "task-b",
        "template": "task-b-template"
      },
      {
        "name": "task-c",
        "template": "task-c-template",
        "dependencies": ["task-a", "task-b"]
      }
    ]
  }
},
{
  "name": "task-a-template",
  "script": {
    "image": "python:3.8",
    "source": "print(\"Executing Task A\")"
  }
},
{
  "name": "task-b-template",
  "script": {
    "image": "python:3.8",
    "source": "print(\"Executing Task B\")"
  }
},
{
  "name": "task-c-template",
  "script": {
    "image": "python:3.8",
    "source": "print(\"Executing Task C\")"
  }
}
]
}
}
```

In the above workflow snippet, tasks A and B can be executed in parallel due to their lack of interdependencies. Task C is dependent on the completion of both tasks A and B.

Effective parallel task execution requires careful resource scheduling to prevent resource starvation or overload. When deploying in a Kubernetes environment, leveraging resource constraints like CPU and memory requests and limits helps maintain cluster stability.

6.1. PARALLEL TASK EXECUTION

```
"resources": {
  "requests": {
    "memory": "64Mi",
    "cpu": "250m"
  },
  "limits": {
    "memory": "128Mi",
    "cpu": "500m"
  }
}
```

Schedulers like Kubernetes also need to address node affinity or anti-affinity, balancing load across computing resources, and prioritizing critical tasks. Advanced features like Horizontal Pod Autoscalers can be utilized to adjust the number of pods executing tasks based on the workload.

Parallel execution scenarios must handle failures without compromising the workflow's integrity. Failure in one parallel branch should not necessarily result in the entire workflow's failure. Instead, workflows should be robust enough to retry failed tasks or implement alternative strategies for task recovery.

In systems like Argo Workflows, retries can be defined alongside back-off strategies to control the frequency and intervals of retries:

```
{
  "retryStrategy": {
    "limit": 3,
    "backoff": {
      "duration": "30s",
      "factor": 2,
      "maxDuration": "5m"
    }
  }
}
```

With this configuration, failed tasks will automatically be retried up to three times, doubling the wait time after each failure until a maximum duration of five minutes.

Efficient parallel task execution must also account for scalability. As the size and complexity of workflows grow, parallel execution frameworks need to efficiently manage increased task counts and data volumes.

Load balancing and dynamic task scheduling play crucial roles in managing resource allocation as workloads increase. Utilizing cloud-native features like auto-scaling helps handle peak loads seamlessly. Additionally, transitioning from batch processing to continuous data streams (stream processing) can offer improved performance for time-sensitive applications.

Continuous integration and continuous delivery (CI/CD) pipelines can benefit significantly from parallel task execution by accelerating testing and deployment cycles, provided the tasks are independent and can be run concurrently without dependencies impacting the results.

Therefore, integrating parallel task execution within workflows can substantially improve throughput and reduce latency, provided that dependencies, resources, and fault tolerance strategies are carefully managed. Efficient parallel task execution supports scalable, resilient, and high-performance workflows, enabling complex systems to handle large volumes of data and execute sophisticated computational tasks efficiently.

6.2 Workflow DAG Patterns

Directed Acyclic Graphs (DAGs) lie at the core of modern workflow management systems, providing a flexible structure for depicting task sequences and dependencies. Within organizations, these workflows enable automation and orchestration of complex sequences of processes in a systematic manner. Understanding and leveraging common DAG patterns enhances the design and execution of complex workflows, allowing efficient parallel execution, load balancing, and resource optimization.

The term 'Directed Acyclic Graph' fundamentally describes a network where nodes (representing tasks or jobs) are interconnected in a directed manner, such that there are no cycles. This structure ensures tasks flow in a single direction—forward—facilitating predictable and determinable workflow progressions.

Pattern Basics: Nodes and Edges

In any DAG-based workflow system, nodes represent distinct units of work or tasks, while the edges reflect dependencies between these tasks. It is crucial that each task defines the dependencies it has on preceding

6.2. WORKFLOW DAG PATTERNS

tasks, ensuring that the task execution order honors these dependencies.

The following are representative JSON structures for a simple workflow defining tasks as nodes and dependencies as edges:

```json
{
  "apiVersion": "v1alpha1",
  "kind": "Workflow",
  "metadata": {
    "generateName": "basic-dag-"
  },
  "spec": {
    "entrypoint": "simple-dag",
    "templates": [
      {
        "name": "simple-dag",
        "dag": {
          "tasks": [
            {
              "name": "task-1",
              "template": "task-1-template"
            },
            {
              "name": "task-2",
              "template": "task-2-template",
              "dependencies": ["task-1"]
            },
            {
              "name": "task-3",
              "template": "task-3-template",
              "dependencies": ["task-1"]
            }
          ]
        }
      },
      {
        "name": "task-1-template",
        "script": {
          "image": "python:3.8",
          "source": "print(\"Executing Task 1\")"
        }
      },
      {
        "name": "task-2-template",
        "script": {
          "image": "python:3.8",
          "source": "print(\"Executing Task 2\")"
        }
      },
      {
        "name": "task-3-template",
        "script": {
          "image": "python:3.8",
          "source": "print(\"Executing Task 3\")"
        }
      }
```

CHAPTER 6. ADVANCED WORKFLOW FEATURES AND PATTERNS

```
    ]
  }
}
```

In this DAG example, 'task-1' is the initial task executed, and both 'task-2' and 'task-3' depend on its completion.

Common DAG Patterns

Fan-out and Fan-in Patterns

The fan-out pattern involves branching a single task into multiple parallel tasks, whereas the fan-in pattern aggregates multiple tasks into a single following task. For instance, one task might initiate several subtasks that compute different components of a data set, which subsequently converge to a final summarization task.

```
{
  "apiVersion": "v1alpha1",
  "kind": "Workflow",
  "metadata": {
    "generateName": "fan-out-fan-in-"
  },
  "spec": {
    "entrypoint": "fan-out-fan-in",
    "templates": [
      {
        "name": "fan-out-fan-in",
        "dag": {
          "tasks": [
            {
              "name": "extract-data",
              "template": "data-extraction-template"
            },
            {
              "name": "transform-data-a",
              "template": "data-transform-template",
              "dependencies": ["extract-data"]
            },
            {
              "name": "transform-data-b",
              "template": "data-transform-template",
              "dependencies": ["extract-data"]
            },
            {
              "name": "aggregate-results",
              "template": "aggregation-template",
              "dependencies": ["transform-data-a", "transform-data-b"]
            }
          ]
        }
      }
    ]
  }
}
```

}

Diamond Pattern

The diamond pattern is a special case of fan-out and fan-in, distinguishing itself by branching several tasks off a single initiation point and then merging them back into a single end task. This pattern is useful in decision graphing and conditional executions where a common task follows multiple decision paths.

```
{
  "tasks": [
    {
      "name": "step-0",
      "template": "start-template"
    },
    {
      "name": "step-1a",
      "template": "step-a-template",
      "dependencies": ["step-0"]
    },
    {
      "name": "step-1b",
      "template": "step-b-template",
      "dependencies": ["step-0"]
    },
    {
      "name": "final-step",
      "template": "aggregate-template",
      "dependencies": ["step-1a", "step-1b"]
    }
  ]
}
```

Pipeline Pattern

Pipelines are linear DAGs where tasks are executed in sequential order. Each task waits for its predecessor to complete before commencing, paving the way for clear and ordered processing steps such as those used within CI/CD pipelines or ETL (Extract, Transform, Load) processes.

```
{
  "tasks": [
    {
      "name": "task-1",
      "template": "task-1-template"
    },
    {
      "name": "task-2",
      "template": "task-2-template",
      "dependencies": ["task-1"]
```

```
    },
    {
      "name": "task-3",
      "template": "task-3-template",
      "dependencies": ["task-2"]
    }
  ]
}
```

Considerations for Designing DAGs

Effective DAG design is crucial for leveraging the full potential of workflow execution engines. Some key considerations include:

- Cycle Avoidance: Acyclicity must be maintained, avoiding circular dependencies to ensure task progress moves forward.
- Optimizing Dependency Chains: Minimizing task interdependencies permits greater parallel task execution, thereby speeding up workflow execution times.
- Error Handling Strategies: Defining strategies for task retries and the cascade of failures are critical for resilient workflows. Use conditional tasks or skippable paths to handle errors gracefully.
- Resource Definitions: Allocating resources for parallel task execution requires careful definition and constant monitoring, especially in shared environments like Kubernetes.
- Scalability: DAG patterns should scale with growing data volumes and complexity, ensuring the system remains responsive and efficient under varying loads.

Advanced Features in DAG Systems

Modern DAG systems provide advanced features that complement basic patterns, including conditional execution paths, loop constructs, and external service integration, making them highly adaptable to various use cases.

Conditional Tasks

Workflows often require conditional execution logic based on the results of preceding tasks. This is particularly prevalent in complex data processing or decision-making automations. Example frameworks like

6.2. WORKFLOW DAG PATTERNS

Argo Workflows allow for 'when' expressions to facilitate these conditions.

```
{
  "name": "conditional-task",
  "template": "evaluate-template",
  "dependencies": ["check-status"],
  "when": "{{tasks.check-status.outputs.result}} == Success"
}
```

Loops and Iterative Constructs

When a task needs to be executed iteratively over a collection of inputs, iterative constructs within a DAG support this need. Loops are crucial in scenarios involving bulk processing and require careful synchronization to maintain task sequence veracity.

```
{
  "name": "process-item",
  "template": "item-template",
  "arguments": {
    "parameters": [
      {
        "name": "item",
        "value": "{{item}}"
      }
    ]
  },
  "withItems": [
    "item1",
    "item2",
    "item3"
  ]
}
```

Integration with External Systems

Complex workflows often interact with external systems such as databases, messaging queues, or cloud services. DAG systems provide mechanisms for such integrations through componentized tasks and extensible template libraries.

```
{
  "name": "fetch-from-db",
  "template": "db-interaction-template",
  "inputs": {
    "artifacts": [
      {
        "name": "db-config",
        "path": "/etc/config/db"
      }
    ]
```

```
  }
}
```

The strategic use of DAG patterns in workflow management fundamentally influences the scalability, efficiency, and reliability of automated tasks. Well-designed DAGs empower organizations to implement profound computational workflows, ensuring they meet both present and future demands. Understanding the nuances of these patterns and the scope of their implementation is key to building high-performance, adaptable workflow systems that successfully navigate complex computational environments. These systems manage dependencies and machine tasks efficiently, maintaining the acyclic nature that guarantees progression towards workflow completion.

6.3   Using Workflow Templates

Workflow templates are a pivotal concept in automating and orchestrating complex business and computational processes. They enable the creation of reusable and modular workflow components that can be instantiated multiple times across various projects, reducing redundancy and enhancing maintenance. The use of workflow templates facilitates consistency in task executions and promotes a streamlined development cycle by abstracting repetitive patterns into reusable forms.

Introduction to Workflow Templates

At its core, a workflow template consists of a predefined set of tasks or steps arranged in a logical order—often using a DAG format—that can be repeatedly employed to accomplish specific functions. This abstraction allows workflows to be defined once and applied broadly across different domains with minimal alteration. Workflow templates enhance flexibility, enabling easy updates and consistent deployment throughout the development pipeline.

```
{
  "apiVersion": "argoproj.io/v1alpha1",
  "kind": "WorkflowTemplate",
  "metadata": {
    "name": "example-template"
```

6.3. USING WORKFLOW TEMPLATES

```
},
"spec": {
  "entrypoint": "example-entry",
  "templates": [
    {
      "name": "example-entry",
      "steps": [
        {
          "name": "example-step",
          "template": "example-step-template"
        }
      ]
    },
    {
      "name": "example-step-template",
      "script": {
        "image": "python:3.8",
        "source": "print(\"Running example step\")"
      }
    }
  ]
}
}
```

Advantages of Workflow Templates

The advantages of integrating workflow templates into process automation cannot be overstated. Templates provide a standard starting point, ensuring that all workflows adhere to organizational policies and best practices. Changes to templates propagate across all derived workflows, simplifying management and updating processes.

- **Reuse**: Templates encapsulate frequently used sequences of tasks, reducing the need to redefine workflows from scratch for every instance.

- **Maintainability**: By updating a template, all workflows using it can inherit improvements or fixes, greatly reducing technical debt.

- **Scalability**: Workflows can be scaled up or down efficiently by leveraging and adapting existing templates to match different use cases.

- **Consistency**: They enforce standards and conventions across workflows, ensuring uniform behavior and outcomes.

Designing Workflow Templates

Parameterization and Customization

Central to the power of workflow templates is parameterization, which allows templates to consume dynamic inputs, adapting their behavior without requiring code modifications. Parameters can be injected at runtime, making the workflows versatile and highly adaptive.

```
{
  "apiVersion": "argoproj.io/v1alpha1",
  "kind": "WorkflowTemplate",
  "metadata": {
    "name": "param-example-template"
  },
  "spec": {
    "entrypoint": "main",
    "templates": [
      {
        "name": "main",
        "steps": [
          [
            {
              "name": "say-hello",
              "template": "say-hello-template",
              "arguments": {
                "parameters": [
                  { "name": "name", "value": "{{workflow.parameters.name}}" }
                ]
              }
            }
          ]
        ]
      },
      {
        "name": "say-hello-template",
        "inputs": {
          "parameters": [
            { "name": "name" }
          ]
        },
        "container": {
          "image": "alpine:latest",
          "command": ["echo"],
          "args": ["Hello, {{inputs.parameters.name}}"]
        }
      }
    ],
    "arguments": {
      "parameters": [
        { "name": "name", "value": "World" }
      ]
    }
  }
}
```

Incorporating Conditional Logic

Templates can include conditional logic to handle different workflow paths based on predetermined conditions. Conditional constructs enhance template flexibility, catering to complex decision-making processes within workflows.

```
{
  "name": "conditional-task",
  "template": "check-status-template",
  "when": "{{tasks.check-status.outputs.result}} == 'OK'"
}
```

Template Nesting and Hierarchies

Complex workflows may necessitate the decomposition of tasks into sub-tasks, which can be abstracted as nested templates. This hierarchical structuring allows smaller templates to be combined, promoting modular design and ease of testing.

```
{
  "name": "parent-template",
  "templates": [
    {
      "name": "child-template",
      "script": {
        "image": "python:3.8",
        "source": "print(\"Running child template\")"
      }
    },
    {
      "name": "parent-workflow",
      "steps": [
        {
          "name": "run-child",
          "template": "child-template"
        }
      ]
    }
  ]
}
```

Best Practices for Template Implementation

- **Modular Design**: Decompose workflows into manageable subcomponents that can be tested and reused independently.

- **Version Control**: Maintain a version history of workflow templates, enabling rollback to stable versions if needed.

- **Documentation**: Clearly document inputs, outputs, and dependencies of each template to facilitate understanding and maintenance.

- **Testing**: Implement automated tests to validate template functionality, ensuring robustness and reliability.

- **Security**: Sanitize inputs and restrict permissions to avoid unauthorized access or executions.

Implementing Workflows with Argo Workflow Templates

Argo Workflows is a Kubernetes-native workflow orchestration tool that supports the use of templates extensively. By storing templates in 'WorkflowTemplate' objects, workflows can be instantiated dynamically, passing parameters and conditions at runtime to tailor their execution.

Dynamic Workflow Instantiation

Argo allows workflows to be dynamically instantiated using predefined templates, and parameters can be injected during submission to customize task behavior.

```
argo submit --from workflowtemplate/example-template -p name=Argo
```

Utilizing Template Libraries

Argo supports the use of template libraries, which consist of collections of predefined templates that can be imported and combined to form larger workflows.

```
{
  "apiVersion": "argoproj.io/v1alpha1",
  "kind": "Workflow",
  "metadata": {
```

6.3. USING WORKFLOW TEMPLATES

```
    "generateName": "library-workflow-"
  },
  "spec": {
    "entrypoint": "main",
    "templates": [
      {
        "name": "main",
        "templateRef": {
          "name": "library-template",
          "template": "standard-step"
        }
      }
    ]
  }
}
```

Workflow Optimization through Templates

The systematic adoption of workflow templates drives optimization in several areas:

- **Resource Management**: Templates can specify resource requirements, allowing workflows to be optimized for CPU and memory allocation.

- **Scalable Execution**: Reutilizing templates for parallel executions can efficiently scale the computation across distributed resources, improving processing throughput.

- **Dynamic Load Balancing**: By leveraging parameterization, workflows can adjust dynamically to fluctuations in input data size and compute requirements, facilitating load balancing.

```
"resources": {
  "requests": {
    "cpu": "500m",
    "memory": "256Mi"
  },
  "limits": {
    "cpu": "1",
    "memory": "512Mi"
  }
}
```

Use Cases and Applications

Workflow templates are employed across a wide variety of domains:

- **Data Processing Pipelines**: In ETL pipelines, templates standardize data extraction, transformation, and loading processes, ensuring consistency across datasets.

- **Continuous Integration/Continuous Deployment (CI/CD)**: CI/CD pipelines use templates to automate testing, building, and deployment processes across various environments.

- **Machine Learning Workflows**: Templates are used for model training, evaluation, and deployment tasks, harmonizing the ML pipeline stages and promoting model reproducibility.

- **Scientific Research**: Researchers use templates to standardize experiment setups, facilitating reproducibility and collaboration across research teams.

Example: CI/CD Workflow Template

A CI/CD pipeline leverages templates to manage dependencies, run tests, build artifacts, and deploy releases consistently.

```
{
  "apiVersion": "argoproj.io/v1alpha1",
  "kind": "WorkflowTemplate",
  "metadata": {
    "name": "ci-cd-template"
  },
  "spec": {
    "entrypoint": "pipeline",
    "templates": [
      {
        "name": "pipeline",
        "steps": [
          {
            "name": "checkout",
            "template": "git-checkout-template"
          },
          {
            "name": "test",
            "template": "unit-test-template"
          },
          {
```

```
            "name": "build",
            "template": "build-artifact-template",
            "depends": "test"
          },
          {
            "name": "deploy",
            "template": "deployment-template",
            "depends": "build"
          }
        ]
      }
    ]
  }
}
```

Ultimately, workflow templates are a powerful abstraction delivering effective management and execution of complex, repeatable processes. As components of the overarching workflow orchestrations, they enable a seamless integration between multiple systems and process automation, fostering agility and productivity in both development and operational environments. Importantly, they facilitate collaboration within and across teams, serving as a shared blueprint that embodies the best practices and standards prescribed within organizations.

6.4 Retry Strategies and Error Handling

Retry strategies and error handling constitute fundamental components of building robust workflow systems. These mechanisms ensure that temporary failures do not permanently disrupt the execution of a workflow, while providing systematic approaches to manage errors and maintain data integrity. This section delves into the methodologies and best practices for implementing retries and error-handling mechanisms, enhancing the reliability and resilience of workflows.

Understanding Errors and Failures

Failures in software systems can arise from numerous sources, including network disruptions, service unavailability, or transient system overloads. Differentiating transient errors from persistent failures is crucial as transient errors often resolve with time, whereas persistent failures require corrective interventions.

- **Transient Errors**: Temporary issues that typically resolve after a short period, such as network latency or temporary unavailability of resources.

- **Persistent Failures**: Critical and often systemic errors that require changes or fixes in the system itself, such as code bugs or misconfigurations.

Identifying the nature of an error helps in deciding the appropriate strategy for retries or invoking error-handling procedures.

Designing Retry Strategies

Retry strategies define the policies and procedures for re-attempting failed operations. These strategies incorporate mechanisms that define when and how retries should occur, thereby strengthening fault tolerance.

Exponential Backoff

Exponential backoff is a widely-used retry strategy that involves progressively increasing the wait time between retries. This approach aims to reduce the load on the system by spacing out retry attempts, mitigating the risk of overwhelming resources.

```
{
  "retryStrategy": {
    "limit": 5,
    "backoff": {
      "duration": "10s",
      "factor": 2,
      "maxDuration": "2m"
    }
  }
}
```

In the above example: - The workflow will attempt retries up to a maximum of five attempts. - The initial wait duration is ten seconds, doubling with each subsequent retry. - The maximum duration between retries is capped at two minutes.

6.4. RETRY STRATEGIES AND ERROR HANDLING

Jittering

Incorporating jitter into retry strategies involves injecting random variability into wait times between retries. This variability helps distribute the retry load more evenly across the system, reducing the potential for simultaneous retry attempts to exacerbate load spikes.

```
import random
import time

def retry_with_jitter():
    base_delay = 1 # start with 1 second
    for attempt in range(5):
        try:
            # Invoke operation here
            pass
        except Exception:
            jitter = random.uniform(0.5, 1.5) # Random jitter factor between 0.5 and 1.5
            time.sleep(base_delay * jitter)
            base_delay *= 2 # Exponential backoff
            continue
```

Fixed Delay

A fixed delay retry strategy attempts to resolve transient failures by retrying at defined intervals, offering simplicity in situations where uniform retry timing is sufficient.

```
{
  "retryStrategy": {
    "limit": 3,
    "backoff": {
      "duration": "15s",
      "factor": 1
    }
  }
}
```

In this scenario, the delays remain consistent across retries, which can be a viable option for lightweight and less complex operations.

Implementing Error Handling Mechanisms

A robust error-handling framework in workflows preemptively addresses potential failures, detailing the response actions to be taken upon encountering errors. Effective error-handling strategies focus on failure isolation, notification, recovery, and resolution to maintain overall workflow stability.

Error Isolation and Context Propagation

Ensuring that errors do not propagate unchecked through the system involves isolating failures to prevent cascading effects that disrupt successive tasks. Propagating error context within workflows allows downstream tasks to make informed decisions based on the status and content of prior steps.

Graceful Degradation

Gracefully degrading functionality involves reducing system performance or capability temporarily, rather than halting entirely, thereby maintaining core functionalities under duress. For example, offering cached data when a live service call fails can sustain service availability despite underlying issues.

Compensation Transactions

Compensation transactions are employed in workflows involving multiple operations that require rolling back changes in the event of failures. This approach is akin to database transactions where changes need reversal when all actions within a predefined scope cannot complete successfully.

```
{
  "name": "compensate-action",
  "template": "compensation-task-template",
  "when": "{{tasks.primary-action.outputs.result}} != 'Success'"
}
```

Notification and Monitoring

Monitoring systems are integral to error handling, offering visibility into workflow performance and failures. Alerts and notifications enable timely intervention when issues arise, allowing operators to assess failures and initiate corrective actions.

Integrating tools such as Prometheus for metrics collection and Grafana for visualization can enhance monitoring capabilities, turning performance data into actionable insight.

```
- alert: WorkflowFailure
  expr: workflows_failed > 0
  for: 5m
  labels:
    severity: high
  annotations:
    summary: "Workflow failure detected"
    description: "Workflow {{ $labels.workflow }} has failed"
```

Case Studies and Application Scenarios

Data Processing Pipelines

In ETL workflows, retry strategies ensure the reprocessing of datasets upon encountering transient data source issues. Compensation mechanisms enable rollback of partial transformations or output verifications to maintain data consistency.

```
{
  "name": "rollback-change",
  "template": "sql-rollback-template",
  "args": [
    "--rollback-script=/path/to/script.sql"
  ]
}
```

Microservices Coordination

Error handling between microservices requires that services handle their failures locally while coordinating with others to maintain system coherency. Asynchronous communication and eventual consistency models, such as those implemented with message brokers or event streaming platforms, provide robustness against service disruptions.

```
{
  "name": "notify-error",
  "template": "kafka-publish-template",
  "inputs": {
```

```
    "parameters": [
      {
        "name": "error-message",
        "value": "{{tasks.handler.outputs.error}}"
      }
    ]
  }
}
```

Machine Learning Operations

In machine learning workflows, retry logic aids in dealing with transient compute errors or service call failures during model training or evaluation phases. Errors during model deployment should trigger rollbacks to previous stable versions and issue alerts for implementation teams.

Scientific Simulations

Complex simulations in scientific workflows benefit from sophisticated error handling where computational errors can be transient or contextual. Employing retries or fallback computation paths helps navigate toward successful simulation results without fully discarding work done in prior steps.

Enhancing Workflow Resilience with Error Strategies

Integrating robust retry and error-handling mechanisms into workflow architectures is vital to ensuring consistent system reliability and uptime. These mechanisms substantially contribute to fault tolerance, making distributed systems more resilient, adaptable, and autonomous.

Streamlined error identification, coupled with intelligent retry logic and comprehensive monitoring, can help transition workflows from failure recovery to anticipatory resilience, thus playing a strategic role in modern system designs that align well with evolving business and technological demands. This foresight not only aids in mitigating immediate disruptions but also furnishes a robust framework to anticipate and adapt to potential challenges, ensuring sustained system performance and agility.

6.5 Workflow Resumability and Recovery

In contemporary computing environments, maintaining continuous operation and swiftly recovering from failures are crucial to the success of automated workflows. Workflow resumability and recovery strategies play a significant role in ensuring that workflows can efficiently handle interruptions caused by system failures, software bugs, or unforeseen contingencies. These strategies allow workflows to pause, persist state, and resume from designated checkpoints, increasing resilience and uptime.

Conceptualizing Resumability in Workflows

Workflow resumability refers to a workflow's capability to pause and later continue from a point of interruption. By capturing state and intermediate outputs at designated checkpoints, workflows can avoid starting from scratch after failures. Resumability not only minimises processing redundancy but also fosters efficient resource utilization, saving time and computational costs.

The resumability mechanism comprises:

- - **Checkpoints**: Well-defined stages within a workflow where state and output are saved securely.

- - **State Persistence**: Mechanisms to store necessary context and data, ensuring restoration accuracy.

- - **Fault Identification**: Techniques to detect failures and decide if resumption is feasible.

Implementing Resumable Workflows

To create resumable workflows, systems must accommodate explicit state management, capture intermediate data, and employ robust failure detection.

Checkpoints and Persistence Strategies

Checkpoints are strategically placed in workflows to capture snapshots of the current state and outputs. Choosing optimal points for checkpoints balances overhead in state persistence against the loss of progress upon failure.

```
{
  "apiVersion": "argoproj.io/v1alpha1",
  "kind": "Workflow",
  "metadata": {
    "generateName": "resumable-workflow-"
  },
  "spec": {
    "entrypoint": "checkpointed-dag",
    "templates": [
      {
        "name": "checkpointed-dag",
        "steps": [
          {
            "name": "step-1",
            "template": "step-1-template"
          },
          {
            "name": "checkpoint",
            "template": "persistence-template"
          },
          {
            "name": "step-2",
            "template": "step-2-template",
            "when": "{{steps.checkpoint.outputs.result}} == 'Success'"
          }
        ]
      }
    ]
  }
}
```

State Persistence Mechanisms

Persisting states involves storing critical workflow data and context securely. Common approaches for persisting state include: -

6.5. WORKFLOW RESUMABILITY AND RECOVERY

Databases: Employing traditional databases such as PostgreSQL for structured state management. - **Object Storage**: Utilizing cloud services like AWS S3 for storing data objects and identifiable markers. - **Cache Systems**: Leveraging distributed caches for temporary state retention during brief tasks.

Data Serialization and Snapshotting

Data serialization transforms complex data structures into formats suitable for storage or transmission, fundamental for accurate workflow recovery. Popular serialization formats include JSON, XML, and Protocol Buffers.

Snapshotting extends beyond simplistic serialization by capturing comprehensive system states, including intermediate processing variables and environmental specifics.

```
import json
import pickle

def serialize_data(data):
    return json.dumps(data)

def snapshot_system():
    system_state = {"var1": "value1", "var2": "value2"}
    with open('snapshot.pkl', 'wb') as snapshot_file:
        pickle.dump(system_state, snapshot_file)
```

Recovery Strategies in Workflows

Workflow recovery involves mechanisms to reload and restore prior state, allowing task continuation, circumventing total workflow restart. Recovery strategies often emphasize efficiency and data consistency, especially in distributed environments.

Orchestration and Fault-tolerant Design

Effective recovery involves orchestrating task resumption, maintaining process continuity, while managing and mitigating side-effects of failures. Sophisticated workflow orchestration platforms, such as

Apache Airflow and Argo Workflows, natively support fault-tolerant paradigms through retry capability and error isolation.

Atomicity and Idempotency

Ensuring atomicity - where a set of operations execute entirely or not at all - and idempotency - the principle of executing actions repeatedly without unexpected results - are foundational to establishing consistency.

```
{
  "name": "check-transaction",
  "template": "transaction-check-template",
  "when": "{{steps.previous-step.outputs.result}} != 'Processed'"
}
```

Task Level Resumption and Backtracking

When a particular task fails, the system should facilitate task-level resumption, confining recovery to the failed task instead of re-executing previously successful processes.

Backtracking, an auxiliary strategy, involves reversing erroneous actions taken post-failure, resetting workflow states accurately to pre-failure conditions.

Monitoring and Handling of States and Errors

Monitoring is vital for stateful systems; it provides visibility into both workflow progression and failure handling. Comprehensive logging, metrics collection, and alert mechanisms underpin operational resilience, allowing agile response to deviations.

```
- alert: WorkflowResumptionFailed
  expr: workflows_resumed_error > 0
  for: 10m
  labels:
    severity: critical
  annotations:
    summary: "Workflow resumption failure detected"
    description: "Check logs for workflow {{ $labels.workflow }} to investigate issues"
```

6.5. WORKFLOW RESUMABILITY AND RECOVERY

Resilient Event Handling

Effective event handling entails adapting and scaling event-driven mechanisms, ensuring consistent message delivery and processing against the backdrop of transient failures.

```
function handleEvent(event) {
  try {
    processEvent(event);
  } catch (error) {
    logError(error);
    enqueueForRetry(event); // Ensure idempotency
  }
}

function enqueueForRetry(event) {
  if (getRetryCount(event) < MAX_RETRIES) {
    scheduleRetry(event);
  } else {
    handleFailedEvent(event); // Eliminate perpetual loops
  }
}
```

Case Studies and Use Cases

Scientific Computing and Simulations

In complex scientific computations, checkpoints allow simulation states to be saved at critical points, minimizing the possibility of extensive recomputation. Storing simulation parameters and environment variables ensures simulations can resume intelligently.

Bulk Data Processing Systems

Workflows for data extraction, transformation, and loading (ETL) use stateful designs to map transformation steps intelligently. Persistent states inform recovery protocols, reconstructing tasks mid-way into batch processing or data extraction procedures without data loss or redundancy.

```
{
  "name": "extract-state",
  "template": "stateful-etl-step",
  "arguments": {
    "parameters": [
```

```
    {
      "name": "previous-state",
      "value": "{{workflow.outputs.state}}"
    }
  ]
 }
}
```

Financial Transactions Systems

Financial systems harness resilient stateful patterns to ensure transactions are atomic and consistent across multi-step processes. Using transactional logs and consistent state checkpoints, errors are isolated, corrected, and systems restored accurately.

Enhancing Workflow Resilience through Resumability and Recovery

The integration of resumability and recovery strategies positions workflows for sustained operation amidst the complexity inherent within distributed systems. This capability bridges system imperatives across automation, operationalization, and resilience—fortifying workflows against the broad expanse of failures and interruptions prevalent in the digital domain.

Optimally placing checkpoints and employing state management practices not only strengthen consistency and accuracy but also streamline system resource allocation, fostering cost efficiency and expeditious recovery paths. By comprehensively addressing and preemptively mitigating error impacts, workflows inherently adapt to dynamic environments, enabling elastic recovery post-crisis and promoting business continuity in the face of adversity.

6.6 Multi-Step Workflow Synchronization

Multi-step workflow synchronization presents crucial challenges and opportunities in the design and execution of complex workflows. As

6.6. MULTI-STEP WORKFLOW SYNCHRONIZATION

workflows grow in complexity, managing the synchronous execution of diverse tasks becomes imperative to ensure all dependencies are satisfied, and data integrity is maintained. This aspect of workflow management not only influences operational efficiency but also affects resource allocation and system reliability.

Understanding Workflow Synchronization

Workflow synchronization concerns itself with coordinating various tasks within a workflow to ensure they execute in the desired sequence, respecting any dependencies or preconditions. Synchronization guarantees that tasks adhere to scheduling constraints and resource availability without leading to deadlocks or data races.

Dependencies and Routing in Workflows

At the core of workflow synchronization lie tasks' dependencies. Tasks often depend on the output of one or more preceding tasks:

- **Open/Closed Dependency Grid**: Tasks defined within a grid that facilitates both independent and sequential task execution by grouping tasks based on shared resources or outputs.

- **Sequential and Parallel Execution**: Balancing sequential dependencies with parallel execution to optimize resource use and minimize processing time.

Workflow systems leverage directed graphs to graphically illustrate these dependencies, utilizing nodes (tasks) and edges (dependencies) for better clarity and management.

```
{
  "apiVersion": "argoproj.io/v1alpha1",
  "kind": "Workflow",
  "spec": {
    "entrypoint": "multi-step-dag",
    "templates": [
      {
        "name": "multi-step-dag",
        "dag": {
          "tasks": [
            { "name": "first-task", "template": "task-template" },
```

```
          {
            "name": "second-task",
            "template": "task-template",
            "dependencies": ["first-task"]
          },
          {
            "name": "third-task",
            "template": "task-template",
            "dependencies": ["first-task"]
          },
          {
            "name": "final-task",
            "template": "task-template",
            "dependencies": ["second-task", "third-task"]
          }
        ]
      }
    }
  ]
}
```

The Role of Synchronization Points

Synchronization points are pivotal stages within a workflow designed to ensure tasks preceding and following them meet certain criteria. They serve as barriers to guarantee that all parallel tasks have completed before subsequent tasks are initiated.

```
from threading import Barrier, Thread

barrier = Barrier(3)

def worker():
    print("Waiting at barrier")
    barrier.wait()
    print("Passed barrier")

for i in range(3):
    Thread(target=worker).start()
```

Architectural Strategies for Synchronization

Architectural strategies facilitate the seamless execution and coordination of workflow tasks, ensuring that system performance remains unaffected by increasing complexity.

6.6. MULTI-STEP WORKFLOW SYNCHRONIZATION

Centrally Controlled Orchestration

Centrally controlled orchestration permits a single point of truth regarding task states and dependencies, allowing for higher-level management and evaluation:

- **Schedule-Driven Synchronization**: Tasks are executed based on a predefined schedule, ensuring all dependencies are resolved methodically. - **Event-Driven Synchronization**: Utilizes events and triggers to initiate tasks as dependencies are completed, enhancing flexibility and responsiveness.

```
{
  "name": "event-triggered-task",
  "template": "task-template",
  "when": "{{tasks.previous-task.outputs.result}} == 'Success'"
}
```

Decentralized Execution Models

In contrast, decentralized models empower individual task nodes to manage their state and execution logic, thereby minimizing central bottlenecks and fostering distributed decision-making.

Hybrid Approaches

Hybrid models blend both centralized and decentralized strategies, allowing architects to leverage their advantages pro rata, adapting to the demands of distinct stages of workflow execution.

Challenges in Workflow Synchronization

Managing synchronization within complex workflows involves tackling several challenges:

- **Deadlock Prevention**: Ensuring resources are allocated in a manner that prevents circular waits and potential execution blockages.

- **Resource Contention**: Balancing resource demand across competing tasks to avoid contention and ensure optimal utilization.

- **Data Consistency**: Guaranteeing data integrity in workflows where multiple tasks access or modify shared datasets.

Example issue: A deadlock scenario arises when Task A waits for Task B's completion while Task B
awaits a resource held by Task A, thus permanently halting both tasks unless external intervention occurs.

Synchronization in Distributed Systems

Distributed workflows exacerbate synchronization complexities as tasks span diverse computational resources and network segments, necessitating advanced strategies for robust management.

- **Consensus Algorithms**: Distributed systems can employ consensus protocols like Paxos or Raft to agree on task completion and state transitions.

- **Quorum-Based Approaches**: These enable confirmation across a majority of nodes to proceed with task synchronization, increasing resiliency.

Inter-node communication requires careful orchestration to maintain low-latency and reliable transmission in environments with significant network variability.

```
{
  "name": "quorum-decision-task",
  "template": "check-consensus-template",
  "when": "{{expressions.quorum_mode}}"
}
```

Use Case Implementation and Analysis

CI/CD Pipelines

Continuous Integration and Continuous Deployment (CI/CD) workflows necessitate precise synchronization across tasks including builds,

6.6. MULTI-STEP WORKFLOW SYNCHRONIZATION

tests, and deployment steps. Here, synchronized gates ensure that each step is predicated on the successful completion of its predecessors.

```
{
  "name": "build-stage",
  "template": "build-template",
  "dependencies": ["checkout-stage"]
}
```

Hierarchical Data Processing Workflows

Data processing pipelines benefit significantly from synchronized task execution, ensuring sequential operations such as data extraction, transformation, and loading abide by transformations' interdependencies.

Machine Learning Model Pipelines

Model training pipelines incorporate synchronization to sequentially unlock tasks post the completion of model validation. This guarantees that only finalized model versions advance toward deployment.

```
{
  "name": "deploy-model",
  "template": "deploy-template",
  "dependencies": ["validate-model"]
}
```

Enhancing Workflow Efficiency through Synchronization

Workflow synchronization extends beyond meeting dependencies; it optimizes system performance and resource use, reducing bottlenecks and preventing systemic delays.

Key Steps for Optimization:

- - **Parallel Resource Management**: Adopting asynchronous execution models where applicable to reduce wait times and enhance throughput.

- - **Dynamic Load Balancing**: Continuously monitoring and adjusting resource allocations to align with task workload variations.

- - **Adaptive Scheduling**: Refining schedules dynamically based on real-time data and task execution metrics, smoothing transitions between sequential tasks.

The judicious selection and implementation of synchronization strategies ensure workflows are well-tuned to address both immediate and evolving business, technical, and environmental needs. By orchestrating task execution with precision, workflows can maintain high throughput rates, safeguard data integrity, and adapt to variations in computational demand, fostering a resilient and responsive system architecture.

Chapter 7

Integrating Argo Workflows with CI/CD Pipelines

This chapter focuses on integrating Argo Workflows within Continuous Integration and Continuous Deployment (CI/CD) pipelines to streamline and automate software delivery processes. It discusses the role of Argo in enhancing CI/CD workflows, providing practical guidance on setting up a suitable environment and managing workflow automation for builds and tests. Readers will learn about implementing continuous deployment strategies with Argo to improve deployment efficiency and reliability. The chapter also covers integration techniques with popular CI/CD tools such as Jenkins, GitHub Actions, and GitLab CI, while managing environment configurations to support dynamic and environment-specific workflows.

7.1 Understanding CI/CD and Its Importance

In modern software engineering, Continuous Integration (CI) and Continuous Deployment (CD) are pivotal practices that transform how software development teams deliver value to stakeholders. CI/CD reduces manual intervention, minimizes errors, and accelerates the feedback loop between code development and production deployment. Initiating with Continuous Integration, we explore its processes, tools, and impact on development workflows, subsequently delving into Continuous Deployment's critical role in automation and the end-user experience.

Continuous Integration is fundamentally about integrating code changes from multiple contributors into a shared repository several times a day. Each integration is verified by an automated build, allowing teams to detect errors quickly and locate them more easily. The foremost advantage of CI is its ability to enhance collaboration among developers, encouraging early communication about potential integration conflicts.

```
# Example command to merge changes from a feature branch to master
git checkout master
git merge feature-branch
```

The concept of CI was popularized with the Agile Manifesto and Extreme Programming principles, emphasizing short cycles of code integration and testing to ensure software health. With CI, each developer's changes are automatically tested and verified, reducing the possibility of integration issues during later stages of the development process. CI enables features such as:

- Automated testing and validation of code as it's integrated into the central repository.

- Rapid feedback for developers, discouraging code conflicts and ensuring high-quality code.

- Immediate detection of system failures and bugs, permitting swift resolutions.

7.1. UNDERSTANDING CI/CD AND ITS IMPORTANCE

In practical terms, implementing CI involves setting up a CI server like Jenkins or Travis CI. This server watches the main repository for changes and triggers build scripts upon finding new commits.

```
pipeline {
    agent any
    stages {
        stage('Build') {
            steps {
                // Shell script to build application
                sh './build.sh'
            }
        }
        stage('Test') {
            steps {
                // Run unit tests
                sh './run_tests.sh'
            }
        }
    }
}
```

Continuous Deployment extends CI by automatically deploying every code change that passes all stages of the production pipeline to the end-users. This process diminishes the need for scheduled releases and traditional deployment waits. Emphasizing Minimal Viable Changes (MVCs), CD benefits organizations by lowering the risk associated with each release.

Several essential components constitute a CD system, including:

- Automated Testing: Beyond unit tests, CD involves integration tests, end-to-end tests, and performance benchmarks to ensure code readiness for deployment.

- Build Automation: Creating deployment artifacts, such as Docker containers or application packages, using scripts that assure consistency across environments.

- Environment Consistency: Infrastructure as Code (IaC) techniques are employed to replicate the production environment across development and testing stages.

- Deployment Automation: Automated scripts or tools such as Kubernetes or Terraform facilitate deploying code with minimal operations team involvement.

A typical deployment script might execute the following commands:

```
# Deploy new version to the development environment
kubectl apply -f deployment.yaml
kubectl rollout status deployment/myapp
```

The importance of CD is manifest in its capability to provide businesses with agility and flexibility in adapting to customer requirements and market changes. The ability to release software rapidly but reliably represents a strategic advantage.

Key benefits include:

- A continuous delivery pipeline shortens the time to market and allows swift reaction to feedback.
- Automation of deployment steps minimizes manual errors and increases repeatability.
- Continuous feedback loops with real users allow teams to iterate and innovate effectively.

Challenges of CI/CD implementation are non-negligible but offer opportunities for optimization. Typical challenges include maintaining comprehensive test suites, ensuring consistency across multiple environments, and managing an ever-growing codebase that must remain compatible with diverse production configurations.

Considerations for integrating a CI/CD pipeline effectively incorporate a mindset shift towards automation culture and integrating DevOps practices. Encouraging collaboration between developers and operations professionals lays the groundwork for a coalesced delivery team.

Moreover, adopting microservices architectures, as opposed to monolithic applications, enhances CI/CD by logically isolating services, allowing independent updates and scaled operations.

A potential microservices deployment might look like this:

```
apiVersion: apps/v1
kind: Deployment
metadata:
  name: microservice
spec:
  replicas: 3
  selector:
```

```
     matchLabels:
       app: mymicroservice
   template:
     metadata:
       labels:
         app: mymicroservice
     spec:
       containers:
       - name: app
         image: mymicroservice:latest
         ports:
         - containerPort: 80
```

In the context of CI/CD, version control systems like Git are indispensable, serving not only as repositories but also as the sources of truth for configuration and automation scripts. CI/CD inherently supports version control-driven development, echoing concepts like feature toggles and dark launches.

Lastly, security and compliance cannot be overlooked within CI/CD systems. Integrating security practices early in the development cycle is vital, ensuring the use of secure code, reliance on trusted dependencies, and adherence to regulatory frameworks.

Adopting DevSecOps, an evolution of DevOps, augments CI/CD pipelines by embedding security at every phase, from initial code writing to deployment. Tools and practices such as dependency management, code scanning, and audit logs become crucial:

```
# Example of a security scan command using a SAST tool
snyk test --docker my_image:latest
```

In summary, embracing CI/CD and recognizing its importance is crucial for teams aiming to enhance productivity, reliability, and delivery efficiency. Organizations that successfully implement CI/CD reap benefits in both technical prowess and market competitiveness.

7.2 Role of Argo Workflows in CI/CD

Argo Workflows is an open-source container-native workflow engine designed to orchestrate parallel jobs on Kubernetes. It is increasingly pivotal in Continuous Integration (CI) and Continuous Deployment (CD) processes for its ability to automate and simplify complex workflows. Argo Workflows provides a robust framework for defining and executing multi-step processes, enabling auto-scalable, fault-tolerant workflows leveraging Kubernetes' inherent advantages.

Argo Workflows operates by defining custom resource definitions (CRDs) within Kubernetes, enabling execution of complex, DAG-based (Directed Acyclic Graph) workflows. Each node in the DAG represents a discrete task specified in a YAML configuration file. This capability allows teams to build intricate pipelines to automate a variety of CI/CD stages, such as code compilation, automated testing, deployment, and validation.

The following snippet depicts a simple example of how a workflow consisting of multiple steps might be structured in a YAML file:

```
apiVersion: argoproj.io/v1alpha1
kind: Workflow
metadata:
  generateName: hello-world-
spec:
  entrypoint: hello-world
  templates:
  - name: hello-world
    container:
      image: alpine:3.7
      command: ["echo", "hello world"]
```

In this example, Argo defines a workflow that runs a container executing an Alpine Linux image, printing "hello world" to the console. This basic setup underpins more complex and interconnected sequences pivotal in CI/CD pipelines.

Integrating Argo Workflows into CI/CD pipelines opens new possibilities for automating and managing tasks with efficiency and scalability. One significant advantage of using Argo is its native Kubernetes integration, allowing several operational activities to be automated with fewer overhead costs.

- **Pipeline Automation:** Argo Workflows supports GitOps principles, whereby code changes trigger CI/CD pipelines depending directly on code repositories. Each workflow becomes executable upon events such as commit pushes, simplifying repeated and labor-intensive tasks. Automation strategies benefit from this by reducing human error and aligning closely with agile development practices.

7.2. ROLE OF ARGO WORKFLOWS IN CI/CD

```
apiVersion: argoproj.io/v1alpha1
kind: Workflow
metadata:
  generateName: github-triggered-
spec:
  entrypoint: build-and-test
  templates:
  - name: build-and-test
    steps:
    - - name: build
        template: build-job
    - - name: test
        template: test-job

  - name: build-job
    container:
      image: maven:3.6.3-jdk-8
      command: ["mvn", "clean", "install"]

  - name: test-job
    container:
      image: maven:3.6.3-jdk-8
      command: ["mvn", "test"]
```

- **Scalability and Efficiency:** Argo provides horizontal scaling by managing node resources efficiently. Within CI/CD, different stages can be parallelized, reducing the total time in processes like test execution, linting, and builds. With cloud-native design, resource utilization aligns tightly with demand, supporting peak loads without excessive provisioning costs.

- **Fault Tolerance and Error Handling:** Workflow execution in Argo is resilient against node failures or other interruptions. Workflows can restart or proceed from failure points, ensuring a consistent and reliable CI/CD process even under adverse conditions. Additional features like retries, timeout scripts, and conditional task execution enhance workflow robustness.

```
apiVersion: argoproj.io/v1alpha1
kind: Workflow
metadata:
  generateName: error-handling-example-
spec:
  entrypoint: main
  templates:
  - name: main
    steps:
    - - name: failing-job
        template: failing-step
```

```
    retryStrategy:
        limit: 3
- name: failing-step
  container:
    image: ubuntu:18.04
    command: ["/bin/sh", "-c"]
    args: ["exit 1"]
```

In this example, a failed job attempts a retry up to three times before the workflow exits, providing mechanisms to handle transitory failures gracefully.

To maximize the benefits of Argo Workflows within CI/CD, specific strategies and configurations elevate performance and reliability:

- **Resource Management:** Assign resource requests and limits per task within the workflow to ensure pipeline stages are performant and cost-effective.

- **Custom Templates and Reusability:** Make use of Argo's templating feature to define reusable components applicable across multiple workflows, thus improving consistency and maintenance.

- **Pipeline A/B Testing and Feature Flags:** Implement dynamic deployment strategies by utilizing configuration files and feature flags to switch functionalities on or off as part of deployment scenarios, all orchestrated by Argo.

As workflows become constituent elements of a broader DevOps strategy, their ability to interlink and communicate with other tools and platforms stands out. Argo seamlessly interacts with tools like Tekton, Jenkins, and Helm, enhancing interoperability and governance within large organizations. Argo's plugin architecture allows easy expansion, integrating additional utilities like notifications and monitoring capabilities.

Security concerns and CI/CD pipelines are intrinsic, and Argo Workflows provides several built-in features that bolster security efforts:

- **Role-Based Access Control (RBAC):** Utilize Kubernetes RBAC to define fine-grained permission levels, ensuring that only authorized users can instantiate or manage workflows.

- **Secrets Management:** Leverage Kubernetes Secrets to store sensitive information, protecting credentials or API keys used in various workflow steps.
- **Security Scanning:** Incorporate static and dynamic security scans as workflow steps to validate builds against known vulnerabilities.

```
apiVersion: argoproj.io/v1alpha1
kind: Workflow
metadata:
  generateName: security-scan-
spec:
  entrypoint: security-tests
  templates:
  - name: security-tests
    container:
      image: snyk/snyk
      command: ["snyk", "test", "--all-projects"]
```

The landscape of CI/CD continues to evolve rapidly, and tools like Argo Workflows are positioned at the forefront, driving innovations through flexibility and extensibility. With Kubernetes as the standard for container orchestration, Argo Workflows can harness ecosystem improvements effectively, benefiting from ongoing advancements in cloud-native computing.

Prospective developments might include deeper integration with AI/ML for predictive analysis or intelligent automation, auto-scaling algorithms driven by real-time usage patterns, and enhanced security features to curtail emerging threats.

Adoption of Argo Workflows within CI/CD aligns seamlessly with modern agile and DevOps methodologies, providing dependability and adaptability as organizational requirements evolve. Ultimately, through leveraging Argo Workflows, teams gain enormous leverage to achieve continuous improvement in deploying applications swiftly, repeatedly, and securely.

7.3 Setting Up a CI/CD Environment

Creating an effective Continuous Integration and Continuous Deployment (CI/CD) environment within Kubernetes requires meticulous planning and execution. This process involves infrastructure preparation, tool integration, environment configuration, and operational scalability to support dynamic software delivery pipelines. The aim is to create an automated, reliable, and scalable system for deploying applications from development to production stages.

- **Infrastructure Preparation:**

Setting up a CI/CD environment begins with preparing the essential infrastructure. Kubernetes serves as a robust platform for orchestrating containerized applications, offering scalability and flexibility critical for CI/CD workflows. Before integrating CI/CD tools like Jenkins, GitLab CI, or Argo Workflows, it is imperative to configure a Kubernetes cluster appropriately.

- **Kubernetes Cluster Setup:** On-premises or cloud-based Kubernetes providers such as AWS EKS, Google GKE, or Azure AKS can be used to set up a cluster. Below is an example of configuring a basic Kubernetes cluster using the kubectl command-line tool.

```
# Create a Kubernetes cluster using minikube for local development
minikube start --cpus=4 --memory=8192
```

This command creates a local Kubernetes cluster with specified CPU and memory resources, useful for development and testing before production deployment.

- **Namespace and Resource Configuration:** Organizing resources within namespaces provides isolation and management of different application environments. Namespaces enable effective resource allocation and limit setting for CPU and memory usage per deployment.

```
# Create a namespace for CI/CD workflows
kubectl create namespace cicd
```

- **Tool Integration:**

7.3. SETTING UP A CI/CD ENVIRONMENT

Integrating the right tools is pivotal for achieving an efficient CI/CD pipeline. A combination of CI servers, container registries, and CD tools orchestrates an end-to-end automated pipeline.

- **Choosing a CI Tool:** Jenkins is one of the widely used CI platforms, offering extensibility through its plugins. GitLab CI and GitHub Actions are other popular choices, integrated seamlessly with repositories for triggering workflows.

- **Jenkins Deployment on Kubernetes:** Deploying Jenkins within the Kubernetes cluster allows the CI server to scale with the cluster. The configuration can be done using Helm, a package manager for Kubernetes.

```
# Add Jenkins Helm repository and install Jenkins
helm repo add jenkinsci https://charts.jenkins.io
helm repo update
helm install jenkins jenkinsci/jenkins --namespace cicd
```

Alternatively, to set up Jenkins using a YAML file, consider the following deployment specification:

```yaml
apiVersion: apps/v1
kind: Deployment
metadata:
  name: jenkins
  namespace: cicd
spec:
  replicas: 1
  selector:
    matchLabels:
      app: jenkins
  template:
    metadata:
      labels:
        app: jenkins
    spec:
      containers:
      - name: jenkins
        image: jenkins/jenkins:lts
        ports:
        - containerPort: 8080
```

- **Container Registry Integration:** Container registries like Docker Hub, Amazon ECR, or Google Container Registry are critical for storing and managing Docker images. They act as central repositories for versioned Docker images, facilitating quick pull and push operations during CI/CD processes.

```
# Push Docker image to Docker Hub
docker login -u username -p password
docker tag local-image:tagname username/repository:tagname
docker push username/repository:tagname
```

- **Environment Configuration:**

A crucial step in setting up a CI/CD environment is tailoring the configuration to specific project needs. This includes understanding deployment strategies, managing secrets, setting environment variables, and organizing configuration files.

- **Deployment Strategies:** Techniques such as Blue-Green and Canary deployments are utilized to minimize downtime and reduce risk during updates. These strategies allow incremental updates and rollback capabilities if necessary.

- **Using ConfigMaps and Secrets in Kubernetes:** Kubernetes ConfigMaps and Secrets help manage environment-specific configurations and sensitive data, ensuring that such values are injected into the pods at runtime without hardcoding them into the application.

```
apiVersion: v1
kind: ConfigMap
metadata:
  name: app-config
  namespace: cicd
data:
  APP_ENV: production
  LOG_LEVEL: info
```

```
apiVersion: v1
kind: Secret
metadata:
  name: db-secret
  namespace: cicd
type: Opaque
data:
  username: dXNlcm5hbWU= # Base64 encoded value
  password: cGFzc3dvcmQ= # Base64 encoded value
```

7.3. SETTING UP A CI/CD ENVIRONMENT

- **Injecting ConfigMaps and Secrets into Pods:**

```
apiVersion: apps/v1
kind: Deployment
metadata:
  name: app-deployment
  namespace: cicd
spec:
  template:
    spec:
      containers:
      - name: myapp
        image: myapp:latest
        envFrom:
        - configMapRef:
            name: app-config
        - secretRef:
            name: db-secret
```

- **Operational Scalability and Monitoring:**

Ensuring operational scalability and maintaining system health are paramount considerations in CI/CD environments. This involves the use of autoscalers and monitoring tools to adapt to load changes.

- **Horizontal Pod Autoscaler (HPA):** Kubernetes' Horizontal Pod Autoscaler automatically adjusts the number of pod replicas based on CPU utilization or custom metrics, allowing the environment to maintain performance under varying load conditions.

```
apiVersion: autoscaling/v2beta2
kind: HorizontalPodAutoscaler
metadata:
  name: app-hpa
  namespace: cicd
spec:
  scaleTargetRef:
    apiVersion: apps/v1
    kind: Deployment
    name: app-deployment
  minReplicas: 1
  maxReplicas: 10
  metrics:
  - type: Resource
    resource:
      name: cpu
      target:
        type: Utilization
        averageUtilization: 50
```

- **Monitoring and Logging:** Tools such as Prometheus, Grafana, and the ELK Stack (ElasticSearch, Logstash, Kibana) provide comprehensive insights by collecting and visualizing logs, metrics, and other system data. Effective monitoring helps in proactively resolving potential issues, optimizing resources, and improving the CI/CD process.

- **Setting Up Prometheus with Kubernetes:**

```
# Deploy Prometheus using Helm
helm repo add prometheus-community https://prometheus-community.github.io/helm-charts
helm repo update
helm install prometheus prometheus-community/kube-prometheus-stack --namespace monitoring
```

- **Continuous Improvement in CI/CD Setup:**

An effective CI/CD environment is not static. It involves continuous monitoring and improvement to retain its relevance and effectiveness in the software development lifecycle. Gathering feedback and incorporating it into pipelines help streamline processes, reduce bottlenecks, and automate repetitive tasks more effectively.

Adopting community best practices, contributing to open-source plugins, and staying informed about emerging trends ensures that the setup remains robust and scalable. Continuous refinement in tooling, processes, and integrations is a collective effort towards achieving an optimal CI/CD environment that adapts to evolving technological demands.

7.4 Automating Builds and Tests with Argo

Automation within Continuous Integration and Continuous Deployment (CI/CD) pipelines represents a major paradigm shift in the way software is developed and delivered. Argo Workflows, a workflow engine for Kubernetes, empowers teams by automating complex build

7.4. AUTOMATING BUILDS AND TESTS WITH ARGO

and test sequences. This alleviates manual intervention, ensures consistency across environment configurations, speeds up feedback cycles, and underpins a robust CI/CD infrastructure.

Introduction to Argo Workflows for Automation

Argo Workflows facilitates the automation of tasks by defining workflows with a Directed Acyclic Graph (DAG). Each node within a DAG is a distinct operation, allowing fine-grained control over dependencies and task execution. This model excels in expressing a range of CI/CD duties, from simple test executions to intricate build processes spread across varied environments.

Automation in Argo begins with defining a YAML configuration file, which specifies the sequence of tasks and the conditions under which they are run. These configurations leverage the containerization offered by Kubernetes, ensuring that tasks are isolated, reproducible, and efficient.

Automating the Build Process

Overview of Build Automation: Build automation involves compiling source code, resolving dependencies, and producing build artifacts such as binaries, executables, or Docker images. Argo automates these steps, ensuring that builds are consistent and deterministic across all development scenarios.

Example of a Simple Automated Build Workflow:

```
apiVersion: argoproj.io/v1alpha1
kind: Workflow
metadata:
  generateName: automated-build-
spec:
  entrypoint: build-project
  templates:
  - name: build-project
    container:
      image: maven:3.6.3-jdk-8
      command: ["/bin/sh", "-c"]
      args:
        - mvn install && echo "Build successful"
```

Advanced Build Pipelines: Complex applications with multiple modules and dependencies can configure multi-stage pipelines using Argo. This method enables individual builds and integrations per module within a shared environment while maintaining clarity and separation of concerns.

```
apiVersion: argoproj.io/v1alpha1
kind: Workflow
metadata:
  generateName: multi-stage-build-
spec:
  entrypoint: build-stages
  templates:
  - name: build-stages
    steps:
    - - name: compile-phase
        template: compile
    - - name: integration-test
        template: test
    - - name: package-binary
        template: package

  - name: compile
    container:
      image: maven:3.6.3-jdk-8
      command: ["mvn", "compile"]

  - name: test
    container:
      image: maven:3.6.3-jdk-8
      command: ["mvn", "verify"]

  - name: package
    container:
      image: maven:3.6.3-jdk-8
      command: ["mvn", "package"]
```

Automating Testing Processes

Testing automation enhances code quality and stability by facilitating continuous testing cycles as code evolves. Argo Workflows streamline testing processes across various layers, including unit, integration, and end-to-end tests.

Unit Testing with Argo: At the unit test level, Argo can execute isolated test functions, ensuring they produce expected outputs. Frequently triggered unit tests provide immediate insights into the codebase integrity after each commit.

7.4. AUTOMATING BUILDS AND TESTS WITH ARGO

```
apiVersion: argoproj.io/v1alpha1
kind: Workflow
metadata:
  generateName: unit-test-
spec:
  entrypoint: run-unit-tests
  templates:
  - name: run-unit-tests
    container:
      image: node:14
      command: ["/bin/sh", "-c"]
      args:
        - npm install && npm test
```

Integration Testing with Argo: Integration tests validate interactions between software modules and dependencies. Argo workflows orchestrate environment setup, data seeding, and complex test scenarios required for accurate integration assessments.

```
apiVersion: argoproj.io/v1alpha1
kind: Workflow
metadata:
  generateName: integration-test-
spec:
  entrypoint: run-integration-tests
  templates:
  - name: run-integration-tests
    container:
      image: python:3.8
      command: ["/bin/sh", "-c"]
      args:
        - pytest tests/integration
```

End-to-End Testing Automation: End-to-end tests mimic user flows across the entire application stack to ensure functionalities behave as intended. By running these tests within the same Kubernetes environment, deployment is faster and more reliable, closely mirroring production setups.

```
apiVersion: argoproj.io/v1alpha1
kind: Workflow
metadata:
  generateName: e2e-test-
spec:
  entrypoint: run-e2e-tests
  templates:
  - name: run-e2e-tests
    container:
      image: cypress/included:6.4.0
      command: ["cypress", "run"]
```

Integration of Builds and Tests in a Unified Workflow

Argo's ability to chain build and test tasks in comprehensive workflows is particularly beneficial. This ensures that each build stage is directly linked to appropriate testing procedures, promoting consistency and error detection across development cycles.

Unified Build and Test Workflow:

```
apiVersion: argoproj.io/v1alpha1
kind: Workflow
metadata:
  generateName: unified-pipeline-
spec:
  entrypoint: pipeline
  templates:
  - name: pipeline
    steps:
    - - name: build
        template: build
    - - name: unit-test
        template: unit-test
    - - name: integration-test
        template: integration-test

  - name: build
    container:
      image: gradle:6.8
      command: ["gradle", "build"]

  - name: unit-test
    container:
      image: gradle:6.8
      command: ["gradle", "test"]

  - name: integration-test
    container:
      image: gradle:6.8
      command: ["gradle", "integrationTest"]
```

Continuous Feedback and Optimization: By receiving automatic feedback through automated processes, developers can identify and correct issues promptly. This streamlines workflows, shortens feedback loops, and leads to more efficient development cycles.

Optimizing Resource Utilization and Execution Time with Argo

Workflow Parallelism Optimization: Argo exploits Kubernetes' scaling capabilities, allowing concurrent execution of non-dependent tasks. This drastically reduces the total execution time of generated workflows, resulting in faster end-to-end processing times.

```
apiVersion: argoproj.io/v1alpha1
kind: Workflow
metadata:
  generateName: parallel-tasks-
spec:
  entrypoint: run-tasks
  templates:
  - name: run-tasks
    steps:
    - - name: task1
        template: task-container
      - name: task2
        template: task-container

  - name: task-container
    container:
      image: ubuntu
      command: ["/bin/sh", "-c"]
      args: ["echo running task"]
```

Cost Efficiency Considerations: Automated workflows greatly reduce the need for manual oversight, cutting down labor costs. In environments where resources are billed by usage, Argo's dynamic resource allocation optimizes expenditure by using resources only when necessary.

Archiving and Cache Strategies: Use of cache strategies to store outputs of build and test processes can further expedite the pipeline, leveraging artifacts from previous executions and minimizing redundant computation.

Security and Reliability in Automated Pipelines

Ensuring security within automated CI/CD processes is crucial:

- **Secure Image Repositories:** Implement authenticated access to Docker image repositories, ensuring that build and test workflows use validated and signed container images.

- **Data Sensitivity and Secret Management:** Employ Kubernetes Secrets to handle sensitive data securely, such as credentials and configuration tokens used during execution.

- **Audit Trails and Compliance:** Maintain detailed logs of automated processes, facilitating auditing and compliance adherence. Argo's integration with logging tools ensures every step is traceable and secure.

```
apiVersion: argoproj.io/v1alpha1
kind: Workflow
metadata:
  generateName: secure-pipeline-
spec:
  entrypoint: secure-build
  templates:
  - name: secure-build
    container:
      image: secure/custom-image:latest
      env:
      - name: DB_PASSWORD
        valueFrom:
          secretKeyRef:
            name: db-secret
            key: password
```

Automating builds and tests using Argo represents a strategic advantage in modern CI/CD environments. This automation leads to reproducible and scalable systems, optimized development workloads, and enhanced delivery speed, capitalizing fully on the capabilities of Kubernetes and containerization technology.

7.5 Continuous Deployment with Argo

Continuous Deployment (CD) practices enable software changes to be automatically deployed to production environments with minimal human intervention. Argo, with its rich orchestration capabilities, is instrumental in implementing robust CD systems that facilitate fast, reliable, and repeatable software delivery. Leveraging Argo within Kubernetes environments optimizes the deployment lifecycle by ensuring consistency, resilience, and agility, pivotal attributes for modern DevOps operations.

Understanding Continuous Deployment in Kubernetes

7.5. CONTINUOUS DEPLOYMENT WITH ARGO

Continuous Deployment automates the release of software changes directly into production after passing the necessary stages in a CI/CD pipeline. The process includes building, testing, containerizing, and eventually deploying applications. Argo integrates with Kubernetes, allowing development teams to streamline deployment strategies using container-based workflows to maintain alignment with the ever-evolving state of application services.

Kubernetes Deployment: In Kubernetes, a deployment describes a desired state of the applications or services being managed. Argo Workflows extends these capabilities by orchestrating deployment steps as defined transitions within workflows.

```
apiVersion: apps/v1
kind: Deployment
metadata:
  name: myapplication
  namespace: production
spec:
  replicas: 3
  selector:
    matchLabels:
      app: myapplication
  template:
    metadata:
      labels:
        app: myapplication
    spec:
      containers:
        - name: application
          image: myapplication:latest
          ports:
            - containerPort: 80
```

Implementing CD with Argo Workflows

Automated Deployment Pipelines: With Argo, deployment processes are expressed in YAML and executed as workflows. These pipelines automate all necessary tasks, from pulling container images, applying configurations, scaling resources, to health-check validations.

Sample Continuous Deployment Workflow:

```
apiVersion: argoproj.io/v1alpha1
kind: Workflow
metadata:
  generateName: continuous-deployment-
spec:
  entrypoint: deploy
```

```
templates:
- name: deploy
  steps:
  - - name: deploy-application
      template: kubectl-apply
  - - name: validate-deployment
      template: probe-endpoint

- name: kubectl-apply
  container:
    image: bitnami/kubectl
    command: ["/bin/sh", "-c"]
    args: ["kubectl apply -f deployment.yaml"]

- name: probe-endpoint
  container:
    image: curlimages/curl
    command: ["curl", "-f", "http://myapplication-service"]
```

The workflow above exemplifies a succinct continuous deployment process involving Kubernetes deployment updates and service validation through HTTP probing.

Advanced Deployment Strategies with Argo

Blue-Green Deployments: This strategy entails maintaining two identical production environments, enabling traffic switching between the 'blue' (current production) and 'green' (the new version) deployments. Argo orchestrates these transitions seamlessly by managing environment shifts as workflow tasks.

```
apiVersion: argoproj.io/v1alpha1
kind: Workflow
metadata:
  generateName: blue-green-deployment-
spec:
  entrypoint: blue-green
  templates:
  - name: blue-green
    steps:
    - - name: deploy-green
        template: kubectl-apply-green
    - - name: switch-traffic
        template: kubectl-patch-service

  - name: kubectl-apply-green
    container:
      image: bitnami/kubectl
      command: ["/bin/sh", "-c"]
      args: ["kubectl apply -f deployment-green.yaml"]

  - name: kubectl-patch-service
    container:
      image: bitnami/kubectl
```

7.5. CONTINUOUS DEPLOYMENT WITH ARGO

```
command: ["/bin/sh", "-c"]
args: ["kubectl patch svc myapplication -p '{\"spec\":{\"selector\":{\"version
    \":\"green\"}}}'"]
```

Canary Deployments: Canary deployments introduce new application versions to a subset of users before full scale rollouts, allowing real-world validation while mitigating risk. Argo orchestrates canary releases using progressive traffic splitting managed through service meshes like Istio for HTTP traffic handling.

```
apiVersion: argoproj.io/v1alpha1
kind: Workflow
metadata:
  generateName: canary-deployment-
spec:
  entrypoint: canary
  templates:
  - name: canary
    steps:
    - - name: deploy-canary
        template: kubectl-apply-canary
    - - name: update-traffic
        template: update-traffic-split

  - name: kubectl-apply-canary
    container:
      image: bitnami/kubectl
      command: ["/bin/sh", "-c"]
      args: ["kubectl apply -f deployment-canary.yaml"]

  - name: update-traffic-split
    container:
      image: curlimages/curl
      command: ["/bin/sh", "-c"]
      args: ["istioctl install -f traffic-split.yaml"]
```

Rolling Updates: Argo supports rolling updates, which incrementally replace instances running the old application version with the new one, ensuring zero downtime. Rolling deployments maintain application availability but should be carefully monitored against stability regressions.

Monitoring and Scaling Continuous Deployments

Comprehensive Monitoring: Integrating monitoring solutions like Prometheus and Grafana enables visualization and alerting for application performance metrics and health indicators during deployments. This facilitates swift action on regressions detected post-deployment.

Setup for Monitoring:

```
# Deploy Prometheus and Grafana using Helm
helm repo add prometheus-community https://prometheus-community.github.io/helm-
    charts
helm repo update
helm install prometheus prometheus-community/kube-prometheus-stack --namespace
    monitoring
```

Autoscaling Deployments: Kubernetes Horizontal Pod Autoscaler (HPA) automates dynamic scaling of pods based on observed CPU utilization or custom metrics. Argo manages HPA configurations within deployment workflows to adapt to varying loads efficiently.

```
apiVersion: autoscaling/v2beta2
kind: HorizontalPodAutoscaler
metadata:
  name: application-hpa
  namespace: production
spec:
  scaleTargetRef:
    apiVersion: apps/v1
    kind: Deployment
    name: myapplication
  minReplicas: 3
  maxReplicas: 10
  metrics:
  - type: Resource
    resource:
      name: cpu
      target:
        type: Utilization
        averageUtilization: 70
```

Error Handling and Rollbacks: Argo Workflows handle deployment errors gracefully by incorporating conditional branches, retries, and rollbacks, all orchestrated through DAG execution. These features ensure resilience and maintain uptime during deployment failures.

```
apiVersion: argoproj.io/v1alpha1
kind: Workflow
metadata:
  generateName: resilient-deployment-
spec:
  entrypoint: safe-deploy
  templates:
  - name: safe-deploy
    steps:
    - - name: deploy-new
        template: deploy-step
      - name: notify-failure
        template: failure-notification
        when: "{{status}} != Succeeded"
```

```yaml
   - name: rollback
     template: rollback-step
     when: "{{status}} != Succeeded"
- name: deploy-step
  container:
    image: bitnami/kubectl
    command: ["/bin/sh", "-c"]
    args: ["kubectl apply -f new-deployment.yaml"]
- name: failure-notification
  container:
    image: alpine
    command: ["echo", "Deployment failed, initiating rollback"]
- name: rollback-step
  container:
    image: bitnami/kubectl
    command: ["/bin/sh", "-c"]
    args: ["kubectl apply -f rollback-deployment.yaml"]
```

Security Considerations in Continuous Deployment

Continuous Deployment necessitates rigorous security measures:

- **Secure Pipeline:** Implement tight access controls using Kubernetes RBAC policies and ensure all resources are accessed by authorized personnel and systems only.

- **Image Security:** Automate container image scanning using tools like Aqua Security or Anchore to detect vulnerabilities or compliance violations before deploying to production.

- **Encryption and Secrets Management:** Use encrypted secrets in Kubernetes via Secrets Management solutions, such as HashiCorp Vault or AWS Secrets Manager, ensuring sensitive information is protected.

Example Command for Image Scanning:

```
# Using Amazon's ECR service for image scanning
aws ecr start-image-scan --repository-name myrepository --image-id imageTag=mytag
```

Continuous Deployment with Argo facilitates rapid, reliable software releases by integrating sophisticated deployment strategies and automations within Kubernetes. The detailed workflows and methodologies herein underscore Argo's capacity to drive innovation, refine delivery processes, and maintain an unwavering focus on operational excellence.

7.6 Integrating Argo with Popular CI/CD Tools

The interoperability of different CI/CD tools enhances software development agility, offering improved workflow automation and efficiency. Argo Workflows, known for its powerful orchestration capabilities within Kubernetes environments, can be effectively integrated with various popular CI/CD tools like Jenkins, GitHub Actions, and GitLab CI. Through such integrations, organizations can leverage robust, container-native processing for complex pipelines, optimizing resource use and ensuring consistent delivery.

Argo Workflows and Jenkins Integration

Jenkins, a mainstay in the CI/CD ecosystem, possesses an inherently flexible architecture that can be augmented with a multitude of plugins, including Argo Workflows. The integration of Argo Workflows into Jenkins provides the ability to run Kubernetes-native workflows alongside traditional pipelines, thereby improving the scalability and flexibility of the existing CI/CD processes.

Configuring Jenkins with Argo:

Integrating with Jenkins typically involves using plugins or creating steps in Jenkinsfiles that interface with Argo via the command line. This connection allows Jenkins to trigger Argo workflows as part of broader CI/CD operations.

```
pipeline {
    agent any
    stages {
        stage('Build') {
            steps {
                sh 'mvn clean install'
            }
        }
        stage('Deploy') {
            steps {
                sh '''
                    argo submit --watch --serviceaccount jenkins-sa workflow.yaml
                '''
```

7.6. INTEGRATING ARGO WITH POPULAR CI/CD TOOLS

```
          }
        }
      }
    }
}
```

In this setup, Jenkins executes a 'mvn' build and subsequently triggers Argo to process the deployment defined in 'workflow.yaml'. The integration ensures smooth transition between pre-existing Jenkins jobs and cloud-native Argo workflows, capitalizing on Kubernetes features.

Using Argo Workflows with GitHub Actions

GitHub Actions provide automation directly within GitHub, enabling event-driven execution of workflows. Integrating Argo with GitHub Actions allows developers to manage Kubernetes workflows in concert with repository events, improving deployment precision and reducing feedback cycles.

GitHub Actions and Argo Integration:

Configuring GitHub Actions with Argo involves creating workflows that use predefined actions to communicate with Argo's API server, enabling the deployment of applications as part of the CI/CD pipeline.

```
name: CI/CD Pipeline

on:
  push:
    branches: [ main ]

jobs:
  deploy:
    runs-on: ubuntu-latest
    steps:
    - uses: actions/checkout@v2
    - name: Set up Kubernetes
      uses: azure/setup-kubectl@v1
    - name: Authenticate to Argo
      uses: stevehipwell/action-argo-credential@v1
    - name: Submit Argo Workflow
      run: |
        argo submit --watch workflow.yaml
      env:
        KUBECONFIG: ${{ secrets.KUBECONFIG }}
```

The above example listens for changes in the 'main' branch, uses actions to configure Kubernetes, authenticate with necessary services, and submits an Argo workflow. This seamless integration facilitates efficient pipeline automation directly influenced by code changes.

Argo Workflows and GitLab CI Integration

GitLab CI, known for its powerful capabilities and built-in Git version control, can integrate efficiently with Argo Workflows. GitLab runners execute jobs defined in '.gitlab-ci.yml', where tasks like building, testing, and deploying are managed.

Configuring Argo with GitLab CI:

GitLab CI runner configurations can cater for Argo CLI invocations, allowing GitLab-managed code changes to trigger corresponding workflows in Kubernetes environments managed by Argo.

```
stages:
  - build
  - deploy

build:
  stage: build
  script:
    - mvn clean package

deploy:
  stage: deploy
  script:
    - argo submit --watch workflow.yaml
    - kubectl apply -f kubernetes/deployment.yaml
  environment:
    name: production
```

This configuration builds Java packages using Maven, submits Argo workflows, and applies Kubernetes resources as required, efficiently bridging GitLab CI capabilities with Argo's orchestration strengths.

Benefits of Integrating Argo with Popular CI/CD Tools

The integration of Argo Workflows with major CI/CD tools like Jenkins, GitHub Actions, and GitLab CI brings about several benefits:

- **Enhanced Automation Capabilities**: The cloud-native features of Argo Workflows complement traditional CI/CD tools, increasing automation efficiencies and reducing manual interventions.

- **Resource Optimization**: Kubernetes-native workflow execution inherently utilizes orchestration and containerization strengths, such as autoscaling and fault tolerance, thus improving resource usage.

7.6. INTEGRATING ARGO WITH POPULAR CI/CD TOOLS

- **Improved Scalability and Flexibility**: Combining Argo with established CI/CD frameworks allows for the execution of highly scalable workflows that dynamically adjust to changing demands and workloads.

- **Broadened Toolchain Capabilities**: Integrating these tools extends the overall toolchain features, providing developers with a unified yet powerful system for end-to-end software deployment.

Example Integration Workflow with Comprehensive Coverage:

```
apiVersion: argoproj.io/v1alpha1
kind: Workflow
metadata:
  generateName: ci-cd-integration-
spec:
  entrypoint: full-pipeline
  templates:
  - name: full-pipeline
    steps:
    - - name: checkout-code
        template: git-checkout
    - - name: run-tests
        template: test-runner
    - - name: build-image
        template: docker-build
    - - name: deploy-app
        template: deploy-k8s

  - name: git-checkout
    container:
      image: alpine/git
      command: ["/bin/sh", "-c"]
      args: ["git clone $GIT_REPO && cd repo-path"]

  - name: test-runner
    container:
      image: maven:3.6.3-jdk-8
      command: ["mvn", "test"]

  - name: docker-build
    container:
      image: docker
      command: ["docker", "build", "-t", "myapp:latest", "."]

  - name: deploy-k8s
    container:
      image: bitnami/kubectl
      command: ["/bin/sh", "-c"]
      args: ["kubectl apply -f kubernetes/deployment.yaml"]
```

Integrating various CI/CD tools with Argo Workflows ensures continuity, agility, and efficiency across software development and deployment pipelines. Such an integrated ecosystem supports innovative practices and sustained improvement, embodying modern DevOps principles.

7.7 Managing Environment Configurations

In modern software development, managing environment configurations is crucial for automating CI/CD pipelines and ensuring that applications are developed, tested, and deployed consistently across different environments. Argo Workflows, when paired with Kubernetes, offers powerful capabilities for managing these configurations effectively. This section discusses various strategies and practices, including versioning, templating, configuration management tools, and secrets handling techniques essential to managing environments efficiently.

Importance of Environment Configurations

Environment configurations encompass the setup details and parameters that a software application requires to run correctly in various stages of its lifecycle—development, testing, staging, and production. Effective handling of these configurations reduces errors caused by environment discrepancies, simplifies the deployment process, and improves operational efficiency.

- **Consistency**: Ensuring identical configurations across all environments prevents bugs related to discrepancies in running conditions.

- **Portability**: Configurations that work for one environment can be swiftly adapted to others without manual intervention.

- **Security**: Proper secrets management safeguards sensitive data like API keys and database passwords.

Configuration Management Strategies

7.7. MANAGING ENVIRONMENT CONFIGURATIONS

Strategies to handle configurations in CI/CD pipelines include hard-coded values, environment variables, and Configuration Management Tools (CMT). Kubernetes natively simplifies management with ConfigMaps and Secrets, while Argo enhances these capabilities through workflows.

Using ConfigMaps in Kubernetes:

ConfigMaps are used for storing non-sensitive configuration data in key-value pairs that Kubernetes applications can consume.

```
apiVersion: v1
kind: ConfigMap
metadata:
  name: app-config
  namespace: dev
data:
  database_url: "jdbc:mysql://db.dev.example:3306/mydb"
  redis_host: "redis.dev.example"
```

Applications access these configurations by referencing the ConfigMap in their deployment specifications, injecting necessary configurations at runtime.

```
apiVersion: apps/v1
kind: Deployment
metadata:
  name: demo-application
  namespace: dev
spec:
  template:
    spec:
      containers:
      - name: app-container
        image: demo-app:latest
        envFrom:
        - configMapRef:
            name: app-config
```

Secret Management in Kubernetes:

Secrets in Kubernetes store sensitive data. These should be base64-encoded and can be used in the same way as ConfigMaps, ensuring secure handling of credentials.

```
apiVersion: v1
kind: Secret
metadata:
  name: db-credentials
  namespace: dev
type: Opaque
```

```
data:
  username: bXlfdXNlcm5hbWU=
  password: bXlfcGFzc3dvcmQ=
```

Injecting Secrets Into Pods:

```
apiVersion: apps/v1
kind: Deployment
metadata:
  name: database-connection
  namespace: dev
spec:
  template:
    spec:
      containers:
      - name: db-connector
        image: db-connector:latest
        env:
        - name: DB_USERNAME
          valueFrom:
            secretKeyRef:
              name: db-credentials
              key: username
        - name: DB_PASSWORD
          valueFrom:
            secretKeyRef:
              name: db-credentials
              key: password
```

Managing Environment Variables across CI/CD Pipelines

Environment variables are essential for parameterizing application behavior without changing code. In CI/CD pipelines, these are set based on the deployment stage, enabling conditional logic.

Handling Dynamic Configurations with Argo:

Argo Workflows can dynamically manage configurations by passing environment variables to tasks. This allows condition-based execution paths and environment-specific setups.

```
apiVersion: argoproj.io/v1alpha1
kind: Workflow
metadata:
  generateName: dynamic-config-
spec:
  entrypoint: config-setup
  templates:
  - name: config-setup
    container:
      image: python:3.8
      env:
      - name: ENV
        value: "{{workflow.parameters.env}}"
```

7.7. MANAGING ENVIRONMENT CONFIGURATIONS

```
      - name: DB_URI
        value: "{{workflow.parameters.db_uri}}"
        command: ["/bin/sh", "-c"]
        args: ["python config_tester.py"]
  arguments:
    parameters:
      - name: env
        value: dev
      - name: db_uri
        value: "jdbc:postgresql://db.dev.example/mydb"
```

Using Templating for Configuration Management

Templating enhances configuration management by abstracting static values into parameters, making templates reusable across different environments. Tools such as Helm and Kustomize in Kubernetes offer sophisticated templating solutions.

Helm for Packaging and Deploying:

Helm uses templates to create deployment charts, which can be configured with custom variables. This facilitates environment-specific installations with minimal effort.

```
apiVersion: v2
name: myapp
description: A Helm chart for Kubernetes
type: application
version: 0.1.0

values:
  image:
    repository: demo/app
    tag: "{{ .Values.appVersion }}"
  config:
    database_url: "{{ .Values.databaseURL }}"
    environment: "{{ .Values.environment }}"
```

Using Kustomize for Dynamic Customizations:

Kustomize allows defining custom overlays for different environments by editing base configurations, offering a simplified way to manage complex configuration hierarchies.

```
apiVersion: apps/v1
kind: Deployment
metadata:
  name: myapp
spec:
  template:
    spec:
      containers:
```

```yaml
    - name: app-container
      image: myapp
      env:
      - name: DATABASE_URI
        value: "jdbc:postgresql://base.db.example:5432/base"
```

```yaml
apiVersion: kustomize.config.k8s.io/v1beta1
kind: Kustomization
resources:
  - ../base
patchesStrategicMerge:
  - patch.yaml
```

```yaml
apiVersion: apps/v1
kind: Deployment
metadata:
  name: myapp
spec:
  template:
    spec:
      containers:
      - name: app-container
        env:
        - name: DATABASE_URI
          value: "jdbc:postgresql://prod.db.example:5432/prod"
```

Versioning and Tracing Configurations

Configuration drift between environments can lead to discrepancies. Versioning configurations helps trace changes and ensures consistency. Integrating version control systems like Git helps manage, audit, and rollback configurations as required.

Version Control Strategy:

Using Git repositories for managing Kubernetes manifests or Helm charts to track changes ensures traceability and provides backup in case of inadvertent modifications.

```
# Initialize git repository for kubernetes manifests
git init
git add deployment.yaml service.yaml configmap.yaml
git commit -m "Initial commit with Kubernetes config"
# Pushing to remote repository
git push origin main
```

Security Considerations in Environment Management

The security of environment configurations is vital:

- **Access Control**: Utilize Kubernetes RBAC to restrict access to sensitive configurations only to necessary users.

- **Encryption**: Use tools like SealedSecrets to encrypt Kubernetes secrets, ensuring data at rest remains secure.
- **Audit Trails**: Implement logging and monitoring solutions to track configuration changes, enabling compliance and security audits.

By managing environment configurations effectively, development teams ensure seamless application functioning across diverse stages. This comprehensive approach safeguards against errors, enhances operational efficiency, and establishes a robust foundation for modern CI/CD practices.

Chapter 8

Monitoring and Debugging Argo Workflows

This chapter delves into the essential practices for monitoring and debugging Argo Workflows to ensure reliable and efficient execution. Readers are introduced to various tools and techniques for overseeing workflow operations, including utilizing the Argo UI for detailed insights and configuring alerts via systems like Prometheus and Grafana. It provides strategies for diagnosing workflow failures, leveraging logs for troubleshooting, and understanding error messages. The chapter also explores the integration of third-party monitoring solutions for enhanced visibility and discusses methods for optimizing workflow performance by addressing identified bottlenecks and inefficiencies.

8.1 Essential Monitoring Practices

In Argo Workflows, effective monitoring constitutes a fundamental pillar upon which reliable execution and efficient use of resources are built. By instituting comprehensive monitoring practices, workflow administrators can achieve a greater degree of oversight and control over their workflow systems. Several tools and methodologies are essential for ensuring visibility into both the execution of workflows and the utilization of resources.

A critical aspect of monitoring within the context of Argo Workflows involves the observation of workflow state transitions and execution timelines. Observing these allows users to identify delays and bottlenecks promptly, which could potentially impede workflow progression. By ensuring that workflows progress smoothly through initiation, processing, and completion phases, operators can ascertain their operational soundness.

```
{
    "metadata": {
        "name": "example-argo-workflow",
        "namespace": "default"
    },
    "status": {
        "phase": "Running",
        "startedAt": "2023-04-20T12:00:00Z"
    }
}
```

In the listings such as the one reflected above, it becomes evident how storing the status in JSON facilitates structured and programmatically accessible data formats. Parsing this information programmatically allows the development of monitoring scripts to automatically detect anomalies or delays, triggering alerts as necessary.

Another important component is resource consumption monitoring. Within Kubernetes, which serves as an orchestration layer for Argo Workflows, resource metrics such as CPU utilization and memory usage are paramount. Kubernetes' native tools like Metrics Server can be leveraged for collecting these metrics, thereby providing a comprehensive view of resource allocation. The following code snippet demonstrates the usage of kubectl to inspect resource utilization:

```
kubectl top pods --namespace=argo
```

8.1. ESSENTIAL MONITORING PRACTICES

The output from the above command is displayed in a tabular form, giving instant insight into which pods might be resource-starved or underutilized:

NAME	CPU(cores)	MEMORY(bytes)
argo-workflow-1234567890-abcde	100m	200Mi
argo-workflow-0987654321-vwxyz	150m	250Mi

Effective monitoring practices also incorporate real-time dashboards, which serve as visual tools for overseeing workflows. By integrating Argo Workflows with visualization frameworks such as Grafana, users can paramountly enhance their ability to interpret complex data via intuitive graphical representations. Grafana, when used in combination with a time-series database like Prometheus, collects and visualizes metrics such as durations of workflow executions, error rates, and throughputs.

Schedulers and cluster scaling behaviors of Argo Workflows are also crucial measures that determine baseline and peak resource requirements. Observing these properties ensures that workflows are running under optimal conditions, avoiding both under-provisioning and overutilization. An automated approach involves setting up custom horizontal pod autoscalers to dynamically adjust the number of replicas based on observed workload conditions:

```
apiVersion: autoscaling/v1
kind: HorizontalPodAutoscaler
metadata:
  name: argo-workflow-autoscaler
  namespace: argo
spec:
  scaleTargetRef:
    apiVersion: apps/v1
    kind: Deployment
    name: argo-workflow-executor
  minReplicas: 1
  maxReplicas: 10
  targetCPUUtilizationPercentage: 75
```

Events form another layer of Argo Workflow monitoring, where observing Kubernetes events allows administrators to track changes or anomalies occurring in the cluster environment. By analyzing event streams, users can detect patterns of failures or inefficiencies and correspondingly adapt workflow configurations to avert such occurrences.

Additionally, the availability and correctness of workflow code and configurations are ensured through the process of validation. This includes verifying YAML syntax of workflow definitions and ensuring compliance with execution policies. The Argo CLI tool is particularly beneficial, providing a means to validate and lint workflow definitions directly:

```
argo lint --namespace my-namespace my-workflow.yaml
```

Successful execution of the command above certifies that the structure and contents of the specified workflow meet all requisite schema requirements and best practices, preempting runtime errors induced by misconfigurations.

Integrating log aggregation features enhances the monitoring experience, presenting the ability to analyze collected logs centrally. Such aggregation solutions, including ELK Stack (Elasticsearch, Logstash, Kibana), correlate logs generated across multiple clusters and environments, aiding in diagnosing anomalies and understanding origin points of failures by scrutinizing aggregated historical logs.

Crucial to effective workflow monitoring is the provision for alerting mechanisms, which immediately inform stakeholders of critical state changes or failures within the workflows. Systems like Prometheus are equipped to define alert rules that specify conditions for triggering alerts. For instance, defining a high latency alert rule ensures timely action is taken should mean execution times extend beyond predetermined thresholds:

```
groups:
- name: argo-workflow-alerts
  rules:
  - alert: WorkflowHighLatency
    expr: histogram_quantile(0.9, sum(rate(argo_workflow_duration_seconds_bucket
      [5m])) by (le)) > 30
    for: 5m
    labels:
      severity: high
    annotations:
      summary: "High execution latency in workflow {{ $labels.workflow_name }}"
      description: "The 90th percentile execution latency of workflow has exceeded 30
        seconds for more than 5 minutes."
```

The rule above continuously evaluates the performance data and generates alerts whenever latencies breaching predefined conditions are detected. Efficient escalation policies necessitate alert notifications be forwarded to communication channels preferred by stakeholders, which may include Slack notifications, emails, or integration with incident management systems like PagerDuty.

Expanding beyond elementary metrics, assessing the health of services utilized by Argo Workflows—such as database connections and message queues—is integral to comprehensive monitoring spheres. Conducting health probes via HTTP checks or incorporating background service monitoring processes increases the robustness of workflow operations.

By implementing these essential monitoring practices, administrators can orchestrate and maintain Argo Workflows with enhanced reliability and visibility. Effective monitoring empowers users to detect, diagnose, and resolve issues before they escalate into critical failures, ensuring workflows remain continuously efficient and accurate in their execution.

8.2 Using Argo UI for Monitoring

The Argo User Interface (UI) is a comprehensive tool integral to the real-time monitoring and management of Argo Workflows. It offers users the capacity to interact with workflows visually, providing insights and telemetry data essential for maintaining operational integrity. Leveraging the Argo UI is an excellent approach for workflow administrators to understand the dynamic states of workflows in execution, view detailed logs, and gain insights by navigating through running tasks.

An initial step in employing the Argo UI includes ensuring its proper installation and configuration within the Kubernetes environment. This requires deploying the Argo Workflows controller, along with its associated UI component, into the desired namespace within the cluster.

The deployment configuration generally resides in a specific YAML file, and it can be executed using the `kubectl` command-line tool, as illustrated in the snippet below:

```
kubectl apply -n argo -f https://raw.githubusercontent.com/argoproj/argo-workflows/stable/manifests/install.yaml
```

Once installed, the Argo UI provides a dedicated web application, accessible within the Kubernetes environment, through which administrators can oversee all workflow-related operations. A common approach to access this UI is by forwarding the service port, making it accessible from a local browser:

```
kubectl -n argo port-forward deployment/argo-server 2746:2746
```

Upon navigating to http://localhost:2746 in a web browser, users access the Argo UI's main dashboard. This interface is comprehensive, containing multiple panes providing an overview of workflows, nodes within the workflows, and detailed status reports—including error states and completion statuses.

The Argo UI is instrumental in interacting visually with the workflow's DAG (Directed Acyclic Graph) structure. This visual representation aids in comprehending complexities within workflows comprising multiple steps and dependencies. Users can analyze factors such as parallel execution paths and conditional branches, gaining insightful visibility into intricate workflow architectures.

Real-time log viewing is another pivotal benefit provided by the UI. Logs offer detailed insights regarding each task executed within the workflow, including success logs and error outputs. Through these logs, developers diagnose unanticipated states or bugs in workflow tasks. The following image representation (Figure **??**) elucidates how logs are demonstrated within the Argo UI:

Further delving into the Argo UI involves navigating through workflows in various execution states such as 'Pending', 'Running', and 'Completed'. Each state is visually distinguishable, allowing users to effortlessly recognize workflows that demand immediate attention. Detailed execution history facilitates retrospective analysis, improving future workflow planning and error anticipation.

Within the UI context, alert and event monitoring components enable real-time feedback about transitional states and errors raised during workflow execution. Aiding decision-making processes during such events assures timely intervention to mitigate potential downtimes or failures.

The integration of these features with advanced filtering options ex-

8.2. USING ARGO UI FOR MONITORING

tends the capability of isolating specific workflows based on labels, phases, and execution times. Users can apply filters using the panel provided within the interface (), thereby narrowing the focus to particular subsets of workflows for deeper inspection:

The utility of the Argo UI is augmented when inspecting specific task events or logs for longitudinal data. This is particularly useful for tasks dependent on variable inputs and outputs, as examining previous completions provides a comparative framework for optimizing these tasks.

Through the Task Details pane, minute details such as inputs, parameter values, and outputs for each executed task within the workflow are accessible. This enables granular-level audits and fine-tuning of task-specific configurations, emphasizing the adaptability of workflows in meeting changing situational requirements.

The feature of retrying or resuming workflows, particularly those interrupted by unexpected states or failures, is effortlessly managed through options in the Argo UI. This feature is indispensable in environments necessitating consistency and completion, where partial success is inadequate, and continuity is paramount. The ability to reset failed tasks or entire workflows ensures that workflows progress efficiently beyond points of interruption.

Moreover, the Argo UI supports users in multi-tenancy settings by provisioning appropriate access controls and role-based access management capabilities. By segregating user permissions, workflows specific to departments, projects, or organizational units are efficiently managed—this aids in maintaining conforming operational policies.

The Argo UI also supports persistent configurations that allow users to manage recurring workflows and templates within the system effectively. These templates offer foundational structuring mechanisms for standardizing workflows, promoting efficiency through reuse, while ensuring compliance with predefined guidelines and policies.

Mastering the Argo UI enables administrators to proficiently monitor and manage workflows in a systematic, organized, and efficient manner. The interface's intuitive features greatly facilitate real-time monitoring, empowering administrative users with holistic oversight capabilities required for resolving issues and promoting the seamless execution of complex workflows within organizational ecosystems.

8.3 Configuring Alerts and Notifications

Configuring alerts and notifications is a vital aspect of managing Argo Workflows, aimed at maintaining a proactive stance in workflow oversight and ensuring that stakeholders are informed about key events and states as they unfold. Alerts are critical for instant recognition of anomalies and workflow states that require human intervention, whereas notifications are used to keep team members updated on standard workflow progressions or completions.

A primary tool employed in the configuration of alerts and notifications is Prometheus, a robust monitoring and alerting toolkit. Prometheus facilitates the collection and querying of metrics within Kubernetes environments, and integrates seamlessly with Argo Workflows for monitoring operational metrics such as workflow duration and error rates. Pairing Prometheus with Alertmanager enables sophisticated routing of alert notifications to designated endpoints.

The first step in implementing alerts with Prometheus is defining alerting rules within a YAML configuration file. These rules set the specific conditions that trigger alerts, which are continuously evaluated against metric data collected from workflows. The following example illustrates how to establish such a rule:

```
groups:
 - name: ArgoWorkflowAlerts
   rules:
   - alert: WorkflowErrorHigh
     expr: rate(argo_workflows_failed_count[5m]) > 1
     for: 10m
     labels:
        severity: critical
     annotations:
        summary: "High failure rate detected for workflows"
        description: "Failure rate exceeds 1 failure per minute over the last 10 minutes."
```

In this configuration, the alert WorkflowErrorHigh activates if the defined error rate threshold is exceeded continuously over a specified duration, allowing for early detection of systematic issues. Once an alert condition is met, Alertmanager takes the responsibility for processing and routing the notification message to selected recipients.

Alerts are typically communicated through various notification channels including email, Slack, PagerDuty, or other webhook endpoints.

8.3. CONFIGURING ALERTS AND NOTIFICATIONS

To configure these channels, Alertmanager utilizes a configuration file where routing rules and receiver configurations are specified:

```
route:
  receiver: slack-notifications

receivers:
- name: slack-notifications
  slack_configs:
  - api_url: 'https://hooks.slack.com/services/T00000000/B00000000/
      XXXXXXXXXXXXXXXXXXXXXXXX'
    channel: '#argo-alerts'
    send_resolved: true
```

In the above configuration, when an alert is triggered, the notification is sent to the #argo-alerts Slack channel. This ensures that the relevant team is immediately informed of critical conditions, facilitating timely corrective actions.

Complementing the use of Prometheus and Alertmanager is Grafana, another powerful tool that provides a flexible dashboarding solution and can be used to visualize alerting rules and state evaluations dynamically. Within Grafana, panels can be constructed to visualize metrics and triggered alerts, streamlining the ability to track alerts visually and corroborate these with additional data streams.

In some scenarios, integrating alerts directly within workflow definitions is both viable and beneficial. Argo Workflows supports webhook triggers embedded within workflow steps, effectively enabling workflows to autonomously signal external systems or applications upon reaching specified states. This is evident in the subsequent workflow example, where a notification webhook is used to inform an external monitoring system of a workflow's completion:

```
apiVersion: argoproj.io/v1alpha1
kind: Workflow
metadata:
  generateName: notify-webhook-
spec:
  entrypoint: main
  templates:
  - name: main
    steps:
    - - name: notify
        template: notify-success
  - name: notify-success
    script:
      image: alpine:3.7
      command: [bash]
```

```
source: |
   curl -X POST https://monitoring.example.com/workflow/completed
```

In this case, upon completion of the workflow, the specified webhook transmits an HTTP POST request to the designated URL, allowing for automated system responses or updates in a third-party monitoring system.

The effectiveness of alerts and notifications depends significantly on their configuration precision and the appropriateness of severity levels defined. Crafting effective alerts requires an understanding of workflow behaviors, resource thresholds, and potential failure points. Equally essential is the crafting of insightful notification messages, inclusive of context sufficient to inform a receiver of action requirements without incurring analysis delays.

Advanced practices also involve integration of Machine Learning (ML) models to anticipate workflow anomalies before traditional metric thresholds are breached. By processing historical data, ML models can derive insights that predict anomalous behavior patterns, heralding preemptive alerts that facilitate proactive measures.

In terms of further extending notification capabilities, event-driven frameworks such as Amazon EventBridge or Google Cloud Pub/Sub could be employed for orchestrating broader event responses in distributed systems, syncing alerts across multifaceted architectures.

Ultimately, configuring alerts and notifications in Argo Workflows is a multipronged strategy involving the careful integration of monitoring tools, automated workflow strategies, and contextual routing of notifications. Establishing a robust alerting and notification infrastructure not only enhances incident response elements but also enriches overall workflow reliability and performance. Consequently, organizations employing these strategies benefit from heightened situational awareness, timely decision-making, and sustained operational efficiency.

8.4 Debugging Failed Workflows

Debugging failed workflows in Argo is a crucial skill for workflow administrators and developers, enabling them to identify and rectify issues that prevent workflows from reaching successful completion. A comprehensive understanding of various debugging methodologies, coupled with the ability to analyze logs and error messages effectively, is fundamental in maintaining the robustness and reliability of the workflows.

One of the primary resources for debugging is the logs generated during workflow execution. These logs furnish a detailed account of each step in the workflow, making it possible to trace how and where errors have occurred. Within the context of Kubernetes, logs can be accessed using the kubectl command-line tool, for tasks executed by individual pods:

```
kubectl logs -n argo <pod-name>
```

By examining these logs, administrators can pinpoint issues such as command failures, incorrect configurations, dependency errors, or resource constraints.

Argo Workflows provide additional capabilities for viewing logs directly via the Argo UI, which is particularly advantageous in complex workflows involving numerous steps. This UI facilitates navigation through the Directed Acyclic Graph (DAG), emphasizing failed nodes, and presenting logs alongside execution details for immediate insights. Upon identifying the log messages corresponding to workflow failures, developers can delineate recovery steps or script corrections.

Error messages emitted during execution further distill the nature of the failure. These may indicate problems like script syntax errors, incorrect file paths, unsupported operations, or external service failures. Understanding the subtleties of these messages is essential, often requiring familiarity with the underlying technologies employed within workflow tasks.

For example, a typical error message might resemble:

```
Error: container has runAsNonRoot and image will run as root
```

This message indicates a container security violation, requiring adjustments in either the container image or the security context defined within the workflow specification:

```
securityContext:
```

CHAPTER 8. MONITORING AND DEBUGGING ARGO WORKFLOWS

```
runAsUser: 1000
runAsGroup: 3000
fsGroup: 2000
```

In addition to analyzing logs and error messages, debugging practices should include the validation of workflow YAML configurations. Errors often result from syntactic mishaps or misconfigurations in these files. The argo lint command is useful for pre-execution tool checks, affirming adherence to schema requirements:

```
argo lint --namespace argo-workflows example-workflow.yaml
```

Upon confirming correct configurations, further validation might involve simulating workflow execution within a controlled environment to better ascertain behavior under variable conditions—this is particularly useful for identifying race conditions or unpredictable state effects intrinsic to specific workload distributions.

For more analytic debugging processes, Argo Workflows can be deployed with tracing methodologies employing OpenTelemetry or Jaeger, enabling extensive distributed tracing of task executions. This allows administrators to trace the entire execution path and interactions between different workflow components, revealing areas where latencies or failures are introduced.

The following YAML section exemplifies a tracing configuration using OpenTelemetry:

```
apiVersion: argoproj.io/v1alpha1
kind: Workflow
metadata:
  generateName: tracing-example-
spec:
  tracingConfig:
    endpoint: http://jaeger-collector:14268/api/traces
    sampler:
      type: const
      param: 1
```

Moreover, debugging failed workflows should integrate thoroughly with rollback strategies. Workflows determined to be interdependent may necessitate backups or checkpoints. By configuring rollback or retry policies within workflows, administrators have the chance to reattempt failed executions post-rectification, crucial for configurations that involve stateful operations or batch processing of large data sets.

The YAML below demonstrates setting retry strategies within a workflow template:

```
retryStrategy:
  limit: 3
  retryPolicy: "Always"
  backoff:
    duration: "20s"
    factor: 2
    maxDuration: "5m"
```

Documenting and archiving failed workflows, along with their remedial responses, is pivotal for long-term operational success. Establishing a knowledge base or error response library harnesses collective learnings and expedites the diagnosis and resolution of future failures. This resource should encapsulate error descriptions, screenshots or logs, causal inferences, corrective actions, and probable impacts of failures.

A regimen of periodic retrospective analyses on workflow failures enhances the capacity to detect patterns indicative of systemic risks or inefficiencies, guiding administrators in proactive adaptation of workflows to accommodate evolving demands or environment changes.

In summary, debugging failed workflows in Argo involves a strategic combination of log analysis, error interpretation, workflow validation, and archival assessment. Each component facilitates an improved understanding of workflow dynamics and aids in establishing frameworks that mitigate risk, enhance adaptability, and foster long-term workflow efficacy. Administrators adopting these practices benefit significantly from sustained operational fidelity and heightened organizational resilience against workflow disruptions.

8.5 Leveraging Workflow Logs

Workflow logs play an essential role in the management and optimization of Argo Workflows, offering a wealth of data that can be leveraged for diagnosing issues, performance tuning, and gaining insights into workflow behavior. Logs provide a detailed chronological record of events that occur within the execution of workflows, serving as a crucial diagnostic tool in understanding where processes might deviate from expected norms or encounter errors.

The primary utility of workflow logs is in the identification and resolution of errors. When workflows fail, logs offer a granular look into the exact operations being performed at various stages, enabling developers to delineate the causes of failures and implement requisite fixes. By systematically analyzing log outputs, administrators can uncover issues such as misconfigurations, missteps in execution, unexpected operational conditions, or resource contention.

Logs for Argo Workflows can be accessed using the Kubernetes command-line tool, kubectl. The following command retrieves logs for a specified pod responsible for a workflow task:

```
kubectl logs -n argo <pod-name>
```

Analyzing log outputs becomes straightforward with integrated tools like Fluentd or Fluent Bit, which enable the aggregation and forwarding of logs to central storage solutions suited for structured queries. Once logs are aggregated, tools such as Elasticsearch, Logstash, and Kibana (ELK Stack) offer the ability to search, analyze, and visualize logs efficiently.

Utilizing Elasticsearch for storing logs is immensely beneficial in creating structured storage that allows for detailed and efficient querying through Lucene query syntax. Logstash processes and transforms log data into formats amenable for detailed analysis, while Kibana provides graphical interfaces for visualizing log data across multiple dimensions.

A typical ELK Stack deployment topology involves configuring Fluentd as a log collector in Kubernetes, forwarding logs to a distant Elasticsearch cluster:

```
<match **>
  @type elasticsearch
  host es-service
  port 9200
  logstash_format true
  flush_interval 5s
</match>
```

Once logs are indexed in Elasticsearch, queries can be executed to derive insights such as the frequency of errors by type, execution duration anomalies, or common litigated processes where workflows repeatedly

8.5. LEVERAGING WORKFLOW LOGS

face bottlenecks.

Kibana visualizations allow workflow administrators to visualize error trends over time, drill down to specific log messages corresponding to error events, and relate these patterns to underlying causes or systemic issues.

In practical applications, logs also serve a dual function in facilitating audits and accountability within systems. By auditing logs, teams can corroborate that workflows were executed in accordance with SLAs (Service Level Agreements) and comply with compliance benchmarks necessary for regulatory standards such as GDPR (General Data Protection Regulation) or HIPAA (Health Insurance Portability and Accountability Act).

Furthermore, leveraging logs for continuous performance tuning ensures workflows operate within optimal parameters, accommodating fluctuating workloads and mitigating resource exhaustion. Analyzing historical logs informs scaling strategies, workflow template refinement, task prioritization, or caching considerations.

In addition, complementary technologies such as Grafana can be synchronized with logging solutions to promote alerts and real-time monitoring based on log-derived metrics. By setting thresholds for specific log messages or error frequency, Grafana dashboards extend situational awareness, complementing the predominantly retrospective function of logs with proactive measures.

The facilitated use of Machine Learning (ML) algorithms for log analysis fosters predictive maintenance. By leveraging anomaly detection models, administrators can identify trends and predict potential failures before they manifest within the actual workflow—enhancing uptime and reliability. ML models may ingest structured log data and apply ensemble learning techniques to identify deviations or fine-tune predictive metrics such as task latency and completion probability.

For improved data sovereignty and compliance assurance, organizations may also opt to use on-premise or hybrid solutions—balancing data security objectives with cloud-native scalability. Storage solutions such as OpenSearch allow for deploying self-managed systems underpinned by consistent log processing, query, and visualization functionalities.

All things considered, workflow logs are a cornerstone in maintaining Argo Workflow efficiency and reliability. They provide groundbreaking opportunities for introspection into operational behavior, identification of redundancies, and unlocking advanced analytical capabilities via integration with cutting-edge data workflows. Administrators leveraging these insights gain a sophisticated understanding of workflow dynamics, bolstering their capability to execute efficient management and rapid problem-solving across complex system architectures.

8.6 Integrating Third-Party Monitoring Tools

Integrating third-party monitoring tools with Argo Workflows enhances observability and analysis capabilities beyond what is typically offered by native tools alone. Through integration with comprehensive monitoring solutions like Prometheus, Grafana, and the ELK Stack (Elasticsearch, Logstash, Kibana), organizations can leverage advanced metrics collection, log analysis, alerting, and visualization features that are necessary in today's complex, multifaceted infrastructures.

Third-party monitoring tools provide functionalities essential for effective system healthcare and performance evaluation, facilitating alerted responses, user-defined dashboards, and long-term storage solutions. The integration process involves setting up toolchains, configuring workflows for metrics and logs collection, and defining data visualization strategies that are coherent across various levels of the Kubernetes and Argo ecosystem.

One of the primary tools for integrating monitoring solutions into Argo Workflows is Prometheus, an open-source systems monitoring and alerting toolkit that pulls in metrics compatible with Kubernetes infrastructure. Prometheus can be configured to scrape metrics from Argo Workflows, storing them in its time-series database. Scraping is typically facilitated by deploying exporters—application-specific endpoints exposing metrics data that Prometheus scrapes at defined intervals.

```
---
apiVersion: v1
```

8.6. INTEGRATING THIRD-PARTY MONITORING TOOLS

```
kind: Service
metadata:
  labels:
    app: argo-metrics
  name: argo-metrics-svc
spec:
  ports:
  - name: http
    port: 80
    targetPort: http
  selector:
    app: argo
---
apiVersion: monitoring.coreos.com/v1
kind: ServiceMonitor
metadata:
  name: argo-metrics
spec:
  endpoints:
  - interval: 30s
    port: http
  selector:
    matchLabels:
      app: argo
```

In this configuration, the ServiceMonitor object is used to configure Prometheus to scrape metrics exposed by the Argo Workflows service, making it capable of collecting data relevant to workflow execution times, task statuses, and resource utilization.

Grafana complements Prometheus by visualizing these metrics through dashboards. Grafana's dynamic query capabilities allow stakeholders to convert raw data into understandable, actionable insights. The integration of Grafana involves importing metrics into Grafana and using the Prometheus data source plugin for displaying metrics through dashboards customized to meet project-specific requirements.

A cohesive monitoring solution is further enhanced by incorporating the ELK Stack for robust log management and analysis. With Elasticsearch at its core, high-volume log data generated by Argo Workflows is indexed and made searchable on a near real-time basis.

Logstash actively parses incoming logs and transforms them into structured content consumable by Elasticsearch. A typical Logstash configuration might include filters for extracting necessary fields from logs, formatting them appropriately, and adding metadata such as timestamps or execution IDs for correlation.

```
input {
  beats {
    port => 5044
  }
}
filter {
  grok {
    match => { "message" => "%{TIMESTAMP_ISO8601:timestamp} %{
        LOGLEVEL:level} %{DATA:workflow} %{GREEDYDATA:msg}" }
  }
  date {
    match => [ "timestamp", "ISO8601" ]
  }
}
output {
  elasticsearch {
    hosts => ["http://localhost:9200"]
    index => "argo-workflows-logs-%{+YYYY.MM.dd}"
  }
}
```

Kibana integrates with Elasticsearch to facilitate interactive visualization of logs through dashboards, graphs, and charts, making it easier for operations teams to spot anomalies, trends, or correlations within workflow executions.

Besides these tools, integrating advanced systems like Splunk or Datadog offers capabilities specifically tailored to enterprise-grade monitoring requirements. Splunk's comprehensive analytics engine allows for the processing and visualization of both logs and metrics, supporting in-depth analyses through sophisticated searches and machine learning algorithms. Alternatively, Datadog combines full-stack visibility with seamless integration to cloud services, offering out-of-the-box dashboards specifically for monitoring and troubleshooting Argo Workflows.

Additionally, practices such as deploying OpenTelemetry enable organizations to gather telemetry data for enhanced monitoring and tracing purposes, further complementing the native functionalities provided by core systems. OpenTelemetry extends support for distributed tracing and metrics collection, capturing and exporting telemetry data to various backends for detailed observability.

```
receivers:
  prometheus:
    config:
      scrape_configs:
        - job_name: 'argo-workflows'
```

8.7. OPTIMIZING WORKFLOW PERFORMANCE

```
        scrape_interval: 30s
        static_configs:
          - targets: ['<ARGO_WORKFLOWS_SERVICE_HOST>']
processors:
  batch:
exporters:
  otlp:
    endpoint: "<BACKEND_ENDPOINT>"

service:
  pipelines:
    metrics:
      receivers: [prometheus]
      processors: [batch]
      exporters: [otlp]
```

The integration of third-party monitoring tools into Argo Workflow environments empowers organizations with comprehensive visibility and analytics capabilities, ensuring that operations remain efficient and any deviations from expected behavior are promptly identified and addressed. Such integrations foster a culture of transparency, accountability, and continuous improvement—key factors in sustaining optimal performance and reliability across dynamically evolving workflow infrastructures.

8.7 Optimizing Workflow Performance

Optimizing the performance of Argo Workflows is a vital consideration for ensuring that workflows execute efficiently, utilize resources effectively, and meet desired performance benchmarks. Achieving optimal performance involves analyzing workflows to identify bottlenecks, implementing best practices in workflow design, and making strategic use of the Kubernetes infrastructure to enhance execution times and resource usage.

A preliminary step in optimizing workflow performance is profiling and analyzing workflow execution times. By leveraging monitoring tools such as Prometheus in conjunction with Grafana dashboards, workflow administrators can gain insights into execution durations for each task and identify irregular patterns or tasks that consistently exceed expected runtimes. Establishing baseline performance metrics enables comparative analysis with ongoing workflow executions, revealing areas for improvement.

The architecture of workflow design significantly influences its performance. Workflows should be designed to maximize concurrency by taking advantage of parallel execution. When tasks are independent and do not have interdependencies, they can be executed simultaneously, reducing overall execution time:

```
apiVersion: argoproj.io/v1alpha1
kind: Workflow
metadata:
  generateName: parallel-template-
spec:
  entrypoint: parallel-example
  templates:
  - name: parallel-example
    steps:
    - - name: task-one
        template: task-template
      - name: task-two
        template: task-template
      - name: task-three
        template: task-template

  - name: task-template
    container:
      image: ubuntu
      command: [echo]
      args: ["Executing task"]
```

Utilizing the parallel execution model optimally leverages underlying resources and minimizes idle time associated with sequential task dependencies.

For tasks that require sequential execution due to dependencies, optimizing the chaining of tasks can reduce overall delays. This may involve evaluating and refining task order to improve data locality, reduce remote calls, or optimize intermediate data processing. The following coding example implies the sequential execution where outputs of preceding tasks are inputs for successive tasks:

```
apiVersion: argoproj.io/v1alpha1
kind: Workflow
metadata:
  generateName: sequential-template-
spec:
  entrypoint: sequential-example
  templates:
  - name: sequential-example
    steps:
    - - name: fetch-data
        template: fetch-template
    - - name: process-data
        template: process-template
```

8.7. OPTIMIZING WORKFLOW PERFORMANCE

```
    - name: store-results
      template: store-template

  - name: fetch-template
    container:
      image: busybox
      command: [sh, -c]
      args: ["echo Fetching data"]

  - name: process-template
    container:
      image: busybox
      command: [sh, -c]
      args: ["echo Processing data"]

  - name: store-template
    container:
      image: busybox
      command: [sh, -c]
      args: ["echo Storing results"]
```

Implementing efficient resource management policies is another key performance consideration. Kubernetes offers horizontal autoscaling to adjust resources dynamically based on workload demand. Configuring Horizontal Pod Autoscalers (HPA) facilitates automatic adjustment of pod replica counts to accommodate peaks in demand, ensuring that workflows are neither starved of resources nor overprovisioned:

```
apiVersion: autoscaling/v1
kind: HorizontalPodAutoscaler
metadata:
  name: argo-workflow-hpa
spec:
  scaleTargetRef:
    apiVersion: apps/v1
    kind: Deployment
    name: argo-workflow-executor
  minReplicas: 2
  maxReplicas: 10
  targetCPUUtilizationPercentage: 70
```

Leveraging caching mechanisms can vastly improve response times in workflows that reuse identical data sets across tasks. By caching outputs of computation-intensive tasks—especially common outputs—subsequent tasks benefit from quicker access times associated with memory or disk caches as opposed to regenerating data.

Moreover, refining container image sizes and base images utilized by workflow tasks is an impactful optimization strategy. Smaller container images reduce startup latency and enhance node packing efficiency. Using optimized base images tailored to the specific needs of tasks enhances performance, often incorporating only essential binaries and libraries needed for execution.

Network latency can be minimized by deploying tasks within regions or zones that are close in proximity to the data they manipulate. Task affinity and anti-affinity rules in Kubernetes can be used to influence pod scheduling decisions favorably for locality and performance considerations:

```
spec:
  affinity:
    podAffinity:
      requiredDuringSchedulingIgnoredDuringExecution:
      - labelSelector:
          matchExpressions:
          - key: app
            operator: In
            values:
            - argo-workflow
        topologyKey: "kubernetes.io/hostname"
```

Incorporating observability practices and establishing feedback loops through continuous monitoring allows for real-time performance audits. Metrics collected from these activities guide iterative optimizations and contextual decision-making. Comprehensive reporting aids in recognizing recurring performance dragons and informs infrastructure upgrades.

A/B testing variations of workflow configurations also introduces empirical evidence into tuning efforts, mitigating guesswork. This could include trials of varied instance types, storage solutions, scaling policies, or code refactoring—all validated through quantifiable improvements in performance metrics.

Ultimately, optimizing Argo Workflow performance extends beyond mere technical adjustments. It requires an understanding of the workflows' purpose, constraints, expected throughput, and stakeholder priorities. By systematically applying evidence-based optimizations, organizations can yield significant improvements in performance—and consequently, better resource allocation, lower operational costs, and enhanced user satisfaction.

Chapter 9

Security and Best Practices in Argo Workflows

This chapter addresses the critical aspects of security and best practices in the deployment and management of Argo Workflows. It covers secure handling of credentials through Kubernetes Secrets and role-based access control (RBAC) to restrict authorization. Readers will learn about enforcing network policies to ensure isolation and secure communication. The chapter also highlights best practices in designing workflows to minimize vulnerabilities, implementing comprehensive audit logging for compliance, and protecting data with encryption techniques for both transit and storage. These strategies are aimed at building secure and resilient workflow infrastructures in Kubernetes environments.

9.1 Understanding Security in Argo Workflows

Argo Workflows is a powerful container-native workflow engine designed to orchestrate parallel jobs on Kubernetes. While it provides extensive functionality, understanding the security implications is crucial to managing and deploying workflows securely. In the context of Argo Workflows, security encompasses securing the execution environment, ensuring data integrity, safeguarding against unauthorized access, and mitigating potential vulnerabilities inherent to distributed systems.

Security in Argo Workflows primarily revolves around three components: securing the workflow execution environment, controlling access, and protecting data. This section explores these components in detail, providing insights into common security risks and strategies for mitigation within Argo Workflows. It is essential for workflow administrators to integrate these security practices to maintain the integrity and availability of their workflows.

- **Workflow Execution Environment**

The workflow execution environment in Argo Workflows is embedded within Kubernetes. Therefore, understanding Kubernetes security principles is a prerequisite. Kubernetes offers layer-based security measures across its ecosystem; these include namespace isolation, Pod Security Policies, and network segmentation.

Namespace isolation helps in segregating different components within Kubernetes to limit the blast radius in the event of a security breach. Administrators should leverage namespaces to separate environments and apply quota limits to protect against resource exhaustion attacks. Utilizing namespaces effectively can prevent workflows from affecting other deployments or services, enhancing the overall security posture.

Consider the following YAML definition for a namespace creation in Kubernetes:

```
apiVersion: v1
kind: Namespace
metadata:
```

9.1. UNDERSTANDING SECURITY IN ARGO WORKFLOWS

```
name: argo-secure
```

Once namespaces are defined, policies such as ResourceQuotas and NetworkPolicies can further constrain the environment, reducing the risk of malicious activities.

Pod Security Policies (PSPs) are another vital aspect of securing the execution environment. They define a set of conditions that a pod must run under, establishing control over aspects like the use of elevated privileges, file system access, and other critical controls. While PodSecurityPolicy is deprecated in favor of Open Policy Agent (OPA) Gatekeeper, it is worthwhile to comprehend its impact.

For instance, a PSP to disallow privileged containers can be structured as follows:

```
apiVersion: policy/v1beta1
kind: PodSecurityPolicy
metadata:
  name: no-privileged
spec:
  privileged: false
  allowPrivilegeEscalation: false
  ...
```

Transitioning to OPA Gatekeeper allows for custom policy creation using a more extensive constraint framework tailored to the specific needs of Argo Workflows.

- **Access Control**

Access control in Argo is primarily managed through Role-Based Access Control (RBAC), which ensures that only authorized users or services can execute or modify workflows. RBAC policies are critical for defining roles and permissions at granular levels, controlling who can execute workflows, view logs, or modify configurations.

Creating effective RBAC policies necessitates a clear understanding of roles and the actions permissible within those roles. For example, the following RBAC configuration grants read access to workflows within the 'argo-secure' namespace:

```
apiVersion: rbac.authorization.k8s.io/v1
kind: Role
metadata:
```

```
  namespace: argo-secure
  name: workflow-reader
rules:
- apiGroups: ["argoproj.io"]
  resources: ["workflows"]
  verbs: ["get", "list", "watch"]
```

Moreover, integrating identity providers with Kubernetes enhances authentication, ensuring secure and dynamic access control mechanisms.

- **Data Protection**

In the lifecycle of a workflow, data often moves across various stages and components. It's vital to protect this data both in transit and at rest to safeguard against unauthorized access and potential breaches. This can be accomplished using encryption techniques and adherence to compliance standards.

Transport Layer Security (TLS) is instrumental in securing data in transit. Ensuring that all communications between Argo Workflow components—such as controller, executor, and user interface—use TLS encryption is a foundational practice. Configuring ingress controllers to enforce TLS termination is common:

```
apiVersion: networking.k8s.io/v1
kind: Ingress
metadata:
  name: argo-ingress
  annotations:
    nginx.ingress.kubernetes.io/ssl-redirect: "true"
spec:
  tls:
  - hosts:
    - argo.example.com
    secretName: argo-tls
...
```

For data at rest, encrypting storage volumes and employing secure secret management solutions is advised. Kubernetes Secrets provide a mechanism to store sensitive information; however, it is critical to employ additional layers such as HashiCorp Vault which offers robust secret management and policy enforcement.

For example, creating a Kubernetes Secret to store API keys can be done using:

```
kubectl create secret generic api-keys --from-literal=key1=VAL
```

Enhancing this with Vault integration allows for dynamic secret generation and rotation, improving security significantly.

- **Mitigating Common Security Risks**

Several common security risks can affect Argo Workflows, including compromised credentials, Denial of Service (DoS) attacks, and vulnerabilities within container images. Mitigation starts with adopting a security-first mindset and implementing routine security updates and audits.

Routine introspection of configuration files is necessary to prevent inadvertent exposure of credentials. Tools like kube-bench and kube-hunter provide automated compliance checks and vulnerability scanning within Kubernetes clusters, thereby enabling proactive security management.

Employing image scanning solutions like Clair or Aqua Security can help ensure that container images remain free of known vulnerabilities before deployment on Kubernetes.

Furthermore, leveraging Kubernetes Network Policies restricts inbound and outbound communications for pods and can be configured to enhance workflow security. A policy example that allows communication only within the 'argo-secure' namespace is given below:

```
apiVersion: networking.k8s.io/v1
kind: NetworkPolicy
metadata:
  name: allow-intra-namespace
  namespace: argo-secure
spec:
  podSelector: {}
  policyTypes:
  - Ingress
  - Egress
  ingress:
  - from:
    - podSelector: {}
  ...
```

Finally, continuous monitoring and logging prove invaluable in detecting anomalous activities. Integration with solutions like Prometheus and Grafana can provide visualization and alerts based on predefined security metrics.

Implementing these methods contributes to a fortified security framework within Argo Workflows, safeguarding workflows from potential exploits and breaches while maintaining operational efficiency and compliance. By understanding and implementing these security measures, organizations can realize the full potential of Argo Workflows, achieving robust and secure automation within Kubernetes.

9.2 Securing Workflow Credentials

Effective credential management is foundational in maintaining the security and integrity of workflows running on Argo Workflows within Kubernetes environments. Workflow credentials, such as API keys, tokens, and other sensitive configurations, can, if exposed, lead to significant security vulnerabilities, including unauthorized access and data breaches. This section explores strategies for securely managing and storing these credentials using Kubernetes tools such as Secrets and advanced secret management solutions like HashiCorp Vault.

Securing credentials in Kubernetes involves understanding how Kubernetes Secrets function, the limitations they present, and how these can be fortified with additional tools and best practices. We will delve into the specifics of creating, managing, and accessing secrets responsibly in a Kubernetes environment running Argo Workflows.

Understanding Kubernetes Secrets

Kubernetes Secrets is a built-in resource that provides a way to store sensitive information such as passwords, OAuth tokens, and SSH keys. It prevents the need to store sensitive data directly within Pod definitions or source code, reducing the risk of accidental exposure. However, by default, Secrets are stored in base64-encoded form in etcd, which is not inherently secure and necessitates further measures to ensure security.

To create a secret, you can use the `kubectl create secret` command. Here is an example of creating a generic secret that stores API keys:

```
kubectl create secret generic api-secrets --from-literal=api-key=1234567890abcdef
```

Instead of using plaintext, secrets should be encrypted and securely managed. The configuration for encrypting secrets at rest in Kubernetes is a critical step. This involves setting up encryption providers in the kube-apiserver.

Example: Encrypting Kubernetes Secrets

To encrypt secrets at rest, configure the kube-apiserver to use a provider configuration file:

```
kind: EncryptionConfiguration
apiVersion: apiserver.config.k8s.io/v1
resources:
  - resources:
      - secrets
    providers:
      - aescbc:
          keys:
            - name: key1
              secret: <base64-secret-here>
      - identity: {}
```

Once the kube-apiserver is configured, secrets are encrypted as they are stored in etcd, offering enhanced security for sensitive data.

Advanced Secret Management with HashiCorp Vault

While Kubernetes Secrets offers a basic level of security, tools like HashiCorp Vault provide more robust secret management solutions, allowing for dynamic secrets, detailed access policies, and automatic rotation, all of which are crucial for improving the security posture.

HashiCorp Vault facilitates advanced capabilities such as leasing and renewal mechanisms for credentials, ensuring they are kept to a minimum duration necessary for operations and reducing the attack window for any potential compromise.

Integrating HashiCorp Vault with Kubernetes

Integrating Vault with Kubernetes enables Argo Workflows to utilize a secure secret management backend. This involves setting up a Vault instance and configuring Kubernetes authentication via Vault. Here's an example setup for enabling Kubernetes authentication in Vault:

- **Enable Kubernetes Authentication in Vault:**

```
vault auth enable kubernetes
```

- **Configure Vault to Recognize the Kubernetes Cluster:**

```
vault write auth/kubernetes/config \
    token_reviewer_jwt="<service-account-jwt>" \
    kubernetes_host="https://<kubernetes-apiserver>" \
    kubernetes_ca_cert=@ca_cert.pem
```

- **Define Roles for Accessing Secrets:**

```
vault write auth/kubernetes/role/argo-role \
    bound_service_account_names=argo-workflow \
    bound_service_account_namespaces=argo-namespace \
    policies=argo-policy \
    ttl=24h
```

This integration allows workflows to access Vault securely to retrieve secrets using service accounts, reducing direct exposure to static credentials.

Policy Management in Vault

Policy management in Vault simplifies defining what specific actions and resources are permissible for an application. These policies help segregate duties, so only necessary operations get access to specified secrets:

```
# Example Vault policy for a workflow
path "secret/data/argo/*" {
  capabilities = ["read"]
}

path "secret/data/database/password" {
  capabilities = ["deny"]
}
```

By creating finely grained policies, Vault minimizes credential risks and unauthorized access, supporting compliance with organizational security protocols and standards.

Accessing Secrets Using Argo Workflows

Argo Workflows can directly access Kubernetes Secrets or leverage solutions like Vault using sidecar containers or init containers. Configuring containers to retrieve secrets at runtime is a secure pattern that ensures minimal exposure:

Consider a YAML definition where an init container fetches the secret:

```
apiVersion: argoproj.io/v1alpha1
kind: Workflow
```

9.2. SECURING WORKFLOW CREDENTIALS

```
metadata:
  generateName: secret-management-example-
spec:
  entrypoint: run
  templates:
  - name: run
    container:
      image: busybox
      command: [sh, -c]
      args: ["echo secret value: $(cat /vault/secrets/api-key)"]
    initContainers:
    - name: vault-agent-init
      image: vault:1.2.3
      volumeMounts:
      - name: vault-secrets
        mountPath: /vault/secrets
    volumes:
    - name: vault-secrets
      emptyDir: {}
```

In this example, the init container fetches secrets from Vault and makes them available to the main container.

Best Practices for Credential Management

- **Use Least Privilege Principle:** When assigning permissions, adhere to the principle of least privilege, ensuring roles and service accounts have only the access necessary to fulfill their functions.

- **Regularly Rotate Credentials:** Regular credential rotation reduces exposure time in the event of compromise.

- **Encrypt Secrets at Rest and in Transit:** Ensure that all path stages preserve secrecy and integrity across networks and storage.

- **Audit Access Logs:** Monitor and audit access logs to detect unauthorized access patterns to credentials, using logs to inform response strategies.

- **Environment Segregation:** Employ different environments for development, testing, and production and ensure secrets are isolated accordingly to reduce exposure and risk.

Employing these best practices within the context of Argo Workflows assures a more secure and resilient framework, attuned to handling sensitive data proactively while maintaining compliance with industry security standards. This forms the backbone of a robust credential management strategy, enabling workflows to operate securely and efficiently.

9.3 Role-Based Access Control (RBAC) in Argo

Role-Based Access Control (RBAC) is an essential security mechanism in Kubernetes used to control access to resources within a cluster. In the context of Argo Workflows, RBAC plays a pivotal role in ensuring that only authorized individuals or services can create, execute, view, or modify workflows. Kubernetes' RBAC offers a flexible and scalable means of managing permissions, which is critical in environments where security and compliance are essential.

RBAC operates by defining permissions through roles and then associating these roles with users or groups. This section provides an in-depth examination of RBAC within Argo Workflows, starting from the basic concepts to more complex configurations, and highlights best practices in designing an effective RBAC policy framework.

Basic Concepts of RBAC in Kubernetes

In Kubernetes, RBAC is used to control access to resources such as pods, services, and nodes. With Argo Workflows, this means controlling access to workflows, workflow templates, and other associated resources.

RBAC in Kubernetes consists of the following key components:

- **Roles and ClusterRoles:** Define a set of permissions. Roles are namespace specific, while ClusterRoles are cluster-wide. - **RoleBindings and ClusterRoleBindings:** Assign a role or cluster role to a user or a set of users. RoleBindings are namespace specific, whereas ClusterRoleBindings are cluster-wide.

The following YAML snippet illustrates a simple Role that grants list and watch permissions for workflows in a specific namespace:

```
apiVersion: rbac.authorization.k8s.io/v1
```

9.3. ROLE-BASED ACCESS CONTROL (RBAC) IN ARGO

```
kind: Role
metadata:
  namespace: argo
  name: workflow-viewer
rules:
- apiGroups: ["argoproj.io"]
  resources: ["workflows"]
  verbs: ["get", "list", "watch"]
```

Implementing RBAC for Argo Workflows

When implementing RBAC for Argo Workflows, it is essential to consider the specific requirements and access patterns of your environment. This can involve multiple roles, each tailored to the duties and responsibilities of particular user groups or services.

1. **Develop User Roles:**

Encountering varied access and interaction patterns necessitates defining user roles for different interaction levels — such as Viewers, Operators, and Administrators.

- Viewers might only need read access to workflows. - Operators could require permissions to execute and manage running workflows. - Administrators necessitate broader access, including altering settings and permissions.

2. **Create RoleBindings:**

Associating these roles with users or groups is achieved through RoleBindings. An example RoleBinding that assigns the workflow-viewer role to a user is illustrated below:

```
apiVersion: rbac.authorization.k8s.io/v1
kind: RoleBinding
metadata:
  name: view-workflows
  namespace: argo
subjects:
- kind: User
  name: jane.doe@example.com
  apiGroup: rbac.authorization.k8s.io
roleRef:
  kind: Role
  name: workflow-viewer
  apiGroup: rbac.authorization.k8s.io
```

3. **ClusterRoles and ClusterRoleBindings:**

For actions requiring cluster-wide permissions, use ClusterRoles and

ClusterRoleBindings. These are particularly useful for managing resources that span multiple namespaces or for overarching administrative access:

```
apiVersion: rbac.authorization.k8s.io/v1
kind: ClusterRole
metadata:
  name: argo-admin
rules:
- apiGroups: ["argoproj.io"]
  resources: ["workflows", "workflowtemplates"]
  verbs: ["*"]
```

```
apiVersion: rbac.authorization.k8s.io/v1
kind: ClusterRoleBinding
metadata:
  name: bind-argo-admin
subjects:
- kind: User
  name: admin@example.com
  apiGroup: rbac.authorization.k8s.io
roleRef:
  kind: ClusterRole
  name: argo-admin
  apiGroup: rbac.authorization.k8s.io
```

Best Practices in Defining RBAC for Argo Workflows

1. **The Principle of Least Privilege:**

RBAC policies should be designed following the principle of least privilege, bestowing only the necessary permissions for users or services to perform their required operations. This reduces the potential security risks of excessive privileges.

2. **Namespace Isolation:**

Use namespaces to isolate applications and enforce granular access controls. Assign roles and rolebindings within specific namespaces to avoid unintended access across the cluster.

3. **Audit and Review:**

Continuously audit and review RBAC policies to ensure they remain aligned with the operational and security requirements of the organization. Kubernetes auditing features can be employed to monitor who accessed what resources and when, aiding in compliance and forensic investigations.

4. **Avoid Cluster-Wide Permissions Where Possible:**

Restrict ClusterRoles and ClusterRoleBindings to strategic needs, primarily for maintaining system operations. It is advisable to use namespace-scoped RBAC roles unless there is a justified need for cluster-wide access.

5. **Tailored Policies for Service Accounts:**

Manually create and manage service accounts for Argo Workflow executions, ensuring these accounts possess only the privileges necessary for executing the workflows they are associated with.

Advanced RBAC Configurations

For environments requiring fine-grained access control and policy enforcement, consider integrating with advanced policy engines such as Open Policy Agent (OPA). OPA provides greater control and visibility by allowing policies to be enforced dynamically based on context beyond what is available with standard RBAC.

Additionally, mapping external identity providers with Kubernetes RBAC—using solutions like Kubernetes's Identity Provider (OIDC)—enables federated identity management. This integration ensures that RBAC policies are dynamically applied based on users' roles received from external identity systems, thereby offering scalability and cohesion across various platforms and systems.

Implementing RBAC Audits and Logging

Auditing RBAC changes and access requests can help detect misconfigurations and unauthorized access that might not align with organizational policies. Enable Kubernetes Audit Logging by configuring the kube-apiserver to audit records of requests that have been authorized, as shown below:

```
--audit-log-path=/var/log/kubernetes/audit.log
--audit-log-maxage=30
--audit-log-maxbackup=10
--audit-log-maxsize=100
--audit-policy-file=/etc/kubernetes/audit-policy.yaml
```

A careful definition of an audit-policy.yaml provides the contexts for logging details, level of verbosity, and specifics on the subject and resource types to be audited.

```
apiVersion: audit.k8s.io/v1
kind: Policy
```

```
rules:
- level: Metadata
  resources:
  - group: ""
    resources: ["secrets", "configmaps"]
    verbs: ["get"]
- level: RequestResponse
  resources:
  - group: ""
    resources: ["pods"]
    verbs: ["create", "delete"]
```

By strategically planning and implementing RBAC with these approaches, Argo Workflows' administrators can ensure robust security configurations that meet both the operational needs and the stringent security requirements of modern cloud-native applications.

9.4 Network Policies and Isolation

In Kubernetes environments, network policies are critical for ensuring secure and efficient communication across pods while preventing unauthorized access and potential network breaches. Network policies enable administrators to specify how pods within a Kubernetes cluster can communicate with each other and with other network entities. Within the context of Argo Workflows, applying network policies ensures that workflows execute in a controlled and secure manner, minimizing the attack surface and isolating components as needed.

This section explores the application of Kubernetes network policies within Argo Workflows, detailing their purpose, implementation, and best practices for securing network traffic.

Understanding Network Policies

Network policies in Kubernetes provide a way to control and secure traffic flows by defining rules that specify which types of traffic are allowed or denied. These rules can specify allowed ingress (incoming) and egress (outgoing) traffic for pods and are usually enforced by the networking plugin used by the Kubernetes cluster, such as Calico, Cilium, or Weave Net.

Network policies use labels to select pods and then define rules based on these selectors. These rules can include specifications for IP blocks,

9.4. NETWORK POLICIES AND ISOLATION

namespaces, and pod selectors, allowing for both broad and granular control over network traffic.

Defining Network Policies

Network policies are defined using Kubernetes resources typically outlined in a YAML file. Below is a simple example of a network policy that only allows traffic between pods that share the same namespace and have a specific label:

```
apiVersion: networking.k8s.io/v1
kind: NetworkPolicy
metadata:
  name: allow-same-namespace
  namespace: argo-workflows
spec:
  podSelector:
    matchLabels:
      app: argo
  policyTypes:
  - Ingress
  - Egress
  ingress:
  - from:
    - podSelector:
        matchLabels:
          app: argo
  egress:
  - to:
    - podSelector:
        matchLabels:
          app: argo
```

In this example, only pods labeled with `app: argo` are permitted to communicate with each other. This fosters a secure communication channel isolated within the namespace argo-workflows.

Applying Network Policies to Argo Workflows

When implementing network policies for Argo Workflows, consider the specific communication patterns required by your workflows. Frequently, workflows need to communicate with external services, databases, or other internal pods, which necessitates careful policy configuration to allow necessary traffic while denying intrusive access.

- **Isolate Workflow Execution Environments:**

  Segregating the network space of workflow execution minimizes the risk of sensitive data exposure and unauthorized access. Restrict Argo Workflow pods to communicate solely within their essential operational components, including internal microservices they depend on, using targeted network policies.

```
apiVersion: networking.k8s.io/v1
kind: NetworkPolicy
metadata:
  name: disallow-external-traffic
  namespace: argo-workflows
spec:
  podSelector:
    matchLabels:
      workflow: secure
  policyTypes:
  - Egress
  egress:
  - to:
    - ipBlock:
        cidr: 10.0.0.0/16
```

This policy prohibits these workflow pods from initiating traffic outside the 10.0.0.0/16 IP range.

- **Restrict Ingress Traffic:**

    Limiting ingress traffic to the Argo UI component is critical for safeguarding against unauthorized access and potential threats. Network policies provide a way to specify allowed ingress sources.

```
apiVersion: networking.k8s.io/v1
kind: NetworkPolicy
metadata:
  name: allow-ui-ingress
  namespace: argo-dashboard
spec:
  podSelector:
    matchLabels:
      component: argo-ui
  policyTypes:
  - Ingress
  ingress:
  - from:
    - namespaceSelector:
        matchLabels:
          argo-access: true
    - ipBlock:
        cidr: 192.168.100.0/24
    ports:
    - protocol: TCP
      port: 2746
```

This configuration allows ingress only from the trusted namespace marked argo-access: true and IP addresses within the specified CIDR block.

Best Practices for Network Isolation in Argo Workflows

- **Adopt Zero Trust Networking:**

    Embrace a Zero Trust model by defaulting to deny all network traffic, granting explicit access only as needed. This model reduces the risk vectors by assuming that every network component, whether inside or outside the network, poses a potential threat.

- **Use Namespace Segmentation:**

    Partition your Kubernetes environment into various namespaces to isolate components that have distinct access and security requirements. Apply namespace-level network policies to control inter-namespace communications.

- **Regularly Review and Update Policies:**

    Network policies should be periodically reviewed and updated to adapt to evolving application architectures, threats, and organization-specific requirements. Continuous monitoring helps detect anomalies and implement timely interventions.

- **Implement Monitoring and Logging:**

    Employ monitoring solutions like Prometheus in conjunction with Grafana and logging frameworks to track network activity across your Argo Workflows deployment. Such observability tools facilitate identifying unexpected traffic patterns and can improve incident response capabilities.

- **Decoupled Network Policy Management:**

    Ensure network policies are maintained separately from application configuration, enabling centralized policy management. This decoupling ensures that changes to network security policies can be applied without disrupting application lifecycle management.

Advanced Isolation Techniques

In complex Kubernetes environments, advanced network isolation techniques include the use of service meshes and encryption for intra-pod communication. Service meshes such as Istio provide an additional abstraction for managing network traffic, enforcing security policies, and offering robust observability features within and across clusters.

Moreover, implementing mTLS (Mutual TLS) ensures encrypted communication and authentication between services, adding an additional layer of security. By configuring a service mesh to control and encrypt traffic between services, Argo Workflows can benefit from enhanced network isolation without sacrificing performance and reliability.

Service meshes also facilitate advanced traffic control features such as load balancing, traffic shaping, and failure recovery strategies, which collectively enhance the resilience of workflow operations.

Network policies and isolation mechanisms are indispensable for securing Argo Workflows and maintaining a robust defensive posture in Kubernetes environments. By defining clear and effective network policies, organizations can safeguard their workflows from unauthorized access and data exfiltration, ensuring reliable and efficient operation of automated tasks.

Administrators are encouraged to continuously fine-tune the policies in place, leveraging the latest technological advancements to mitigate emergent threats and maximize the benefits afforded by Kubernetes' network configuration capabilities. With a comprehensive and proactive approach to network security, organizations can smoothly orchestrate sophisticated workflows, achieve seamless integration and secure interaction between diverse system components, while fortifying their cloud-native infrastructure against potential threats.

9.5 Best Practices for Workflow Design

Designing efficient and secure workflows in Argo Workflows not only enhances operational robustness but also minimizes security vulnerabilities inherent to distributed systems. This section aims to elucidate best practices in workflow design that can lead to improved performance, maintainability, and security. By adhering to these practices, DevOps and engineering teams can leverage the full capabilities of Argo Workflows within Kubernetes while ensuring scalability and reliability.

Modular Workflow Architecture

One of the foundational principles in designing workflows is adhering to modular architecture. Breaking down a complex workflow into smaller, reusable components or templates promotes better readability, easier troubleshooting, and maintenance. This componentization aligns with the microservices approach, allowing different segments of a workflow to be developed, tested, and scaled independently.

For instance, consider a workflow that processes data through a series of transformations. Instead of a single monolithic workflow, it can be divided into distinct steps, each handling a specific transformation:

```
apiVersion: argoproj.io/v1alpha1
kind: Workflow
metadata:
  generateName: modular-example-
spec:
  entrypoint: data-processing
  templates:
  - name: data-processing
    steps:
    - - name: fetch-data
        template: fetch
    - - name: transform-a
        template: transform
        arguments:
          parameters:
          - name: step
            value: "A"
    - - name: transform-b
        template: transform
        arguments:
          parameters:
          - name: step
            value: "B"
  - name: fetch
    container:
      image: busybox
      command: ["sh", "-c"]
      args: ["wget http://example.com/data"]
  - name: transform
    inputs:
      parameters:
      - name: step
    container:
      image: busybox
      command: ["sh", "-c"]
      args: ["echo Transform ${{inputs.parameters.step}} data"]
```

This structure also facilitates the reuse of components across multiple workflows, further optimizing development efforts and maintaining consistency.

Parameterization for Flexibility

Parameterization involves abstracting specifics of a workflow segment, allowing varied input values to be supplied when the workflow is executed. It increases the flexibility and reusability of workflows by enabling them to adapt dynamically based on input parameters without hardcoding specifics.

Within Argo Workflows, parameterization is achieved using the inputs.parameters under each template. Consider a workflow that processes files of different formats; parameterization could be used to handle the file type:

```
apiVersion: argoproj.io/v1alpha1
kind: Workflow
metadata:
  generateName: parameterized-example-
spec:
  entrypoint: file-processing
  arguments:
    parameters:
    - name: filetype
      value: csv
  templates:
  - name: file-processing
    inputs:
      parameters:
      - name: filetype
    container:
      image: busybox
      command: ["sh", "-c"]
      args: ["echo Processing ${{inputs.parameters.filetype}} file"]
```

Such parameterization is vital for enabling workflows to be triggered with differing input configurations, thus maximizing the workflow's utility and adaptability in differing scenarios.

Implementing Workflow Agility

Workflow agility refers to the capacity of workflows to be modified, interrupted, or resumed with minimal overhead, empowering teams to rapidly accommodate changes in business requirements or environmental conditions. This agility is often realized through careful design choices such as integrating workflow lifecycle hooks, which monitor

9.5. BEST PRACTICES FOR WORKFLOW DESIGN

the state of workflows and enable runtime adjustments.

Utilizing hooks in Argo Workflows can aid in better control and flexibility. Hooks can be implemented for various stages such as completion, success, or failure of a workflow. Here is an example of a lifecycle hook that sends notifications upon workflow completion:

```
apiVersion: argoproj.io/v1alpha1
kind: Workflow
metadata:
  generateName: hooks-example-
spec:
  entrypoint: main-steps
  hooks:
    exit:
      template: notify
  templates:
  - name: main-steps
    steps:
    - - name: execute-something
        template: exec
  - name: exec
    container:
      image: busybox
      command: ["sh", "-c"]
      args: ["echo Performing primary work"]
  - name: notify
    container:
      image: busybox
      command: ["sh", "-c"]
      args: ["echo Notification sent upon completion"]
```

These patterns make workflows resilient and adaptable, allowing new operation needs to be seamlessly integrated.

Ensuring Workflow Security

Security is an integrated concern that must be woven into the very fabric of workflow design. Some essential security practices include:

- **Minimize Privileges and Isolate Execution:** Design workflows to operate with the least privileged accounts and clearly map necessary permissions. Use namespaces, roles, and policies to enforce isolation and constraint access.

- **Secure Handling of Sensitive Data:** Employ environment variables, secrets management (e.g., Kubernetes Secrets, HashiCorp Vault), or other secure methods to manage sensitive data inputs, ensuring it is never embedded within workflow manifests.

- **Ingress and Egress Policies:** Network policies should be defined to control ingress and egress of data, further reducing the attack surfaces.

```
apiVersion: networking.k8s.io/v1
kind: NetworkPolicy
metadata:
  name: secure-egress
  namespace: argo-workflows
spec:
  podSelector:
    matchLabels:
      workflow: secure
  policyTypes:
  - Egress
  egress:
  - to:
    - ipBlock:
        cidr: 10.244.0.0/16
```

Robust Error Handling

Designing workflows to handle errors gracefully is crucial for maintaining operational continuity. This can be achieved via retry and timeout mechanisms, as well as incorporating specific tasks to handle failures and clean-up resources.

In Argo Workflows, retries can be specified at the template level. This retry mechanism helps prevent transient network or service failures from causing a workflow to fail entirely:

```
apiVersion: argoproj.io/v1alpha1
kind: Workflow
metadata:
  generateName: retry-example-
spec:
  entrypoint: fault-tolerant-step
  templates:
  - name: fault-tolerant-step
    retryStrategy:
      limit: 3
    container:
      image: busybox
      command: ["sh", "-c"]
      args: ["echo Attempt && false"]
```

Workflows should monitor exit statuses and employ conditional logic to branch execution paths upon encountering failures, thus facilitating intelligent recovery strategies.

Documentation and Testing

Comprehensive documentation is indispensable for workflow clarity and maintainability. Descriptive comments and metadata annotations can convey the purpose and functionality of workflow steps and templates.

Constant testing and validation of workflows within isolated environments ensure they behave as expected under various conditions. This can be achieved by maintaining a separate development namespace where changes are deployed and tested before moving to production.

Scalability Considerations

Workflow design must account for varying loads, especially in environments with unpredictable processing requirements. Implement concurrency controls via parallelism and resource quotas to optimize resource utilization. Use Kubernetes' native scaling features to adjust workflow execution environments in response to demand dynamics.

By adhering to these best practices for workflow design in Argo Workflows, organizations can create structures that are secure, scalable, and maintainable, providing a robust foundation for delivering diverse computational or business processes. Adopting workflow designs that anticipate change, while maintaining strict security and performance standards, ensures that organizational operations remain resilient and responsive to future innovation.

9.6 Audit Logging and Compliance

Audit logging is a critical component of system security and compliance, particularly in environments orchestrated by Kubernetes where tools like Argo Workflows operate. The significance of audit logging cannot be overstated, as it provides the means to track changes, identify security incidents, and ensure adherence to regulatory standards. This section discusses the principles and implementation of audit logging within Argo Workflows, detailing how logs can be leveraged for compliance and security purposes.

Purpose of Audit Logging

Audit logs are detailed records of events or activities within a system. In the context of Kubernetes and Argo Workflows, they document actions such as the creation, modification, and deletion of workflows, changes to permissions, and access to secrets. These logs serve various purposes:

- **Security Monitoring:** Audit logs help detect unauthorized access and anomalous behavior, alerting administrators to potential security threats.

- **Forensic Analysis:** In the event of a security incident, audit logs provide the data necessary to reconstruct actions and understand the implications.

- **Compliance Verification:** Many regulatory frameworks, such as GDPR, HIPAA, and FINRA, require organizations to maintain detailed logs of system activity. Audit logs support these compliance requirements by providing verifiable records of operations.

Configuring Audit Logging in Kubernetes

Kubernetes provides a built-in audit logging feature that captures requests reaching the API server. To start using audit logging, configure the API server by specifying an audit policy and log destinations.

Audit Policy Specification

An audit policy file defines how different requests are logged based on their attributes. Below is a sample audit policy configuration:

```
apiVersion: audit.k8s.io/v1
kind: Policy
rules:
- level: Metadata
  namespaces:
  - argo-workflows
  resources:
  - group: "argoproj.io"
    resources: ["workflows"]
    verbs: ["create", "update", "delete"]
- level: RequestResponse
  resources:
  - group: "core"
    resources: ["pods", "configmaps"]
    verbs: ["get", "list"]
  omitStages:
  - "RequestReceived"
```

Levels of Logging:

9.6. AUDIT LOGGING AND COMPLIANCE

- **None:** No logs are recorded.
- **Metadata:** Includes information such as the operation type, user, resource, and timestamp.
- **Request:** Captures metadata and the request body.
- **RequestResponse:** Logs metadata, request, and response bodies.

The choice of logging level depends on the necessary balance between resource consumption and the detail required for compliance and security monitoring.

Enabling and Managing Audit Logs

To enable audit logging, include the '–audit-policy-file' and '–audit-log-path' flags in the API server configuration:

```
--audit-policy-file=/etc/kubernetes/audit-policy.yaml
--audit-log-path=/var/log/kubernetes/audit.log
```

Consider using a structured log management solution such as Elasticsearch, Fluentd, and Kibana (EFK) stack or Prometheus to efficiently store, query, and visualize logs. These tools facilitate advanced log analysis and can be configured to generate alerts for predefined anomaly patterns.

```
output.elasticsearch:
  hosts: ["http://elasticsearch.example.com:9200"]
output.logstash:
  hosts: ["localhost:5044"]
```

Integrating Argo Workflows with Audit Logging

In Argo Workflows, audit logging extends to capturing the lifecycle events of workflows, including submission, execution, and results. The integration allows for comprehensive insights into workflow operations and adherence to data governance policies.

Instrumentation for Detailed Logging

Argo Workflows can be equipped with custom logging outputs for each task. Using workflow annotations and log customization, users can consolidate logs related to specific workflow executions, facilitating detailed audit trails:

```yaml
apiVersion: argoproj.io/v1alpha1
kind: Workflow
metadata:
  annotations:
    logging.compliance.enabled: "true"
  generateName: audit-log-example-
spec:
  entrypoint: log-task
  templates:
  - name: log-task
    container:
      image: busybox
      command: ["sh", "-c"]
      args: ["echo Task execution details"]
```

Custom logging mechanisms can categorize and output logs relevant for compliance, storing them externally for easier aggregation and analysis.

Multi-Tenancy and Segregation

When deploying Argo Workflows in a multi-tenant environment, ensuring audit logs are segregated and tenant-awareness is crucial. Use namespace-specific logging routes or tagged identifiers that align with tenant boundaries in your logging solution to maintain isolation and data integrity.

Audit Trails for Compliance

Audit trails are indispensable for compliance audits, offering a chronological record of actions performed on workflows. This includes user identification, permissions, and timestamps, among others.

Regulatory frameworks frequently mandate that organizations maintain comprehensive audit trails corresponding to all operations that touch on sensitive data. In alignment with standards, organizations must ensure that logs not only persist but are protected against tampering and unauthorized access. To achieve this, employ:

- **Immutable Logs:** Implement technical controls for immutable logs that cannot be altered post-creation, ensuring log integrity. Solutions include append-only log stores or signed log hashes which can be verified independently.

- **Data Anonymization and Redaction:** Ensure sensitive personal data is anonymized or redacted within logs, especially when

9.6. AUDIT LOGGING AND COMPLIANCE

handling sensitive information protected by privacy laws.

- **Retention Policies:** Establish policies for log retention that abide by regulatory timelines. Time-box log retention reduces storage overhead while complying with standards.

- **Regular Integrity Verification:** Scheduled cryptographic verification of log integrity preserves non-repudiability.

Efficient Log Management

Efficiency and scalability in log management are paramount when operating at cloud and enterprise scales. Consider adopting centralized log aggregation and visualization platforms that allow for data normalization, deduplication, and correlation:

- Implement tagging and structured formats (e.g., JSON) to accommodate machine parsing and query optimizations.

- Use indexing and partitioning strategies to hasten query performance when dealing with large datasets.

- Deploy analysis tools that leverage machine learning to identify correlations and detect anomalies autonomously from the log data.

Alerting and Real-Time Monitoring

Real-time monitoring and alerting are crucial for proactive security postures and immediate response to suspicious events. Integrate systems such as Prometheus Alertmanager or Elastic's Alerting feature to define alert rules that trigger notifications or automations based on log analysis. For instance:

Set up an alert for unexpected workflow termination:

```
alert:
  conditions:
    - type: Workflow
      condition: "status.phase == Failed"
  actions:
    - type: "email"
      email:
        to: "security-team@example.com"
        subject: "Argo Workflow Failure Alert"
        body: "A workflow has unexpectedly failed and requires attention."
```

By thoroughly understanding audit logging and its significance beyond compliance into proactive security, organizations can ensure that their Argo Workflows remain robust against threats and aligned with operational and regulatory policies. Audit logs are not merely records of history; they are actionable insights when managed effectively, influencing decisions and enhancing an organization's ability to achieve secure and reliable automated operations.

9.7 Securing Data in Transit and at Rest

Data security is a crucial consideration in any system, particularly within cloud-native environments like Kubernetes where Argo Workflows operate. Securing data in transit and at rest helps protect sensitive information from unauthorized access and breaches, ensuring data integrity, confidentiality, and compliance with regulations. This section elaborates on strategies and best practices for securing data across its lifecycle in Argo Workflows, with a detailed focus on encryption techniques and access controls.

Understanding Data Security Requirements

Data security involves protecting data both as it moves through the system (in transit) and when stored (at rest):

- **Data in Transit:** Refers to any data actively moving from one location to another, such as across the internet or through a private network. Secure transport protocols are necessary to prevent interception and ensure the confidentiality and integrity of data.

- **Data at Rest:** Refers to inactive data stored on any device, whether records in a database, files within a storage system, or data backups. Encryption and stringent access controls prevent unauthorized access in this state.

Securing Data in Transit

TLS (Transport Layer Security) is the standard protocol for encrypting data traveling over the network, providing security against eavesdropping and tampering. To secure data in transit within Kubernetes and

9.7. SECURING DATA IN TRANSIT AND AT REST

Argo Workflows, you must ensure TLS is enabled for all inter-service communication:

- **Enable TLS for Service Communications:**

    Configure encryption for services by enabling TLS on ingress and internal services, ensuring that data moving through the network carries encryption headers. Consider the following Kubernetes Ingress configuration for TLS:

    ```
    apiVersion: networking.k8s.io/v1
    kind: Ingress
    metadata:
      name: argo-ingress
      annotations:
        nginx.ingress.kubernetes.io/force-ssl-redirect: "true"
    spec:
      tls:
      - hosts:
        - argo.example.com
        secretName: argo-tls-secret
      rules:
      - host: argo.example.com
        http:
          paths:
          - path: /
            backend:
              serviceName: argo-service
              servicePort: 443
    ```

    This configuration uses a pre-provisioned TLS secret to establish secure connections.

- **Mutual TLS (mTLS):**

    Implement mTLS for internal pod-to-pod communications, enhancing security by requiring both the client and server to authenticate each other. This verification helps prevent man-in-the-middle attacks within the Kubernetes network.

    Service meshes like Istio can automate mTLS configurations, making it manageable without extensive overhead. When configured, Istio injects sidecars that handle encryption between services transparently:

    ```
    apiVersion: security.istio.io/v1beta1
    kind: PeerAuthentication
    metadata:
      name: strict-mtls
      namespace: argo
    ```

```
spec:
  mtls:
    mode: STRICT
```

- **Encrypting Secrets and Configurations:**

    Use Kubernetes Secrets and ConfigMaps with caution. Employ TLS while transferring any sensitive data within Secrets for secure transport over the network. For enhanced management, deploy tools like SecrecyOperator or SOPS to encrypt Secrets further.

Securing Data at Rest

Ensuring data security at rest involves data encryption and access control mechanisms that protect stored data from unauthorized access and modifications.

- **Encryption with Storage Solutions:**

    Integrate persistent storage solutions with Kubernetes that support data encryption at rest. Use encryption features provided by cloud services like AWS EBS, GCP Persistent Disks, or Azure Disk Storage, and enable them as part of your storage class definitions:

    ```
    apiVersion: storage.k8s.io/v1
    kind: StorageClass
    metadata:
      name: secure-storage-class
    provisioner: kubernetes.io/aws-ebs
    parameters:
      encrypted: "true"
      kmsKeyId: "arn:aws:kms:region:account-id:key/key-id"
    ```

    Integrating with cloud-native encryption services reduces overhead by automatically managing encryption keys and lifecycle.

- **Database Encryption:**

    If your workflows interact with databases, activate both column-level and tablespace encryption using DBMS native capabilities. Moreover, using TDE (Transparent Data Encryption) ensures that DBAs and unauthorized users can't read the data without decrypting it first.

9.7. SECURING DATA IN TRANSIT AND AT REST

- **Secrets Management:**

  Employ dedicated secret management systems such as HashiCorp Vault for encryption and access policy management. Vault enables dynamic secrets, automatic expiration, and manages revocation, substantially increasing the level of security and control over confidential information.

  Configuration of dynamic secret engine with database access may look as follows:

  ```
  vault secrets enable database
  vault write database/config/my-db \
      plugin_name=mysql-database-plugin \
      connection_url="{{username}}:{{password}}@tcp(mydb:3306)/" \
      allowed_roles="db-roles"
  ```

- **Encryption Key Management:** Ensure robust key management practices, including key rotation, loss prevention, and secure storage, using HSMs (Hardware Security Modules) or cloud KMS services for enhanced security.

Implementing Access Controls

Restricting access to sensitive data is as crucial as encryption. Access restrictions should be enforced contextually, ensuring only authorized users and applications can access the data:

- **Role-Based Access Control (RBAC):**

  Implement RBAC rigorously for workflows, ensuring that different roles have distinct permissions set according to their needs:

  ```
  apiVersion: rbac.authorization.k8s.io/v1
  kind: Role
  metadata:
    namespace: argo-secure
    name: read-secrets
  rules:
  - apiGroups: [""]
    resources: ["secrets"]
    verbs: ["get"]
  ```

- **Network Policies:**

  Utilize network policies to restrict pod communication, allowing only necessary traffic to and from pods that manage or process sensitive data, thereby reducing exposure to potential attackers.

- **Auditing Access:**
  Maintain extensive logging and auditing of all access requests to sensitive data, leveraging tools like Prometheus, Fluentd, and Elasticsearch to analyze usage patterns and detect anomalies.

Compliance Considerations

Data protection laws (GDPR, CCPA, HIPAA, etc.) mandate strict control over how sensitive data is handled, stored, and transferred:

- Ensure encryption techniques are compliant with relevant standards (e.g., AES-256, RSA-2048).

- Use geo-location policies to ensure data does not transit through regions with less stringent data protection laws.

- Regular audits and compliance checks should verify adherence to policies and controls, ensuring readiness for external audits.

By thoroughly understanding and implementing encrypted communications and stringent controls for both data in transit and at rest, Argo Workflows can operate in a secure manner, meeting high security and compliance standards. Through such protections, organizations are better equipped to defend against breaches, ensuring the maintenance of their customers' trust and service integrity.

Chapter 10

Real-World Use Cases and Examples

This chapter showcases practical applications of Argo Workflows through real-world use cases across various industries. It illustrates how workflows can be utilized for data processing and ETL pipelines, highlighting each phase of data transformation. Readers will explore examples such as orchestrating machine learning model training, managing microservices, and facilitating continuous deployment in production settings. The chapter also demonstrates the automation of compliance and auditing tasks, efficient batch processing, and the management of real-time data streaming pipelines, providing comprehensive insights into the implementation of Argo Workflows in dynamic and complex scenarios.

10.1 Data Processing and ETL Pipelines

In modern data-driven enterprises, the extraction, transformation, and loading (ETL) processes are essential to converting raw data into valuable insights. Argo Workflows provides a robust framework for orchestrating complex data processing pipelines, leveraging declarative configuration and comprehensive orchestration capabilities to enable seamless automation of ETL tasks. In this section, we will explore a sophisticated example that demonstrates the practical application of Argo Workflows in automating and managing data processing and ETL pipelines, detailing each stage of the workflow and highlighting the benefits of using Argo.

The ETL process broadly involves three critical stages: data extraction, data transformation, and data loading. Each step requires meticulous handling to ensure data integrity and optimal performance. Argo Workflows excels in coordinating these stages by providing a structured workflow, where each task is encapsulated in a containerized format, ensuring compatibility across diverse computing environments.

Data Extraction:

Data extraction is the initial phase of the ETL process, where data is sourced from various origins such as databases, cloud storage, application programming interfaces (APIs), or flat files. The goal is to gather relevant data for further processing. Argo Workflows facilitates the automation of this phase by managing data extraction tasks concurrently, ensuring rapid data accumulation from multiple sources.

To illustrate, consider an e-commerce platform that needs to collect sales data from multiple regional databases for centralized analysis. Utilizing Argo, each extraction task can query a database and export data to a common storage location, such as an Amazon S3 bucket.

```
apiVersion: argoproj.io/v1alpha1
kind: Workflow
metadata:
  generateName: data-extraction-
spec:
  entrypoint: extract-dag
  templates:
    - name: extract-dag
      dag:
        tasks:
          - name: extract-region1
            template: extract
            arguments:
              parameters: [{name: "region", value: "region1"}]
          - name: extract-region2
            template: extract
            arguments:
              parameters: [{name: "region", value: "region2"}]
```

10.1. DATA PROCESSING AND ETL PIPELINES

```yaml
- name: extract
  inputs:
    parameters:
      - name: region
  container:
    image: python:3.8
    command: [sh, -c]
    args: ["python extract_data.py --region {{inputs.parameters.region}}"]
```

In this YAML configuration, the workflow is defined with a Directed Acyclic Graph (DAG) structure, specifying tasks for data extraction from different regions. The use of parameters facilitates task customization, allowing the same 'extract' template to be reused for multiple regions.

Data Transformation:

Once data is extracted, it enters the transformation phase, in which it is cleansed, enriched, and structured to meet organizational requirements. This phase may involve procedures such as filtering out duplicates, normalizing data formats, and aggregating information across datasets.

Argo Workflows can integrate with data transformation tools like Apache Spark or pandas running within containers. By enabling intricate dependency management and condition-based task execution, Argo ensures that transformation tasks are executed in the correct sequence and only when prerequisite data is available.

```yaml
apiVersion: argoproj.io/v1alpha1
kind: Workflow
metadata:
  generateName: data-transformation-
spec:
  entrypoint: transform-dag
  templates:
    - name: transform-dag
      dag:
        tasks:
          - name: clean-data
            template: spark-transform
            dependencies: [extract-region1, extract-region2]
          - name: aggregate-data
            template: pandas-transform
            dependencies: [clean-data]

    - name: spark-transform
      container:
        image: spark:latest
        command: [sh, -c]
        args: ["spark-submit --class com.example.TransformJob transform_job.jar"]
```

```
- name: pandas-transform
  container:
    image: python:3.8
    command: [sh, -c]
    args: ["python transform_script.py"]
```

This segment showcases a two-step transformation sequence where 'spark-transform' cleans the extracted data and 'pandas-transform' performs subsequent data aggregation. The dependencies ensure tasks are executed in an orderly fashion, only commencing when the required tasks are complete.

Data Loading:

The final stage of the ETL process is loading the transformed data into a target data warehouse, database, or analytics tool, such as Amazon Redshift, Google BigQuery, or a custom SQL server. The loading phase is critical for ensuring that transformed data is accessible for business intelligence and analytical tasks.

Argo Workflows can efficiently handle data loading operations, coordinating the logistics of moving large volumes of data into a target system while maintaining performance and reliability.

```
apiVersion: argoproj.io/v1alpha1
kind: Workflow
metadata:
  generateName: data-loading-
spec:
  entrypoint: load-dag
  templates:
    - name: load-dag
      dag:
        tasks:
          - name: load-to-warehouse
            template: load
            dependencies: [aggregate-data]

    - name: load
      container:
        image: mysql:latest
        command: [sh, -c]
        args: ["python load_to_db.py"]
```

In this configuration, the 'load-to-warehouse' task initiates once the data aggregation is complete. Implementing Argo in this manner ensures seamless data ingestion with minimal manual intervention.

10.1. DATA PROCESSING AND ETL PIPELINES

Benefits of Using Argo Workflows for ETL:

The deployment of Argo Workflows in orchestrating ETL pipelines presents several advantages:

- **Scalability:** Argo Workflows excels in scaling operations across multiple environments, handling large datasets with ease, and allowing dynamic scaling of computational resources as needed.

- **Reusability:** Declarative YAML configurations and templated tasks promote reusability across different pipeline implementations, reducing development time and promoting consistency.

- **Resilience and Fault Tolerance:** By leveraging Argo's DAG execution model, ETL jobs can gracefully handle failures, retrying task executions while maintaining data integrity.

- **Visibility and Monitoring:** Argo provides real-time workflow execution visibility through its web user interface, allowing for effective monitoring and troubleshooting.

- **Containerization:** The use of container images for each task ensures compatibility across various platforms and environments, leveraging the flexibility and isolation provided by container technology.

The integration of Argo Workflows with ETL processes significantly optimizes resource utilization, reducing operational costs while enhancing the agility and responsiveness of data-driven decisions. Furthermore, as data landscapes evolve, Argo's flexible architecture accommodates emerging data sources and transformation tools, providing a future-proof solution for modern ETL pipelines.

By employing Argo Workflows in data processing and ETL routines, organizations gain the ability to swiftly adapt to changing data needs and maintain a competitive edge in an increasingly data-centric marketplace. This robust orchestration framework not only supports current data initiatives but also sets the foundation for future scalability and innovation, making it an indispensable tool in the toolkit of data professionals.

10.2 Machine Learning Model Training

Machine learning (ML) has become an integral part of many business processes, powering applications from predictive analytics to autonomous systems. The process of training a machine learning model involves a series of interdependent tasks, including data preparation, model training, hyperparameter tuning, and evaluation. Argo Workflows can automate and orchestrate these tasks, providing a structured and efficient means to manage the complexity inherent in machine learning pipelines. This section delves into how Argo Workflows can facilitate the orchestration of machine learning model training, incorporating each vital task into a cohesive workflow.

The machine learning model training pipeline can be broadly outlined in the following phases: data preparation, model training, hyperparameter optimization, and model evaluation. Each phase not only requires computational resources but also meticulous coordination to ensure the integrity and performance of the resultant models.

Data Preparation:

The foundation of successful machine learning is robust data preparation. This phase involves aggregating, cleaning, and preprocessing raw data into a format suitable for model training. Argo Workflows can coordinate data retrieval from multiple sources, ensure data quality through cleaning processes, and split datasets into training, validation, and test datasets.

For example, consider a scenario where we need to train a model on customer purchase data stored across various data silos. Argo Workflows can orchestrate the extraction and preprocessing tasks as illustrated in the following YAML configuration:

```yaml
apiVersion: argoproj.io/v1alpha1
kind: Workflow
metadata:
  generateName: data-preparation-
spec:
  entrypoint: prepare-data
  templates:
    - name: prepare-data
      dag:
        tasks:
          - name: fetch-dataset
            template: fetch
```

10.2. MACHINE LEARNING MODEL TRAINING

```
        - name: clean-dataset
          template: clean
          dependencies: [fetch-dataset]
        - name: split-dataset
          template: split
          dependencies: [clean-dataset]

  - name: fetch
    container:
      image: python:3.8
      command: [sh, -c]
      args: ["python fetch_data.py"]

  - name: clean
    container:
      image: python:3.8
      command: [sh, -c]
      args: ["python clean_data.py"]

  - name: split
    container:
      image: python:3.8
      command: [sh, -c]
      args: ["python split_data.py"]
```

This workflow fetches the dataset, cleans it by removing anomalies and inconsistencies, and subsequently splits it into subsets (training, validation, and test sets), setting the stage for model training.

Model Training:

Model training is the core phase where algorithms learn patterns from data. The selection of algorithms and architectures is crucial, depending on the problem context. Argo Workflows can parallelize model training experiments, support various frameworks such as TensorFlow and PyTorch, and streamline the integration of pre-trained models for transfer learning.

```
apiVersion: argoproj.io/v1alpha1
kind: Workflow
metadata:
  generateName: train-model-
spec:
  entrypoint: train-dag
  templates:
    - name: train-dag
      dag:
        tasks:
          - name: train-logistic-regression
            template: train
            arguments:
              parameters: [{name: "model-type", value: "logistic\_regression"}]
          - name: train-neural-network
```

```
            template: train
            arguments:
                parameters: [{name: "model-type", value: "neural\_network"}]
  - name: train
    inputs:
      parameters:
        - name: model-type
    container:
      image: python:3.8
      command: [sh, -c]
      args: ["python train_model.py --model {{inputs.parameters.model-type}}"]
```

Here, the workflow initiates parallel training of two distinct models: a logistic regression model and a neural network model. Each training task utilizes a separate container, encapsulating the dependencies and execution environment necessary for the respective model.

Hyperparameter Optimization:

Optimal hyperparameter settings significantly impact the performance of machine learning models. Argo Workflows supports orchestrating hyperparameter tuning processes, employing techniques like grid search or Bayesian optimization to systematically explore parameter spaces.

```
apiVersion: argoproj.io/v1alpha1
kind: Workflow
metadata:
  generateName: hyperparameter-tuning-
spec:
  entrypoint: tune-dag
  templates:
    - name: tune-dag
      steps:
        - - name: grid-search-param
            template: grid-search

    - name: grid-search
      container:
        image: python:3.8
        command: [sh, -c]
        args: ["python grid_search.py"]
```

This example configures a grid search to identify the best hyperparameter combination. The search iterates over a predefined parameter grid, evaluating each configuration to identify optimal settings that enhance model performance.

Model Evaluation:

10.2. MACHINE LEARNING MODEL TRAINING

The final evaluation phase assesses the model's performance using metrics pertinent to the specific application context. This phase may include accuracy, precision, recall, F1-score, or others, depending on whether it is a classification or regression problem. Argo Workflows can automate the evaluation of multiple models, facilitating a comparative analysis to select the best model for production deployment.

```
apiVersion: argoproj.io/v1alpha1
kind: Workflow
metadata:
  generateName: model-evaluation-
spec:
  entrypoint: evaluate-dag
  templates:
    - name: evaluate-dag
      dag:
        tasks:
          - name: evaluate-logistic-regression
            template: evaluate
            arguments:
              parameters: [{name: "model-type", value: "logistic\_regression"}]
            dependencies: [train-logistic-regression]
          - name: evaluate-neural-network
            template: evaluate
            arguments:
              parameters: [{name: "model-type", value: "neural\_network"}]
            dependencies: [train-neural-network]

    - name: evaluate
      inputs:
        parameters:
          - name: model-type
      container:
        image: python:3.8
        command: [sh, -c]
        args: ["python evaluate_model.py --model {{inputs.parameters.model-type}}"]
```

After training, each model undergoes an evaluation process. The results guide the selection of the most proficient model based on predefined performance criteria.

Benefits of Using Argo Workflows in ML Pipelines:

Deploying Argo Workflows in the orchestration of machine learning training pipelines introduces several advantages:

- **Automation:** Reduces manual effort by automating repetitive tasks, ensuring consistency in pipeline execution and boosting productivity.
- **Parallelism:** Enhances experiment throughput by paralleliz-

ing model training and evaluation tasks, accelerating time-to-insight.

- **Flexibility:** Allows dynamic execution of complex workflows, adapting to various model types, data formats, and computing environments.

- **Reproducibility:** Facilitates reproducible research through declarative workflow definitions, preserving the exact configurations for future iterations.

- **Scalability:** Leverages cloud-native infrastructure to scale pipelines according to data size and computational intensity, optimizing resource utilization.

Argo Workflow's integration with machine learning processes is pivotal for scaling AI initiatives across organizations. By managing model training workflows efficiently, Argo drives innovation and speeds up the transformation of ideas into actionable business outcomes. This synergy between workflow orchestration and machine learning underpins the advancement of intelligent systems and broadens the horizon for data science and artificial intelligence applications.

10.3 Microservices and Serverless Orchestration

The rise of microservices and serverless architectures has revolutionized the way applications are designed, built, and deployed. These architectural paradigms enhance modularity, scalability, and resource efficiency, allowing developers to focus on specific functionalities encapsulated within services. However, orchestrating numerous independent services to work seamlessly as a cohesive application poses significant challenges. Argo Workflows provides a comprehensive framework to address these challenges, enabling streamlined orchestration of microservices and serverless functions.

Microservices are independently deployable services, each responsible for a specific business capability, often communicating through

10.3. MICROSERVICES AND SERVERLESS ORCHESTRATION

lightweight protocols such as HTTP or message queues. Meanwhile, serverless functions (also known as Functions as a Service, FaaS) abstract away infrastructure management, allowing developers to write and execute code without provisioning servers. Both architectures support highly distributed systems, but orchestration is essential to manage their interactions effectively.

Microservices Orchestration:

Orchestrating microservices involves managing service interactions to ensure communication flow aligns with business logic. Argo Workflows can be employed to manage these interactions through task dependencies and event triggers, enabling complex workflows that span multiple services.

Consider a hypothetical e-commerce application comprising services like order processing, payment handling, inventory management, and shipping. Using Argo Workflows, a typical order processing workflow might be configured as follows:

```
apiVersion: argoproj.io/v1alpha1
kind: Workflow
metadata:
  generateName: microservice-orchestration-
spec:
  entrypoint: order-process
  templates:
    - name: order-process
      dag:
        tasks:
          - name: create-order
            template: http
            arguments:
              parameters: [{name: "service-url", value: "http://order-service/create"}]
          - name: process-payment
            template: http
            dependencies: [create-order]
            arguments:
              parameters: [{name: "service-url", value: "http://payment-service/process"}]
          - name: update-inventory
            template: http
            dependencies: [process-payment]
            arguments:
              parameters: [{name: "service-url", value: "http://inventory-service/update"}]
          - name: arrange-shipment
            template: http
            dependencies: [update-inventory]
            arguments:
              parameters: [{name: "service-url", value: "http://shipping-service/arrange"}]
```

```
- name: http
  inputs:
    parameters:
      - name: service-url
  container:
    image: curlimages/curl
    command: [sh, -c]
    args: ["curl -X POST {{inputs.parameters.service-url}}"]
```

In this workflow, the orchestration begins by creating an order, processes payment, updates inventory levels, and finally arranges shipment. Each task is a call to a separate microservice endpoint, leveraging HTTP through the 'curl' command in a containerized execution environment.

Serverless Orchestration:

Serverless functions allow for fine-grained task execution, where each function can be seen as an event-driven microservice. Orchestrating these functions ensures that business processes are executed in sequence or concurrently as needed, with Argo Workflows providing the necessary infrastructure for dependency management and error handling.

Let's consider the same e-commerce application transformed into a serverless model. Each function corresponds to a step in the order lifecycle, capable of scaling dynamically based on demand. An Argo workflow to orchestrate these functions follows a similar pattern to microservices:

```
apiVersion: argoproj.io/v1alpha1
kind: Workflow
metadata:
  generateName: serverless-orchestration-
spec:
  entrypoint: serverless-order
  templates:
    - name: serverless-order
      dag:
        tasks:
          - name: invoke-create-order
            template: aws-lambda
            arguments:
              parameters: [{name: "function", value: "createOrder"}]
          - name: invoke-process-payment
            template: aws-lambda
            dependencies: [invoke-create-order]
            arguments:
              parameters: [{name: "function", value: "processPayment"}]
```

10.3. MICROSERVICES AND SERVERLESS ORCHESTRATION

```
    - name: invoke-update-inventory
      template: aws-lambda
      dependencies: [invoke-process-payment]
      arguments:
        parameters: [{name: "function", value: "updateInventory"}]
    - name: invoke-arrange-shipment
      template: aws-lambda
      dependencies: [invoke-update-inventory]
      arguments:
        parameters: [{name: "function", value: "arrangeShipment"}]

 - name: aws-lambda
   inputs:
     parameters:
       - name: function
   container:
     image: amazon/aws-cli
     command: [sh, -c]
     args: ["aws lambda invoke --function-name {{inputs.parameters.function}}
            result.json && cat result.json"]
```

This workflow uses Amazon Web Services (AWS) Lambda to execute serverless functions. Each function call is managed as an independent task, facilitating clear and manageable orchestration of an otherwise complex set of interdependencies.

Handling Communication and State:

One critical challenge in orchestrating microservices and serverless functions is managing communication and maintaining state. Statelessness is a hallmark of these architectures, prompting the need for external systems (like databases or message queues) to maintain state across workflow executions.

Argo Workflows, through its DAG model, inherently supports the management of state across tasks. Furthermore, using centralized data stores, such as Redis or Amazon DynamoDB, can facilitate data sharing and state management efficiently.

For example, using a Redis container to handle temporary state storage might be implemented as follows:

```
apiVersion: argoproj.io/v1alpha1
kind: Workflow
metadata:
  generateName: stateful-orchestration-
spec:
  entrypoint: redis-workflow
  templates:
    - name: redis-workflow
      dag:
```

```
    tasks:
      - name: set-state
        template: redis-set
      - name: get-state
        template: redis-get
        dependencies: [set-state]
- name: redis-set
  container:
    image: redis
    command: [sh, -c]
    args: ["redis-cli SET workflow_state completed"]
- name: redis-get
  container:
    image: redis
    command: [sh, -c]
    args: ["redis-cli GET workflow_state"]
```

In this example, a Redis service acts as a temporary state repository, capable of storing and retrieving workflow state across executions.

Benefits of Argo Workflows in Orchestrating Microservices and Serverless:

- **Simplified Management:** Provides a high-level abstraction over complex interactions, reducing the cognitive load associated with managing distributed service communication.

- **Concurrency Control:** Manages parallelism and concurrency effectively, enabling tasks to run in parallel or sequentially based on defined dependencies.

- **Resilience and Recovery:** Ensures seamless recovery from failures through retry policies and detailed failure logs, maximizing uptime and reliability.

- **Scalability:** Leverages Kubernetes' native scalability, allowing workflows to automatically adapt to fluctuating loads.

- **Decoupled Architecture:** Promotes decoupled, event-driven design principles, leading to highly maintainable and adaptable systems.

By leveraging Argo Workflows, organizations can efficiently orchestrate microservices and serverless applications, ensuring robust service coordination and superior process execution. This agility is instrumental as enterprises continue to evolve their cloud-native approaches, driving competitive advantages through iterative delivery cycles and rapid adaptation to market demands.

The adoption of Argo Workflows in microservices and serverless architectures exemplifies next-generation IT operations, standing at the forefront of digital transformation by facilitating fine-tuned orchestration and empowering teams to build scalable, resilient, and responsive systems.

10.4 Continuous Deployment in Production

Continuous Deployment (CD) is a crucial aspect of modern DevOps practices, where code changes are automatically built, tested, and deployed to production environments. This practice ensures that software can be delivered frequently and reliably, reducing time to market and enhancing product quality. Argo Workflows provides a robust framework to facilitate continuous deployment, offering capabilities that integrate seamlessly with existing CI/CD pipelines, thereby automating code delivery and infrastructure changes in production environments.

CD in production is a complex process that involves multiple stages, including code integration, automated testing, containerization, deployment, and monitoring. Each stage requires careful orchestration to ensure smooth operations without human intervention. Argo Workflows excels at managing these stages through its comprehensive orchestration and automation capabilities.

- **Code Integration and Automated Testing:**

In a continuous deployment pipeline, code changes are frequently merged from feature branches into the main branch. Automated testing is crucial to ensure code quality and functionality before deployment. Argo Workflows can automate this process by integrating with

Continuous Integration (CI) tools like Jenkins or GitHub Actions to trigger workflows upon changes in the code repository.

For instance, the following YAML configuration demonstrates a workflow that runs unit tests and integration tests every time there is a code change:

```yaml
apiVersion: argoproj.io/v1alpha1
kind: Workflow
metadata:
  generateName: code-integration-
spec:
  entrypoint: test-dag
  templates:
    - name: test-dag
      dag:
        tasks:
          - name: run-unit-tests
            template: unittest
          - name: run-integration-tests
            template: integrationtest
            dependencies: [run-unit-tests]

    - name: unittest
      container:
        image: maven:3.6.3-jdk-8
        command: [sh, -c]
        args: ["mvn test"]

    - name: integrationtest
      container:
        image: maven:3.6.3-jdk-8
        command: [sh, -c]
        args: ["mvn verify"]
```

This workflow first executes unit tests using a Docker container running Maven and JDK, ensuring code correctness. Once unit tests pass, integration tests verify that components work together as expected.

- **Containerization and Deployment:**

After successful testing, the application is packaged into containers for consistent deployment across various environments. Containerization provides an isolated environment for applications, ensuring that they run the same way regardless of where they are deployed.

Argo Workflows can automate the build and deployment of containers using tools like Docker and Kubernetes. The following YAML configuration illustrates a workflow that builds a Docker image and deploys it to a Kubernetes cluster:

10.4. CONTINUOUS DEPLOYMENT IN PRODUCTION

```
apiVersion: argoproj.io/v1alpha1
kind: Workflow
metadata:
  generateName: deploy-container-
spec:
  entrypoint: deploy-dag
  templates:
  - name: deploy-dag
    dag:
      tasks:
        - name: build-docker-image
          template: docker-build
        - name: deploy-to-kubernetes
          template: kubernetes-deploy
          dependencies: [build-docker-image]

  - name: docker-build
    container:
      image: docker:19.03.8
      command: [sh, -c]
      args: ["docker build -t myapp:latest ."]

  - name: kubernetes-deploy
    container:
      image: bitnami/kubectl:1.18
      command: [sh, -c]
      args: ["kubectl apply -f deployment.yaml"]
```

This workflow builds the Docker image using a Docker container, ensuring that the application is consistently packaged. It then uses 'kubectl' to apply a deployment configuration to the Kubernetes cluster, facilitating the release to production.

- **Infrastructure as Code and Configuration Management:**

Infrastructure as Code (IaC) is a key practice in managing and provisioning infrastructure through code, promoting reproducibility and reducing configuration drift. Configuration management involves defining and maintaining consistent environments across development, testing, and production.

Argo Workflows can orchestrate IaC tools such as Terraform or Ansible to ensure infrastructure is provisioned and managed as part of the deployment pipeline. The following example demonstrates using Argo to apply Terraform configurations:

```
apiVersion: argoproj.io/v1alpha1
kind: Workflow
```

317

```yaml
metadata:
  generateName: iac-terraform-
spec:
  entrypoint: terraform-dag
  templates:
    - name: terraform-dag
      dag:
        tasks:
          - name: plan-infrastructure
            template: terraform-plan
          - name: apply-infrastructure
            template: terraform-apply
            dependencies: [plan-infrastructure]

    - name: terraform-plan
      container:
        image: hashicorp/terraform:latest
        command: [sh, -c]
        args: ["terraform init && terraform plan"]

    - name: terraform-apply
      container:
        image: hashicorp/terraform:latest
        command: [sh, -c]
        args: ["terraform apply --auto-approve"]
```

In this workflow, Terraform is used to plan and apply infrastructure changes. This ensures that infrastructure is version-controlled and changes are traceable, supporting robust production environments.

- **Monitoring, Logging, and Rollbacks:**

Continuous monitoring and logging are imperative for maintaining application health and diagnosing issues. Argo Workflows can trigger monitoring tools and alerting mechanisms, ensuring prompt detection of anomalies in production. Rollbacks provide a safety net, allowing applications to revert to previous stable states in case of failure.

Using Prometheus and Grafana for monitoring and Fluentd for logging are common practices. Argo can integrate with these tools to initiate automated rollbacks if metrics indicate a malfunction post-deployment.

```yaml
apiVersion: argoproj.io/v1alpha1
kind: Workflow
metadata:
  generateName: monitoring-rollback-
spec:
  entrypoint: monitor-rollback-dag
  templates:
```

10.4. CONTINUOUS DEPLOYMENT IN PRODUCTION

```yaml
- name: monitor-rollback-dag
  dag:
    tasks:
      - name: monitor-application
        template: prometheus-monitor
      - name: rollback-deployment
        template: rollback
        dependencies: [monitor-application]
        when: "{{tasks.monitor-application.outputs.parameters.failed}} == true"

- name: prometheus-monitor
  container:
    image: prom/prometheus
    command: [sh, -c]
    args: ["promtool check metrics"]

- name: rollback
  container:
    image: bitnami/kubectl:1.18
    command: [sh, -c]
    args: ["kubectl rollout undo deployment/myapp"]
```

Here, Prometheus monitors application metrics. If an anomaly is detected (set via workflow conditions), the workflow triggers a rollback using 'kubectl'.

- **Benefits of Argo Workflows in Continuous Deployment:**

- End-to-End Automation: Argo streamlines the entire deployment pipeline, from code integration to production rollout, fostering rapid and reliable delivery cycles.

- Scalability: Integrated with Kubernetes, Argo Workflows scales effortlessly, accommodating the demands of large-scale applications and extensive deployment operations.

- Consistency and Reproducibility: By defining deployment processes as code, Argo reduces configuration drift, ensuring consistent environments across deployments.

- Auditability and Compliance: Detailed logging and traceability provided by workflows support compliance requirements and facilitate audits.

- Resilience: Automated rollback and monitoring mechanisms enhance system resilience, reducing downtime and mitigating potential disruptions.

Argo Workflows revolutionizes continuous deployment by providing a structured, flexible, and scalable architecture tailored to the dynamic needs of modern production environments. Its integration into DevOps strategies accelerates the deployment of innovative features, enhances collaboration across teams, and sets the stage for improved software quality and customer satisfaction.

By utilizing Argo for continuous deployment, organizations can achieve greater agility, responsiveness, and operational excellence, establishing a resilient foundation for future-proofing their technology stacks. The seamless orchestration of pipelines ensures that technology continuously evolves alongside business objectives, marking a significant stride toward digital transformation and competitive advantage.

10.5 Compliance and Auditing Automation

In today's rapidly evolving business landscape, compliance and auditing have become critical components of organizational governance. Organizations must adhere to various regulatory frameworks, such as GDPR, HIPAA, and SOX, to protect sensitive data and maintain integrity in financial reporting. Automation of compliance and auditing processes can significantly reduce the risk of non-compliance and enhance operational efficiency. Argo Workflows offers a sophisticated framework that automates these tasks, ensuring that necessary checks and balances are in place for regulatory adherence and internal auditing.

Compliance and auditing processes generally encompass data collection, policy enforcement, anomaly detection, reporting, and evidence management. Each of these stages can be orchestrated and automated using Argo Workflows, which provides a systematic approach to managing these processes within a cohesive workflow structure.

Automated Data Collection and Validation:

The foundation of compliance automation lies in the systematic collection and validation of pertinent data. This data is essential for gen-

10.5. COMPLIANCE AND AUDITING AUTOMATION

erating accurate reports and demonstrating adherence to regulatory standards. Argo Workflows can automate data collection from various sources, ensuring data integrity through validation checks.

Consider an organization that needs to gather access logs from multiple applications for compliance reporting. The following YAML configuration demonstrates how Argo Workflows can automate the data collection process:

```yaml
apiVersion: argoproj.io/v1alpha1
kind: Workflow
metadata:
  generateName: compliance-data-collection-
spec:
  entrypoint: collect-validate-data
  templates:
    - name: collect-validate-data
      dag:
        tasks:
          - name: collect-access-logs
            template: collect-logs
          - name: validate-logs
            template: validate-logs
            dependencies: [collect-access-logs]

    - name: collect-logs
      container:
        image: python:3.8
        command: [sh, -c]
        args: ["python collect_logs.py"]

    - name: validate-logs
      container:
        image: python:3.8
        command: [sh, -c]
        args: ["python validate_logs.py"]
```

This workflow fetches access logs from predefined sources and subsequently validates them by checking for completeness and accuracy.

Policy Enforcement and Anomaly Detection:

Enforcing policies and detecting anomalies are crucial for maintaining compliance and mitigating risks. Automated checks can identify deviations from standard operating procedures, enabling timely remedial actions.

Argo Workflows can encapsulate policy enforcement and anomaly detection tasks, leveraging custom scripts or integrating with external policy engines:

CHAPTER 10. REAL-WORLD USE CASES AND EXAMPLES

```
apiVersion: argoproj.io/v1alpha1
kind: Workflow
metadata:
  generateName: compliance-policy-enforcement-
spec:
  entrypoint: enforce-policies
  templates:
    - name: enforce-policies
      dag:
        tasks:
          - name: check-policy-compliance
            template: policy-check
          - name: detect-anomalies
            template: anomaly-detection
            dependencies: [check-policy-compliance]

    - name: policy-check
      container:
        image: python:3.8
        command: [sh, -c]
        args: ["python check_policy.py"]

    - name: anomaly-detection
      container:
        image: python:3.8
        command: [sh, -c]
        args: ["python detect_anomalies.py"]
```

In this scenario, policy-check assesses compliance against established protocols, while anomaly-detection monitors for irregularities that could indicate potential breaches or errors.

Automated Reporting and Audit Trail Generation:

Generating comprehensive reports and maintaining an audit trail are integral to demonstrating compliance. Argo Workflows can automate the creation of detailed reports, compiling data from various stages to provide a coherent view of compliance status.

The following YAML configuration illustrates an automated reporting process using Argo:

```
apiVersion: argoproj.io/v1alpha1
kind: Workflow
metadata:
  generateName: compliance-reporting-
spec:
  entrypoint: generate-report
  templates:
    - name: generate-report
      dag:
        tasks:
          - name: compile-data
            template: compile
```

10.5. COMPLIANCE AND AUDITING AUTOMATION

```
      - name: create-report
        template: report
        dependencies: [compile-data]
  - name: compile
    container:
      image: python:3.8
      command: [sh, -c]
      args: ["python compile_data.py"]

  - name: report
    container:
      image: python:3.8
      command: [sh, -c]
      args: ["python create_report.py"]
```

This workflow compiles data from the compliance checks and subsequently generates a detailed report that can be used internally or provided to auditors.

Evidence Management and Storage:

Efficient management and storage of evidence are requirements for compliance audits. Evidence, such as log files, test results, or policy documents, must be systematically preserved for verification by auditors.

Argo Workflows can automate evidence collection and storage procedures, integrating with cloud storage solutions like AWS S3 or Google Cloud Storage:

```
apiVersion: argoproj.io/v1alpha1
kind: Workflow
metadata:
  generateName: evidence-management-
spec:
  entrypoint: collect-evidence
  templates:
    - name: collect-evidence
      dag:
        tasks:
          - name: store-logs
            template: store
          - name: archive-logs
            template: archive
            dependencies: [store-logs]

    - name: store
      container:
        image: amazon/aws-cli
        command: [sh, -c]
        args: ["aws s3 cp logs/ s3://compliance-evidence/logs/ --recursive"]
```

```yaml
- name: archive
  container:
    image: amazon/aws-cli
    command: [sh, -c]
    args: ["aws s3 cp logs/ s3://compliance-evidence/archive/ --recursive"]
```

Here, all logs are stored and archived in an S3 bucket, providing a centralized repository for compliance evidence.

Benefits of Argo Workflows in Compliance Automation:

- **Efficiency:** Streamlines repetitive compliance tasks, reducing the time and effort required to maintain regulatory adherence.

- **Accuracy:** Minimizes human errors by automating data collection, validation, and reporting processes, enhancing the reliability of compliance efforts.

- **Real-time Monitoring:** Facilitates continuous monitoring of compliance status, enabling prompt detection and remediation of potential breaches.

- **Scalability:** Supports scaling of compliance operations to accommodate growing organizational needs and regulatory changes.

- **Traceability:** Maintains comprehensive records and audit trails, essential for demonstrating compliance during regulatory inspections and audits.

The automation of compliance and auditing processes through Argo Workflows empowers organizations to maintain a robust governance framework. By leveraging automation, organizations can focus on strategic initiatives, confident in their compliance posture and readiness for audits.

Argo Workflows thus acts as a catalyst for compliance in the era of digital transformation, helping organizations navigate complex regulatory landscapes with precision and agility. It enables a culture of continuous compliance, where automation drives consistency and integrity across business functions, safeguarding the organization against regulatory risks and fostering trust among stakeholders.

10.6 Batch Processing and Scheduling

Batch processing remains a cornerstone in the realm of data management, particularly in scenarios involving the handling of large volumes of data where throughput is prioritized over latency. Typical use cases span data warehousing, ETL (Extract, Transform, Load) operations, financial transactions processing, and more. Adequate scheduling of these batch tasks ensures optimized resource utilization and timely execution. Argo Workflows serves as a robust orchestration framework, facilitating automated batch processing and scheduling within Kubernetes environments.

Argo Workflows capitalizes on Kubernetes' inherent scalability and resource management capabilities, providing a container-native solution that orchestrates intricate batch processing tasks seamlessly. It allows for the decomposition of complex jobs into manageable tasks, coordinating their execution according to defined dependencies.

Defining Batch Jobs:

Defining batch jobs involves specifying the tasks that comprise the job, understanding the dependencies between them, and orchestrating their execution. Argo Workflows manages these tasks in a Directed Acyclic Graph (DAG) structure, where each node represents a task, and edges denote dependencies.

Consider a data pipeline that involves extracting data from multiple sources, transforming the data, and aggregating the results into a data warehouse. The following YAML configuration exemplifies how this can be set up in an Argo Workflow:

```
apiVersion: argoproj.io/v1alpha1
kind: Workflow
metadata:
  generateName: data-processing-batch-
spec:
  entrypoint: batch-pipeline
  templates:
    - name: batch-pipeline
      dag:
        tasks:
          - name: extract-data-source1
            template: extract
            arguments:
              parameters: [{name: "source", value: "source1"}]
          - name: extract-data-source2
```

```
            template: extract
            arguments:
              parameters: [{name: "source", value: "source2"}]
        - name: transform-data
          template: transform
          dependencies: [extract-data-source1, extract-data-source2]
        - name: aggregate-results
          template: aggregate
          dependencies: [transform-data]

    - name: extract
      inputs:
        parameters:
          - name: source
      container:
        image: python:3.8
        command: [sh, -c]
        args: ["python extract.py --source {{inputs.parameters.source}}"]

    - name: transform
      container:
        image: python:3.8
        command: [sh, -c]
        args: ["python transform.py"]

    - name: aggregate
      container:
        image: python:3.8
        command: [sh, -c]
        args: ["python aggregate.py"]
```

This workflow defines a multi-step batch job, beginning with the extraction of data from two sources, followed by a transformation phase, and concluding with aggregation. Each task runs within a container, ensuring isolation and repeatability.

Scheduling Batch Jobs:

Efficient scheduling is paramount to ensure that batch processing tasks run during periods of low resource demand or at specific intervals. Argo Workflows supports cron-based scheduling, akin to the Unix 'cron' system, which allows workflows to execute at predefined times.

The following example demonstrates the scheduling of a nightly data processing job using Argo's cron workflow feature:

```
apiVersion: argoproj.io/v1alpha1
kind: CronWorkflow
metadata:
  name: nightly-data-processing
spec:
  schedule: "0 2 * * *" # Executes daily at 2 AM
  concurrencyPolicy: "Allow"
```

10.6. BATCH PROCESSING AND SCHEDULING

```
      successfulJobsHistoryLimit: 3
      failedJobsHistoryLimit: 1
      jobTemplate:
        spec:
          entrypoint: batch-pipeline
          templates:
            # Templates similar to the previous example
```

In this configuration, the batch job is scheduled to run every day at 2 AM, ensuring that it executes during off-peak hours, thereby optimizing resource usage and minimizing potential impact on other operational workloads.

Error Handling and Retry Policies:

Handling errors and incorporating retry logic is crucial in batch processing to enhance robustness and reliability. Argo Workflows supports specifying retry strategies at the task level, allowing workflows to automatically attempt task re-execution upon failure.

```
apiVersion: argoproj.io/v1alpha1
kind: Workflow
metadata:
  generateName: retry-batch-job-
spec:
  entrypoint: batch-pipeline
  templates:
    - name: batch-pipeline
      dag:
        tasks:
          # Define task with retry strategy
          - name: extract-data-with-retry
            template: extract
            retryStrategy:
              limit: 3
              backoff:
                duration: "10s"
                factor: 2
            arguments:
              parameters: [{name: "source", value: "source1"}]

    # Define extract template as before
```

This configuration incorporates a retry strategy that limits retries to three attempts, with exponential backoff, providing resilience in handling transient failures without manual intervention.

Resource Optimization:

Effective resource allocation is essential for optimizing batch processing tasks, ensuring that they utilize computational resources efficiently without monopolizing them. Argo Workflows leverages Kubernetes' resource management features, allowing resource requests and limits to be specified for individual tasks.

```
apiVersion: argoproj.io/v1alpha1
kind: Workflow
metadata:
  generateName: resource-optimized-batch-job-
spec:
  entrypoint: batch-pipeline
  templates:
    - name: extract
      inputs:
        parameters:
          - name: source
      container:
        image: python:3.8
        command: [sh, -c]
        args: ["python extract.py --source {{inputs.parameters.source}}"]
        resources:
          requests:
            memory: "256Mi"
            cpu: "500m"
          limits:
            memory: "512Mi"
            cpu: "1"
```

Resource specifications allow Argo Workflows to request appropriate allocations, optimizing execution performance while preventing resource contention with other tasks or applications.

Monitoring and Logging:

Monitoring the status of batch jobs and capturing logs are indispensable for maintaining observability and diagnosing issues. Argo Workflows integrates with Kubernetes' native logging and monitoring solutions, facilitating comprehensive oversight of batch execution.

Log management can be further streamlined by integrating with tools such as ELK (Elasticsearch, Logstash, Kibana) stacks or Fluentd, providing centralized log aggregation and analysis. Additionally, Prometheus and Grafana can be employed to capture and visualize metrics, offering real-time insights into workflow performance and resource utilization.

Benefits of Argo Workflows in Batch Processing and Scheduling:

- **Scalability:** Leverages Kubernetes to scale batch jobs dynamically in response to varying workload demands, ensuring optimal execution performance.

- **Automation and Efficiency:** Automates the orchestration and scheduling of batch processes, minimizing manual intervention and maximizing throughput.

- **Resilience:** Integrates error handling and retry logic, ensuring batch processes are robust against intermittent failures and transient conditions.

- **Resource Management:** Employs Kubernetes' resource controls, optimizing the allocation and usage of computational resources for batch workloads.

- **Observability:** Provides integration with observability tools, ensuring high visibility and traceability into batch processing operations.

The automation and orchestration provided by Argo Workflows transform batch processing into a highly efficient and manageable operation, aligning with the demands of modern enterprise environments. By integrating seamlessly with containerized and cloud-native architectures, it empowers organizations to harness the full potential of their data at scale, paving the way for enhanced decision-making and innovation.

10.7 Real-Time Data Streaming Pipelines

In the era of big data, the need for processing and analyzing information as it flows in real-time has given rise to data streaming pipelines. These pipelines empower organizations to respond to events instantaneously, providing capabilities that are critical in areas such as fraud detection, recommendation systems, financial trading, and operational monitoring. Argo Workflows, with its powerful orchestration capabilities, is an ideal choice for configuring real-time data streaming pipelines, ensuring efficient data ingestion, processing, and analytics.

Real-time data streaming pipelines involve the continuous flow of data streams, which are processed and analyzed to extract actionable insights almost instantaneously. The architecture typically includes components for data ingestion, processing, storage, and analytics. Argo Workflows facilitates the orchestration of these components, ensuring seamless integration and execution.

Data Ingestion:

The first stage in a real-time streaming pipeline is data ingestion, where streams of data are captured from various sources. These sources can include IoT devices, user interactions, log data, social media platforms, or financial transactions. Apache Kafka, Apache Pulsar, and AWS Kinesis are widely used technologies for building robust data ingestion layers.

Argo Workflows can automate the configuration and management of data ingestion components, triggering workflows to start data collection as new streams arrive. Consider the following YAML configuration for integrating Kafka-based ingestion within an Argo workflow:

```
apiVersion: argoproj.io/v1alpha1
kind: Workflow
metadata:
  generateName: kafka-ingestion-
spec:
  entrypoint: ingest
  templates:
    - name: ingest
      container:
        image: confluentinc/cp-kafka:latest
        command: [sh, -c]
        args: ["kafka-console-consumer --bootstrap-server broker:9092 --topic my-topic --from-beginning"]
```

This workflow initiates a Kafka consumer to read data from the specified topic, ensuring continuous data flow into the processing pipeline.

Data Processing:

Once ingested, the data undergoes real-time processing, where transformations, filtering, aggregation, and enrichment take place. This processing is often managed through stream processing frameworks like Apache Flink, Apache Storm, or Apache Spark Streaming, which offer capabilities to handle large volumes of data with low latency.

Argo Workflows can orchestrate these processing tasks, coordinating

10.7. REAL-TIME DATA STREAMING PIPELINES

multiple stages of transformation and ensuring that they execute concurrently or sequentially as required. Consider the orchestration of a Spark Streaming job:

```
apiVersion: argoproj.io/v1alpha1
kind: Workflow
metadata:
  generateName: spark-streaming-process-
spec:
  entrypoint: stream-process
  templates:
    - name: stream-process
      container:
        image: spark:latest
        command: [sh, -c]
        args: ["spark-submit --class org.example.StreamingJob streaming-job.jar"]
```

This configuration submits a Spark Streaming job, processing incoming streams with high throughput and fault tolerance.

Data Storage:

Processed data is often stored in real-time databases or data lakes, where it remains accessible for further analysis or querying. Technologies like Apache Cassandra, Amazon DynamoDB, and Elasticsearch offer capabilities suited for handling real-time workloads.

Argo Workflows can manage data persistence tasks, automating the integration with storage solutions to ensure processed data is reliably stored and indexed:

```
apiVersion: argoproj.io/v1alpha1
kind: Workflow
metadata:
  generateName: data-storage-
spec:
  entrypoint: store-data
  templates:
    - name: store-data
      container:
        image: cassandra:latest
        command: [sh, -c]
        args: ["cqlsh -e 'COPY my_keyspace.my_table FROM my_stream WITH
               HEADER = TRUE;'"]
```

This workflow demonstrates using Apache Cassandra to handle the storage of processed data, applying CQL commands to ingest data directly from streaming sources.

Real-Time Analytics and Visualization:

The ultimate goal of real-time data streaming pipelines is to extract insights and generate analytics in near real-time. These insights drive business decision-making, impacting areas such as customer engagement and operational efficiency. Tools like Apache Druid, Elasticsearch, and Grafana are often employed to query and visualize data promptly.

Argo Workflows can orchestrate the execution of analytics jobs and trigger visualization updates based on processed data metrics. The following workflow uses Elasticsearch to index and analyze data:

```
apiVersion: argoproj.io/v1alpha1
kind: Workflow
metadata:
  generateName: realtime-analytics-
spec:
  entrypoint: analyze-data
  templates:
    - name: analyze-data
      container:
        image: docker.elastic.co/elasticsearch/elasticsearch:latest
        command: [sh, -c]
        args: ["curl -X POST 'localhost:9200/my_index/_search' -H 'Content-Type: application/json' -d @search_query.json"]
```

By employing Elasticsearch, this workflow performs real-time indexing and analytics, ensuring data remains actionable and readily available for insights generation.

Benefits of Argo Workflows in Real-Time Data Streaming:

- **Scalability:** Capitalizes on Kubernetes orchestration to scale components dynamically, optimizing performance as data volumes fluctuate.

- **Flexibility:** Encourages modularity, allowing independent scaling and management of ingestion, processing, storage, and analytics components.

- **Resilience:** Incorporates fault tolerance through containerized execution, ensuring workflows are robust against interruptions and failures.

- **Integration:** Seamlessly integrates stream processing technologies and storage solutions, supporting diverse environments and datasets.

10.7. REAL-TIME DATA STREAMING PIPELINES

- **Speed:** Reduces latency through automated orchestration, enabling rapid response to events and facilitating real-time insights.

Argo Workflows transforms real-time data streaming pipelines by orchestrating the myriad tasks that underlie data ingestion, processing, and analysis. Its container-native design, coupled with the robust resource management of Kubernetes, ensures that streaming workflows are efficient, scalable, and resilient, underpinning the foundational capabilities of data-driven organizations.

By automating and streamlining these processes, Argo enables enterprises to harness the full potential of their data in real-time, fostering innovation and securing competitive advantage in increasingly dynamic markets. The strategic insights derived from real-time analytics empower businesses to make informed decisions, enhancing customer experiences, optimizing operations, and driving growth.

www.ingramcontent.com/pod-product-compliance
Lightning Source LLC
Chambersburg PA
CBHW052140220526
45471CB00004B/1459